INFORMATION ACCESS

Capabilities and Limitations of Printed and Computerized Sources

Richard Joseph Hyman

AMERICAN LIBRARY ASSOCIATION

Chicago and London 1989

Cover designed by Harriett Banner

Composed by Impressions, Inc.
in Baskerville on a Penta-driven
Autologic APS-μ5 phototypesetting
system

Printed on 50-pound Glatfelter,
a pH-neutral stock, and bound
in 10-point Carolina cover stock
by Edwards Brothers, Inc.

The paper used in this publication meets the minimum requirements of American National Standard for Information Sciences—Permanence of Paper for Printed Library Materials, ANSI Z39.48–1984. ♾

Library of Congress Cataloging-in-Publication Data

Hyman, Richard Joseph.
Information access: capabilities and limitations of printed and computerized sources / by Richard J. Hyman.
p. cm.
Bibliography: p.
Includes index.
ISBN 0-8389-0512-9 (alk. paper)
1. Information retrieval. 2. Cataloging—History. 3. Cataloging—Data processing. 4. Machine-readable bibliographic data. 5. Online bibliographic searching. 6. Bibliographic services.
I. Title.
Z699.H96 1989
025.3—dc19 89-6477

93 92 91 90 89 5 4 3 2 1

CONTENTS

Acknowledgments

My pleasant duty is to thank all those who read at least parts of this book while it was in process: Herbert Bloom, senior editor, ALA Books, who also enlisted outside advisors; Professor Laurel Franklin, chief, Catalog Division, City College of New York Library; Professor Frederick Low, technical services librarian, Fiorello H. La Guardia Community College Library; and Joseph Hohendahl, account representative, Utlas International Canada, who helped much with the pages on Utlas. I wish also to thank my friends in the library profession whose ideas I have not always acknowledged—all the better for them since any errors in the text are of my own making and library colleagues must be held blameless. Finally, a thank-you to the splendid library of the Columbia University Graduate School of Library Service and to its friendly staff and librarian, Olha della Cava, without whose aid this book could not have been written.

Introduction

This writer's original intention was to prepare a searcher's guide for the end user. It soon became obvious, however, that changes in descriptive cataloging and subject analysis were too numerous—and apparently too confusing—for end users to engage in any but simple searching tasks. The knowledge and experience of a professional librarian usually seemed mandatory. INFORMATION ACCESS details these changes and their effect on access to information through bibliographic records. It shows the scope—and the limits—of these records when they are used to identify or locate sources of information. Hence this book aims to assess the effectiveness of the records (or surrogates) that represent the informational content of collections. The book is directed to the practitioner and library school student, though it is also intended to be readable, at least in large part, by the interested layperson.

Of prime importance is to recognize that a bibliographic surrogate only *refers* to an original text. Sometimes the surrogate can substitute for the original, such as summaries of books or newspaper-index items. Also, because of its growing popularity, full-text display in automated sources, though in fact not a surrogate, has been included in the chapter on analytical database searching.

Our study focuses on the retrieval of information whose surrogates have been organized by descriptive cataloging and subject analysis (traditional subject headings and classification), as well as by thesaurus and computerized indexing techniques which have developed from descriptive cataloging and subject analysis. This organization creates access points through which the user can obtain desired information, from either printed or machine-readable records.

Definitions, even if preliminary or fragmentary, are presented here to help the reader understand this book's scope.[1] *Bibliographic surrogates* include records of whole books and serials, volumes as parts of sets and series, and the physical identification and content analysis of shorter items, such as journal articles, technical reports, and units in collections and compilations. Entries for smaller pieces of information, such as back-of-the-book indexes, can be even more specific surrogates. Although they are not considered in detail like print items, nonprint works like audio-visuals, sound recordings, films, video products, and graphics may be expected to follow the same patterns of surrogation. Certainly their basic problems of identification and retrieval do not differ from those of the print media.

Access point in this publication incorporates not only the definition in the revised second edition of *Anglo-American Cataloguing Rules* (*AACR2*, revised)—"A name, term, code, etc., under which a bibliographic record may be searched and identified"[2]—but also any label or handle that helps us locate and retrieve original texts, even when the surrogation comes from subject analysis which, strictly speaking, is not the responsibility of *AACR2*, revised.

These definitions of bibliographic surrogate and access points subsume data in the Library of Congress (LC) Machine-Readable Cataloging (MARC) communications format that is identified by MARC content designators.[3] Although descriptions of the work's physical characteristics (e.g., pagination, presence and kinds of illustrative matter, height in centimeters) are not directly related to the intellectual contents—and are indeed considered "anachronistic" by some critics—they may be useful in combination with other access points for searching and verification in printed and computerized bibliographic records. The MARC format includes these physical details and codes, including subject headings and contents notes, the last being the province actually of descriptive cataloging rather than of subject analysis.

In this book, *analytical entry* leading to *analytical access* is given a broader interpretation than in *AACR2*, revised. The Glossary of *AACR2*, revised defines analytical entry as "an entry for a part of an item for which a comprehensive entry has been made." The comprehensive entry, of course, would have been made in accordance with the descriptive

1. Some terms may be unfamiliar to readers or require formal definition. The Bibliography includes dictionaries and glossaries as well as general texts and specialized works on information organization.

2. *Anglo-American Cataloguing Rules*, 2nd ed., 1988 revision, Michael Gorman and Paul W. Winkler, eds. (Chicago: ALA, 1988), 615.

3. Walt Crawford, *MARC for Library Use: Understanding Integrated USMARC*, 2nd ed. (Boston: G.K. Hall, 1989).

cataloging rules of *AACR2*, revised. The very short Chapter 13 of *AACR2*, revised, suggests rules for the construction of analytical entries: "Analytics of Monographic Series and Multipart Monographs," " 'In' Analytics" and "Multilevel Description."[4] By extension, analytical access through analytics can provide access points not only through entries for substantial or significant parts of works cataloged as wholes by the descriptive cataloging rules of *AACR2*, revised. It can also provide access through printed indexes for anthologies and compilations (e.g., of poems, short stories, or dramas), through back-of-the-book indexes, and through surrogates for information within serial literature which are furnished in printed or computerized records. (*Serials*, *periodicals*, and *journals* are often used by this writer, doubtless incorrectly, as equivalents.) Analytical access is thus made possible in this book by applying the rules of both descriptive cataloging and subject analysis.

This book does not aim to teach practitioners how to catalog, classify, and index, but instead how to use the results of these techniques to obtain information and thus be alert to the difficulties. (As they use this work, practitioners will become familiar with technical services procedures generally. Ideally, the librarian will have experience in both technical and reader services.) The reasons are many for treating information access by its use and not by its production. First of all, the need for original (that is, first-time local) cataloging has lessened precipitously during the last two decades with the growth of national bibliographic utilities, such as the Online Computer Library Center, Inc. (OCLC), the Research Libraries Group, Inc. (RLG), and Research Libraries Information Network, Inc. (RLIN). The trend to centralized catalog-record distribution in this country goes back at least to the beginning of the century when the Library of Congress (LC) began to sell copies of its printed catalog cards in 1901. Charles Ammi Cutter (1837–1903), in the posthumous 1904 edition of his *Rules for a Dictionary Catalog*, expressed misgivings on the effects of these sales on local catalogers. Cutter was moved to a well-known prophecy whose irony, probably unintended, lingers:

> Still I can not help thinking that the golden age of cataloging is over and that the difficulties and discussions which have furnished an innocent pleasure to so many will interest them no more. Another lost art.[5]

For many years smaller public and school libraries could purchase catalog cards from commercial sources, e.g., the now defunct catalog

4. *Anglo-American Cataloguing Rules*, 2nd ed., revised, 299–302, 615.

5. Charles Ammi Cutter, *Rules for a Dictionary Catalog*, 4th ed., rewritten (Washington: Govt. Print. Off., 1904), 5.

card service of the H. W. Wilson Company. Some other vendors still supply catalog records to such customers, though in a less coordinated centralized fashion. The 1961 LC Books-with-Cards program encouraged book suppliers to enclose LC catalog cards with orders. The successor 1971 Cataloging-in-Publication (CIP) program strengthened local library dependence on LC but without LC itself supplying the CIP cards.

The influence of the 1966 LC National Program for Acquisitions and Cataloging (NPAC) on local academic libraries' cataloging was documented in a 1973 article which found a steep decline in the number of cataloging personnel.[6] Expansion of the NPAC, now called the National Coordinated Cataloging Program (NCCP), was officially announced by LC in 1986. Later, a pilot project was announced for early 1988.[7] Just because of all these stand-ins for original cataloging, most librarians use these products of cataloging and classification in their ordinary routines.

Information seekers, either practitioners or end users, usually are not concerned with the mechanics that make a successful search or "hit" feasible. Diners in a restaurant, for example, are concerned only with how food tastes, not how those in the kitchen had to prepare it. Accommodating this lack of user concern can be seen in "transparent" computer access systems that do not require user knowledge of what goes on within the machine. High-level or natural-language computer software and commands that are easy to use are now standard for consumers. Menu-driven systems are designed to aid the layperson. The searcher's need to know *how* to program instructions has been eliminated in a user-friendly milieu, though introductory programming knowledge remains meaningful for the librarian and end user. Practitioners in particular should know enough about programming to communicate intelligently with technicians and salespeople. Users of computerized information far outnumber technicians and programmers.

User-friendly environments, transparent systems, menu-driven programs, and high-level, natural language computer commands still do not change the role of the librarian in searching requests for computerized information. The end user may be able to search fairly adequately in printed sources or in the Online Public Access Catalog (OPAC) that replaces the old card catalog. The end user may also be able to search

6. Carol F. Ishimoto, "The National Program for Acquisitions and Cataloging: Its Impact on University Libraries," *College & Research Libraries* 34 (Mar. 1973):126–36, especially 134.

7. "Semiannual Report on Developments at the Library of Congress, April 1 through September 30, 1986 (Continued) . . . Processing Services," *Library of Congress Information Service Bulletin* 46 (Jan. 12, 1987): 21; Henriette D. Avram and Breacher Wiggins, "The National Coordinated Cataloging Program," *Library Resources & Technical Services* 32 (Apr. 1988):111–15.

automated sources from a terminal at home or in the office. The benefits of direct online access should not be withheld from end users, but less complicated applications, such as OPAC, are remote from the sophisticated computer searching that librarians can perform. The limitations of typical end users' direct searching are made evident as this text develops. Analogously, also discussed is the need for subject and database specialization by searchers—in other words, the relationships between the professional librarian and the end user.

This writer's opinion, based on experience as a practitioner and instructor in the technical services, is that the organization of information in any form represents the probity of librarianship, to paraphrase the French painter Jean-Auguste-Dominique Ingres (1780–1867). Information organization is surely a prime candidate for the discriminating characteristic of librarianship as a profession.[8] Courses in cataloging, classification, and indexing can be seen as the litmus paper tests for those seeking a career in professional librarianship. Literacy is not enough!

Library school students' complaints about courses in cataloging, classification, and indexing may to some extent be justified by how these subjects are traditionally taught. Instead of presenting them as interrelated elements within a system comprising all library functions, from acquisition to reference work, the courses often introduce the principles of information organization as discrete unrelated units. Also lending support to student complaints is the unavoidable reality that the subjects are not sciences but arts which cannot be mastered without fairly long supervised professional experience (true of almost all professions). No experienced practitioner would agree that a textbook or introductory course will produce a finished cataloger, classifier or indexer. However, the need of the library professional to interpret the organizational methodology is ever present.

Librarians, including those who are not exclusively catalogers, find most of their workday taken up with answering requests for information from end users as well as colleagues. A basic understanding of the elements of information organization is essential for effective search and retrieval. This understanding is based not on knowing how to organize information through its surrogates—the production function—but on recognizing what access points have been provided by the various Anglo-American cataloging codes, subject authorities, and indexing systems to facilitate the use function: searching for the original behind the surrogate.

8. Richard Joseph Hyman, "Professionalism in Librarianship: Professions of an Educator," *Urban Academic Librarian* 5 (Fall/Winter 1986/87):35–38.

INFORMATION ACCESS discusses many of the problems caused by the changes in codes. Though some of these problems are seemingly intractable, the text offers realistic solutions or recommends measures to deal with them in a manageable way.

An important step in solving any problem is to recognize that the problem exists and to explain its implications. Two points are stressed in this text: first, the necessity of retaining older printed records, and second, how automated access relies on established principles of bibliographic organization. The convenience of computerized searching must be weighed against a user's request that may make an automated search inappropriate. Earlier printed surrogates both help the practitioner understand current computerized search methodology and also remain a useful and sometimes an exclusive source for information. Although an automated search may provide many additional access points, we should not discount the records not yet made machine-readable. Neither printed nor computerized surrogation has answered the age-old dilemmas of bibliographic organization, such as the corpus of an author's works written under different or varying forms of names, or the time-bound products of subject analysis. The limitations of both manual and machine searching must be understood for them to be fully effective. Very often, as will be pointed out, a union of the two is desirable.

Another important issue that is addressed is that many bibliographic surrogates, whether automated or printed, have yet to be changed to conform *completely* with newer codes and rules. This need for recataloging and reclassification is examined. A related matter is the frequent conflict between the requirements of standardization and those of local libraries.

Chapter titles were chosen for convenient reference. The index is also a good data source. After a first reading, particular attention can be given those chapters describing problems in practice. It is not to be expected that professionals remember all the changes in codes, only that they be aware of the changes and be able to find guides detailing them.

The book begins with a historical survey of bibliographic organization in the first two chapters to show how librarians through the ages have relied on descriptive cataloging and subject analysis techniques—the "two approaches to library organization"—to order their collections and to prepare catalog surrogates. These two approaches must confront access problems still with us and, with little change of basics, have remained the major ways to describe and arrange libraries.

The codes for descriptive cataloging and subject analysis became necessarily more detailed, culminating in efforts at standardization during the nineteenth and twentieth centuries. The rise of national libraries, the conflict between scientific and library classifications and its effects on shelving, the American neglect of the classified catalog and the equating of classification and subject headings, the collocative qualities of the main-entry heading and of filing procedures, all gathered force. In our times, despite the computerizing of bibliographic surrogates, the obstacles facing descriptive cataloging and subject access continue.

The next two chapters concern the use of printed bibliographic surrogates to retrieve information through access points supplied by descriptive cataloging and subject analysis, respectively. These chapters differentiate between looking for cataloging information in such printed sources as the *National Union Catalog (NUC)* and individual library inventories and looking for non-cataloging data in periodical indexes and reference tools.

Chapter 5 then covers automated searching—descriptive cataloging and subject analysis access points combined—in union catalogs such as the Online Union Catalog (OLUC) of OCLC and in OPAC examples, e.g., the Columbia Libraries Information Online (CLIO).

Again combining descriptive cataloging and subject analysis, Chapter 6 discusses searching for information in automated periodical indexes such as the analytical databases distributed by DIALOG. The final chapter recaps the book, reviews state-of-the-art research and discusses unmet bibliographic organization needs.

Because this book is directed to a wide audience, some of it may seem *déja vu* to the experienced. It is hoped, however, that as the text develops the reader will gain useful insights on some or all of the topics.

If this text were chiefly concerned with the content of recorded knowledge in its original form, the subject would become hopelessly diffuse. By emphasizing the organizational system used to create surrogates, the topic becomes more tractable. The user may come to the librarian or information manager for assistance because the latter knows more not about the field but about how its subject matter is organized for access.

In summary, this book relates accepted principles of information organization to the requirements of users who must locate, through printed or automated surrogates, recorded knowledge in available formats. If the book succeeds in this principal goal, the permanent validity of the principles of bibliographic organization for defining librarianship as a profession will be reaffirmed.

1 ORGANIZATION of INFORMATION before the NINETEENTH CENTURY

The earliest extant library catalogs of our Western world reflect the rationale that catalogs are designed to give to the collection access points that are most useful for—which is to say, most expected by—the beneficiaries of the collection. These access points are based on answers to two questions about the physical containers of information in the collection: (1) what is the item? and (2) what is the item about? Two approaches are used to produce the answers; they are, respectively, to employ modern terms, (1) descriptive cataloging and (2) subject analysis.

As not uncommon in library terminology, these terms are not precise. The two may overlap, making the purpose of the catalog less definite as the size of the collection increases. Furthermore, the two approaches have been accommodated by librarians more frequently for works as wholes than for the smaller units of information these works may contain, what we call today "indexing" or supplying analytical access. Ancient librarians gave some indications of recognizing the necessity for analytical access, but until the eighteenth-century rise in journal-article indexing, the challenges were largely ignored. The difficulties of adequately indexing bits of information within books and making these access points generally available in the same way as for books as wholes have still to be resolved.

We can benefit from a review of how librarians historically employed these two approaches to information in their cataloging. Such a review is, first, psychologically therapeutic. It is reassuring to learn that our ancestors had the same problems, recognized the same access needs, and in their own way provided for them. Second, an understanding of the age-old dilemmas in our own bibliographical controls is of practical current value. Over centuries there have been many descriptive cataloging and subject analysis codes and techniques. Inevitably these rules and procedures have changed, but vestiges of them remain. For that reason, today's searchers should anticipate inconsistencies, even contradictions, in the same or different bibliographical apparatuses. Discarded or forgotten measures may have been revived or transformed. The limitations of these measures will be clearer to those aware of their history.

Our earliest librarians were more concerned with a subject analysis approach than an author approach to whole works, which is a province of descriptive cataloging. A late third-millennium temple library has been discovered at Nippur in southern Babylon. Some 25,000 cuneiform tablets were arranged by subject in rooms and on shelves. Evidence suggests an accompanying classified catalog.[1]

Ancient classified catalogs differed from modern versions based on hierarchical schemes, like the Dewey Decimal Classification (DDC) created by Melvil Dewey (1851–1931). The very old classified catalogs were written groupings of topical descriptions like our modern subject headings, except that the groupings must have followed some logical, not strictly alphabetical, order. Though this book is chiefly about bibliographical and not bibliothecal access to collections (that is, searching surrogates rather than shelves), evidence is unmistakable that written surrogates served as bibliothecal guides, regardless of patron admission to the stacks.

For millennia thereafter, until the era of Greek and Roman libraries, authorship was not considered a prime access point. Only as the Western concept of individualism grew stronger did the need for author identification arise. Also, for many millennia up to the latter part of the nineteenth century, a congruence was expected between shelf and catalog organization—that is, the order on the shelves was to be the same as in the catalog. This attempt at congruence was to plague Enlightenment classificationists.

The Assyrian Nineveh library, developed by the royal family during the first part of the first millennium, added descriptive cataloging elements to the subject analysis of the Nippur library.

> Though authorities differ, the majority believe that the tablets were arranged on the shelves in systematic subject order. Many familiar modern techniques assured access to related items among the estimated tens of thousands of tablets. Content descriptions and locational signs were added on labels or to the

1. The brief history of bibliographic organization in this and the next chapter is drawn from standard secondary sources, which are not individually referenced unless opinions or texts are quoted. For the sources, see Richard Joseph Hyman, *Shelf Access in Libraries* (Chicago: ALA, 1982), 6, footnote 2.

> exteriors of the tablets. Tablets in series were identified by the series title, and numbered as parts of the series. Each series tablet had at its top the ending line of the previous tablet and at its bottom the first line of the next, a device similar to modern printers' signatures. Catalogs, probably classified, gave bibliographical access. At least some were carved on the wall or doorway of the subject room. For each work, the catalog entries included its title or first line, number of lines on the tablet, number of tablets for a multi-unit work—many of the descriptive cataloging elements of our own records.[2]

Since Nineveh, librarians have endeavored to fill out bibliographic records so that fuller surrogates may be consulted by readers to determine whether library items meet their needs. A modern surrogate, such as an entry with summary, may fill these needs by itself. Despite the efforts at the Nineveh library to group the collections by subject, the cataloging techniques were largely bibliothecal, not bibliographical. The following Savage quotation, perhaps too laudatory, makes this same point.

> How oddly it must strike us modern librarians to learn that some of the features of library management on which they pride themselves today—their general catalogues, their list of best or popular books, their methodical arrangement of books, even their classification by subject—were practices on the banks of the Tigris and Euphrates several thousand years before the Christian era.[3]

Savage perhaps repeats the obvious. Organization of recorded information and provision of access points to that information follow a pattern set in antiquity. The two basic approaches to seeking information persist because evidently that is the way the human mind operates. A history of information organization confirms that belief. The physical containers of recorded knowledge changed over the centuries, from clay tablets to papyrus and animal-skin rolls to vellum manuscripts to printed paper books to microform to machine-readable data. The kinds of information sought, however, did not change nor did the fundamental means of implementing the two approaches to information retrieval. Ancient Egyptian libraries, probably as old as any in the Near East, maintained the concept of a subject-organized catalog mirroring the shelf order. Such a catalog was carved on the walls of the much later temple library at Edfu, the "House of Papyrus." Egyptian libraries also had subject-spe-

2. Ibid., 7.

3. Ernest A. Savage, *The Story of Libraries and Book-Collecting* (1909; reprint ed., New York: B. Franklin, 1969), 3. See also *Encyclopaedia Britannica*, 11th ed., s.v. "Libraries," by Henry Richard Tedder and James Duff Brown.

cialized collections, e.g., the temple library of Ptah in Memphis that contained only medical literature.

In Greek and Hellenistic libraries, personal author identification became a prominent access point. The Alexandrian Library, center of the Silver Age of Greek literature, was founded by the Ptolemies (320–30 B.C.) and at its height was said to have housed more than a half million papyrus scrolls. (Like modern libraries, it had a very large cataloging backlog.) Its lost catalog, partially reconstructed from cited excerpts, was divided into 120 *Pinakes* or books (perhaps classes) attributed to Callimachus of Cyrene (ca. 300–ca. 240 B.C.). The catalog followed the shelf arrangement. The *Pinakes* appeared to be organized by type of author, e.g., poets, lawmakers, and subdivided by period. Miscellaneous short subjects (one subject was cheesecakes!) were arranged alphabetically by author. Descriptive cataloging data on the scrolls included author, title or first words, number of lines, date, place, and sometimes even an annotation for the author.

The organization of Roman collections copied that of Greek and Hellenistic libraries. Bibliotheca Ulpiana, begun by Trajan (A.D. 98–117), was divided into Greek and Latin wings, and like its Alexandrian predecessor, its scrolls were probably arranged in a subject order that agreed with its catalog.

Medieval European librarianship added little new in access to these classical prototypes. In fact, Dorothy May Norris in her 1939 history of largely English cataloging and catalogs from 1100 to 1850 points out that such a history cannot show evolutionary development because the ancients were as proficient as we, differing from us only in their methods.[4] Although medieval libraries were much smaller than the gigantic Greek, Hellenistic, and Roman ones, a new bibliographic and bibliothecal division was needed. Volumes were arranged not only in Greek and Latin but also in Christian literature groups. Monastic libraries used subject groupings for physical placement and the shelflist for a locational guide. Within the class of sacred writings, the Church Fathers were arranged by name. Thus, also in medieval libraries the two approaches were not forgotten.

Medieval university libraries organized their books and catalogs according to the system of instruction: the liberal arts and faculties. (Today's most used American classification schemes, the Library of Congress Classification (LCC) and Dewey, follow a not dissimilar plan based on the academic disciplines.) Chained libraries with their *libri catenati*, where the collection was physically chained down, became common at the beginning

4. Dorothy May Norris, *A History of Cataloguing and Cataloguing Methods 1100–1850; With an Introductory Survey of Ancient Times* (1939; reprint ed., Detroit: Gale, 1969), vii.

of the fourteenth century and merged their reading and storage areas. The motivation for chaining was economic since handwritten copies were very expensive, and replacements were sometimes unobtainable. (Suspicion of user pilferage continues to our day. Publicly available books like telephone directories are often chained to prevent removal.) In medieval chained libraries, shelflists (or catalog frames) were placed by or on each lectern or stall. As in Mesopotamia and Egypt, library patrons—perhaps only the librarians themselves in the ancient Near East—could determine from the frames what was to be found in the designated subject area.

Renaissance libraries continued the subject analysis approach by further developing subject classification schemes for catalog and shelf. In his *Pandectarium* (1548–49), Conrad Gesner (1516–65), the "German Pliny," offered a classification scheme for the items in his *Bibliotheca Universalis* (1545), which was an attempted universal listing of Greek, Latin, and Hebrew authors. *Bibliotheca Universalis* was to be used by all libraries for records of their holdings, much as the LC *National Union Catalog* (*NUC*) is used today in American libraries. *Bibliotheca Universalis* could also be used by Renaissance librarians for collection development. *Pandectarium*, likewise, was the equivalent of our LCC or DDC assignments on *NUC* surrogates.

In 1560 Florian Trefler (1483–1565), a Benedictine German monk, published his own classification scheme, which included color as a component! The first of his five recommended catalogs (indexes in the broad sense) was an alphabetical author listing with shelf marks. The purpose of Trefler's family of catalogs was to offer multiple access points to the collection. By the end of the Renaissance, increased attention to classified organization of information could not eliminate the need for access by authors' names.

Seventeenth-century libraries continued to accentuate subject classification, but found it increasingly difficult to use the same scheme for both shelf and catalog. They continued to give both subject and author access to their collections. Debate on the kind of classification needed for libraries resulted in the formation of two treatments, one theoretical and the other, practical. The first was based on the scheme of Francis Bacon (1561–1621) as included in his 1605 *Advancement of Learning*. The second was represented by the schemes of Jean Garnier (1612–81), published in 1678, and Ismael Boulliau (1605–94), published in 1679. These schemes were based on the divisions of the medieval university faculties. In modified forms they vied for supremacy against Bacon-influenced schemes in American libraries through the early nineteenth century.

The distinction between practical and theoretical or scientific library classifications can blur, and the two classifications may overlap. The distinction has not been definitively worked out to this day. In general, a practical library classification is designed to facilitate the usage of books. A theoretical or scientific library classification emphasizes the organization of knowledge as perceived by scholarly observation of the world around us—that is, scientific organization, usually the most up-to-date.

A theoretical classification can start from a practical point of view. Bacon's psychological classification had obvious roots in the medieval curriculum divisions of the trivium and quadrivium, an eminently practical grouping of academic disciplines. Yet it was Bacon's mental framework for these medieval practical divisions which made his classification theoretical. If Bacon's classification were to be adopted by libraries, the world of recorded knowledge had to be organized in accordance with his subjective theory. Bacon had not intended his classification for library materials, but the more that library classificationists absorbed nonlibrary concepts, the more theoretical or "scientific" their classifications became. An ideal combination of the practical and theoretical or scientific approaches has yet to be attained.

The catalogs of Oxford's Bodleian Library offer obvious examples of the equivocal status of classification for library shelves. The first catalog of the Bodleian, published in 1605, essentially reproduced the tables or shelflists placed on the ends of the library presses. Although the subject classes were not subdivided, within each class the books were arranged alphabetically by author. (Author subarrangement is still used by LCC and DDC.) The second Bodleian catalog of 1620 abandoned classified order and, like the later catalogs of the British Museum and the *NUC*, was arranged whenever possible by author. The compiler of this second Bodleian catalog, Thomas James (1573?–1629), did believe in classified catalogs (based on the university faculties) with author indexes, but not in classified shelving. Later national bibliographies and catalogs in France and Germany, like those in England and the United States, used the author as the principal means of arrangement.

Seventeenth-century American libraries were small and librarians, usually moonlighting custodians, not patron- and service-oriented professionals, followed European principles of bibliographic and shelf organization. Not until the latter part of the nineteenth century did American information organization become significant at home and abroad.

During the eighteenth century, European methods of bibliographic and shelf organization continued as models for American libraries. European models tended to the traditional shelf and catalog equivalent of scientific classification schemes, which had yet to be replaced by their more practical rivals. European thinkers, however, were seeking more useful nontheoretical methods. The German philosopher Gottfried Wilhelm von Leibniz (1646–1716) proposed a practical library classification based on the divisions of the medieval university faculties, a type of classification advocated by the Frenchmen Garnier and Boulliau and by the later Gabriel Naudé (1600–53), librarian for the Cardinals Richelieu and Mazarin. Leibniz's advice was followed in the organization of the Göttingen University library.

Especially remarkable in Leibniz's advocacy was its opposition to the later Enlightenment's stress on scientific theoretical principles of hierarchical classification. (Interestingly, Leibniz was expert in the science of mathematics.) In the nineteenth century a respectable classification had to be based on a scientific theory of knowledge. The evolutionary order in nature (not to be confused with Darwinism) structured the classification schemes of Cutter and of Ernest Cushing Richardson (1860–1939) in the United States. The spirit of the Enlightenment did not die!

Analytical access was not forgotten by eighteenth-century European librarians. The need for bibliographic control of serial, that is, journal literature was recognized. In 1775 the Abbé Rozier (François Rozier) (1754–93)—perhaps the inventor of the catalog card—proposed a card index of the Paris Académie des Sciences publications, 1660–1770. The Abbé recommended author entry as well as multiple entries for title-word subjects. The card index was to supplement a printed general index for tables of contents.[5]

Today's information seekers benefit as well as suffer from the historical development of access points. Benefits are not hard to identify: users needed access points, for both the physical nature and the subject content of the information container. Another benefit was the progressive recognition by librarians of the need for a standardized transferable methodology for creating these access points. By the end of the Renaissance, Gesner had proposed such a universal model.

Standardization and centralization of bibliographic information continue as goals for the current suppliers of surrogates, including standard descriptive cataloging codes, lists of verbal subject descriptions, and classification schemes. All emanate from a central authority, usually a national bibliographic service, and are intended for national (and international) use through networking and other cooperative bibliographic projects. Analytical access, unfortunately, has not been given equal attention, though theoretical interest has recently increased.

The disadvantages for present-day information seekers also appeared in embryonic form as access points developed over the centuries. The nineteenth century saw seeds of contradiction sprout and produce a

5. Richard B. Prosser, "The Origin of the Card Catalogue: A Brief Note," *Library Association Record* 2 (Dec. 1900):651. See also Richard Joseph Hyman, *Analytical Access: History, Resources, Needs* (Flushing, N.Y.: Queens College Press, 1978), 21–22.

bibliographic jungle, which had to be cut through by national facilities in the United States and Great Britain—to mention only those countries that are this book's principal concern regarding modern information search and retrieval. In the latter decades of the twentieth century, the expansion of computerized services from many sources complicated, not simplified, information organization in numerous local libraries. One step forward and two back!

Bibliographic organization of information in libraries before the nineteenth century began with identifying and arranging the works on shelves by subject. The attribution of classic works to subject rather than author was a characteristic of non-Western scholarship in its earliest days. (Perhaps only with the Renaissance did the Western world itself stress the individual and the individual's production. Even into the nineteenth century the identification of people was not that specific and was made by patronymic, by place of origin, or by trade.)

It is tempting to apply the modern term *libraries* to the most ancient collections, e.g., in Sumeria. The oldest libraries in the Western world were what we would now call archives or repositories, containing written records on such matters as law, business, religion, medicine, and magic. Such archives were frequently connected to temples, under the care of priests. (Before—sometimes despite—the invention of writing, literature was orally transmitted. The professions of bard and priest were thus protected from outsiders.) It should come as no surprise that the chief access to archaic depositories was by subject not author.

With the rise of Greek civilization, the creator was celebrated and the name became important as an access point after the subject or type of the work was assigned. We have become familiar with the names of Greek philosopher-scientists, dramatists and poets since the dawn of Hellenic recorded culture. In the Western world, the growth of *belles lettres* has been slow. Fictional narrative became common with the Renaissance. The novel became a genre in Europe in the sixteenth or seventeenth century. It took many centuries for authorship to become significant in terms of search and retrieval in European collections. A sociocultural history could well be written on how different civilizations stressed subject access to recorded information by subject heading, classified order, or title-catchword entry. A similar history could document the separation of ecclesiastical and lay management of information.

Although identification by both subject and author was being practiced in later libraries, there soon arose a conflict between the verbalization of content, what we now designate as subject headings, and the hierarchical arrangement of these topics in classification schemes. Nineteenth-century practitioners passed on the concurrent use of subject headings and classification, even though the latter is commonly employed in American libraries as a shelf-locational, not subject-revelatory device. The complications multiplied when librarians, influenced by contemporary scientists, tried to make the shelf arrangement follow the order of the classification scheme. The most recent compromise is the thesaurus, which purportedly combines classification with subject terms.

The quantitative growth of information did not alone cause our present problems. After all, if more and more books were printed on unchanging subjects, the chore of bibliographic control would still be with us, though in much smaller dimensions. A major cause was qualitative growth: new approaches to old subjects, new subjects written about, new interdisciplinary relations established. Librarians have always prided themselves on keeping up with science, which created continuously new frameworks for ordering the record of human culture. Specialized bibliographic information sources for different subject areas are inconsistent with overall conformity—a perpetual difficulty magnified in our times. Already, in the early nineteenth century, standardization issues in bibliographic organization had come to a head both for descriptive cataloging and subject analysis. Anthony Panizzi (1797–1879) in the nineteenth century was faced with these controversies, as the next chapter shows.

2 ORGANIZATION of INFORMATION in the NINETEENTH CENTURY

Anthony Panizzi, in his battle to catalog the British Museum holdings and make them accessible to patrons, confronted inherited predicaments. His 1841 "Ninety-One Rules" for constructing the British Museum catalog became the source for all Anglo-American cataloging codes—and for many of our present difficulties.[1] The problems confronting Panizzi were foreshadowed in bibliographic methodology and had to be dealt with, sometimes by omission, in his rules. Not necessarily in order of importance, such problems include: (1) finding list versus bibliographic collating purpose of the catalog; (2) completeness of the catalog record; (3) validity of subject classification for libraries; (4) inconsistency of title-catchword entry; and (5) shelf equivalence of subject classification order.

Increasingly sophisticated "scientific" classification schemes could not be reproduced on the shelves. In theory, the classification scheme as used in the catalog does not need to match the shelf arrangement. In 1912 and 1913 Georg Leyh (1877–1968) proposed a classified catalog, complete with multiple subject analytics and cross references, that was independent of subject-locational placement for the shelves.[2] Any kind of classified catalog is rare today in America.

1. Anthony Panizzi, *et al.*, comps., "Rules for the Compilation of the Catalogue of Printed Books in the British Museum," in British Museum, Department of Printed Books, *The Catalogue of Printed Books in the British Museum* (London: Printed by Order of the Trustees, 1841), 1:v–ix. Suspended publication with volume 1.

2. Georg Leyh, "Das Dogma von der systematischen Aufstellung," *Zeitblatt für Bibliotekswesen* 29 (1912):241–59; 30 (1913):98–136.

Panizzi disbelieved in classified catalogs and even in subject classification for libraries. He had been left with the expensive failure of Thomas Horne (1780–1862) who compiled a classified catalog for the British Museum library and reclassified the shelves according to his own scheme. Classified stacks did not mean direct patron access. The large European scholarly libraries had mostly closed stacks; only practitioners and attendants could benefit from any orderly physical arrangement. Books were grouped in subject presses and on subject shelves. The most specific classification subdivision was for the shelf, not for the books on that shelf. Only after Melvil Dewey (1851–1931) published his 1876 scheme, which featured relative location, was classifying the book rather than the shelf acceptable.[3] Panizzi solved the problem of classified catalog and shelf equivalence by rejecting classification for library materials, although he did not think it worthwhile to change Horne's faulty physical arrangement.

Panizzi had more than one practical reason for not endorsing library classification. He felt that every classification scheme was subject to continuous change, because scientific and intellectual activities were always changing. (The continuous changes in all bibliographical controls remain a serious problem.) He observed that scholars in European libraries found classified catalogs unsatisfactory.[4]

Panizzi's rejection of subject classification for libraries did not discourage nineteenth-century classificationists. Ernest Cushing Richardson (1860–1939), in his chronological listing of 162 classification schemes from Plato (428–347 B.C.) to 1910, described 85 schemes created in the nineteenth century, compared to 69 in all the preceding centuries.[5] American schemes have been numerous, especially since 1876. Dewey, as noted above, published the first edition of his classification in 1876. Charles Ammi Cutter (1837–1903) in 1879 issued the first expansion of his Expansive Classification (EC).[6] Richardson, who had constructed a classification scheme for the Hartford Theological Seminary in Connecticut, left for Princeton University in 1890 and started to develop his own

3. Melvil Dewey, *A Classification and Subject Index for Cataloguing and Arranging the Books and Pamphlets of a Library* (Amherst, Mass.: G. K. Hall, 1876).

4. Dorothy May Norris, *A History of Cataloguing and Cataloguing Methods 1100–1850; with an Introductory Survey of Ancient Times* (1939; reprint ed.: Detroit: Gale, 1969), 205, 211.

5. Ernest Cushing Richardson, *Classification, Theoretical and Practical, Together with an Appendix Containing an Essay towards a Bibliographical History of Systems of Classification*, 3rd ed. (New York: Wilson, 1930), 48–88.

6. Charles Ammi Cutter, *Expansive Classification, Part 1: The First Six Classifications* (Boston: C. A. Cutter, 1891–93).

subject classification.[7] The Library of Congress began to study the need for reclassification in 1897 and adopted its Library of Congress Classification in 1898.[8] American schemes, such as those of Cutter and Richardson, were strong on evolutionary order from primitive to perfect, and on structural hierarchy.

Panizzi chose authorship as the organizing principle of his recommended catalog. Entries were alphabetical by author or, if necessary, by a substitute for personal authorship. A fundamental problem confronting Panizzi was consistency. He knew that thorough consistency in descriptive cataloging was possible, if at all, only when one cataloger was responsible—an impossible situation in a large library. He tried to reduce the inevitable inconsistency through his rules. For the authoritative source of cataloging data he selected the title page, which would offer the same data to all catalogers to be interpreted strictly in accordance with his rules. But what was to be done with a book whose title page revealed no author? Panizzi believed that, for descriptive cataloging purposes, entering the work by the first word of the title (disregarding any preliminary article), not by the first substantive word, was the only way to insure desired cataloging consistency.

As far back as Nineveh, the title was judged important enough to be recorded on identification labels. The *Pinakes* arrangement for the Alexandrian Library included catchword or title-keyword (the German *Schlagwort*) information on the scrolls. Through the centuries librarians used this catchword approach not only for physical identification but also for description of the subject content of the work. Because the title did not have to be completely transcribed, only enough could be extracted to jog the memory or to suggest the topic of the work. Since each book title had its own wording, catchword entries were not consistent or collocative. Panizzi's rules aimed to do away with such catchword titles for the main-entry headings in catalogs.

Panizzi rejected subject classification for the British Museum catalog, but he did favor a subject guide, that is, a list of topical headings under which the relevant works were arranged. In 1886 the first volume of the guide was published by the Trustees (note that Panizzi had died in 1879!). The Trustees included in their three guides only works published after 1879. Later subject indexes superseded the earlier volumes and included

7. Ernest Cushing Richardson, *Location of Books in the Library of Princeton University* (Princeton, N.J.: Princeton Univ. Library, 1901). "Abstract of Classification" is on 11–22. A fuller treatment appears in Richardson, *Princeton University Library Classification System, 1900–1920* . . . (Yardley, Pa.: F. S. Cook & Son, 1929).

8. U.S. Library of Congress, Classification Division, *Classification* (Washington: Publishers vary, 1902–).

works published before 1880.[9] The Trustees' indexes, incorporated into the superseding issues, are especially difficult to use. Headings are not very specific, there are many subheadings, and catchword entries are not uncommon. We can easily see how modern subject headings evolved from catchword elements, but it was only when Cutter published his 1876 *Rules for a Dictionary Catalog* that a code was proposed to stabilize the use of verbal subject indicators.[10]

Though Panizzi was a feisty spokesman for his cataloging methodology, his "Ninety-One Rules" were not completely of his own making. First, the rules themselves were prepared after he consulted with his assistants, and then, in their final form, the rules were sometimes changed by a supervising Parliamentary Select Committee. Later commentators have called the committee's revisions "meddling." Although there is copious documentation of Panizzi's committee testimony on the kind of cataloging he thought the British Museum needed, it is not always easy to infer from the record his unqualified opinion on basic cataloging policies. On one matter, Panizzi was definite. He wished the British Museum catalog to be more than a finding catalog with only enough descriptive cataloging information to identify and retrieve a desired item known by its author's name. He envisioned the catalog as a national bibliographical reference source for future generations. To achieve this, the catalog had to group all works by the same author, no matter what the form of the name on the title page. Cross-references for unused forms and considerable research to identify the chosen form would be necessary.[11] The controversy on the finding list versus collocation role of the catalog continues even in the latest Anglo-American cataloging code.

Edward Edwards (1812–86), a prominent British librarian and a believer in Panizzi's ideas, later wrote that though the finding catalog concept was frequently discussed, no definition could be found for it. He concluded that the concept depended on the kind of role to be played by the particular catalog—rather begging the question—since, in a literal sense, all catalogs were expected to find an item for their users.[12]

Another problem involved the physical difference between the finding catalog and the bibliographic reference source catalog. If the catalog

9. For the subject indexes to the printed books in the British Museum library, see Eugene P. Sheehy, comp., *Guide to Reference Books*, 10th ed. (Chicago: ALA, 1986), AA135–36. For updatings to the *Guide*, see the January and July issues of *College & Research Libraries*.

10. Charles Ammi Cutter, *Rules for a Printed Dictionary Catalog*, in U.S. Bureau of Education, *Public Libraries in the United States of America; Their History, Condition, and Management; Special Report; Part 2*, 2 vols. in 1 (Washington: Govt. Print. Off., 1876).

11. Seymour Lubetzky, "Panizzi vs. the 'Finding Catalog'," *Journal of Cataloging and Classification* 12 (July 1956):152–56.

12. Ibid., 156.

were to be only a finding list, abbreviated records would suffice for identification and retrieval. Panizzi favored more than this skeleton description for future scholars to benefit. As an anticlimax, only the first volume of a printed catalog was produced under Panizzi.[13]

Scholarly attention to endless additions clashed with the exigencies of an inflexible printed format. Much of Panizzi's philosophy of cataloging was violated in practice. The degree of detail in the British Museum catalog has varied with time. Early volumes, to be incorporated in much later printed issues, did not have information on publisher, pagination, or size. After Panizzi's vividly expressed views on the collocative role of the catalog, main-entry headings in the catalog oddly lacked authors' birth and death dates.

Panizzi, busy with more than cataloging chores, did not live to see his principles implemented, but he was among the first in the modern English-speaking world to essay a standardization of cataloging rules. All later catalogers started with Panizzi to compose their codes, and though the debates of his time are still with us, suggested solutions are largely expansions or refinements of the "Ninety-One Rules."

Charles Coffin Jewett (1816–68), a very active and influential American librarian of his time, is today only of historical importance. He was the link between Panizzi and Cutter, the latter rivaling Dewey as the most significant American librarian of the final quarter of the nineteenth century. Like Panizzi, Jewett stressed usefulness as a catalog criterion and strove to reduce cataloging inconsistency through a list of rules. Panizzi wrote his rules for the British Museum, and may have hoped for their wider influence, but Jewett from the start meant his for all American libraries.

In 1852 Jewett published *On the Construction of Catalogues of Libraries and of a General Catalogue, and Their Publication by Means of Separate Stereotype Titles. With Rules and Examples.*[14] These thirty-three rules were based on the "Ninety-One Rules" of Panizzi, which Jewett revised in some respects. Like Panizzi, Jewett wanted an author listing for the general catalog to be supplemented by an alphabetical list of subjects. Thus he took into account the two approaches to information. His later work from 1857 at the Boston Public Library contributed a pattern for the dictionary catalog and the verbal subject-heading techniques advocated by Cutter in 1876.

13. For the catalogs of printed books in the British Museum library (made part of the British Library in 1973), see Sheehy, *Guide*, AA132–34, 791.

14. Charles Coffin Jewett, *On the Construction of Catalogues of Libraries and of a General Catalogue, and Their Publication by Means of Separate Stereotype Titles. With Rules and Examples* (Washington: Smithsonian Institution, 1852).

Jewett is most remembered as an early proponent of centralized cooperative cataloging and of an international union catalog. Those ideals were not to be realized during his lifetime. Only in 1901 did his first ideal come to partial fruition when LC began to sell sets of its printed catalog cards. (Jewett was fired from the Smithsonian after the mechanical failure of his stereotype plate project, a failure reputed as welcome to his superior.) His universal union catalog, not unlike Gesner's *Bibliotheca Universalis,* is still not achieved.

In 1876 Cutter, continuing the efforts towards cataloging standardization of Panizzi and Jewett, first published his *Rules.* The fourth edition appeared in 1904, a year after Cutter's death. The fourth edition combined rules for author and title entry, descriptive cataloging, subject headings and filing. No other American code has had so long-lasting an influence. Today's library users, both practitioners and patrons, still have to cope with its effects on bibliographic records and access to recorded information. Especially in traditional subject heading work, there has been little change since Cutter's *Rules.* Early in his *Rules* he described the general nature of any catalog, that is, the roles of access points in retrieving the information needed by users. Cutter's now familiar list included "Objects" (that is, "Purposes") and "Means" (that is, "Access Points") of the library's dictionary catalog. The *Rules* were originally written for printed bookform catalogs but are mostly still applicable for card and online catalogs.

Objects

1. To enable a person to find a book of which either
   (A) the author
   (B) the title } is known
   (C) the subject
2. To show what the library has
   (D) by a given author
   (E) on a given subject
   (F) in a given kind of literature
3. To assist in the choice of a book
   (G) as to its edition (bibliographically)
   (H) as to its character (literary or topical)

Means

1. Author-entry with the necessary references (for A and D)
2. Title-entry or title-reference (for B)
3. Subject-entry, cross-references and classed subject table (for C and E)
4. Form-entry and language entry (for F)

5. Giving edition and imprint, with notes when necessary (for G)
6. Notes (for H)[15]

Cutter's *Rules* endeavored to show how a library's dictionary catalog in one unbroken alphabetical sequence could provide both approaches to information. Though generally acceptable for the latest applications of descriptive cataloging and subject analysis, Cutter's listing incorporates a multitude of specific problems, especially in subject-heading work, that still concern practitioners and end users. Cutter, aware of most of these problems, was unable to offer final solutions. In his *Rules* Cutter mandated only one part of subject analysis, the use of standardized verbalizations in alphabetical order. He tried hard to minimize the classificatory aspect in this subject approach, although he had already begun his own Expansive Classification (EC) at the Boston Athenaeum and, indeed, devoted much of his time to it thereafter. His rules for subject headings probably impressed American librarians of the time more than any other part of his *Rules* and fundamentally affected how they and their clients accepted the verbalized subject approach to information. Today this acceptance has been strengthened by thesaurus availability and the latest computerized techniques.

The imprecision of library terminology, which is still with us, is demonstrated in Cutter's listing of objects and means. Everything on the bibliographic record except for subject headings and classification notation are currently the responsibilities of the descriptive cataloger. All Cutter's objects except for 1C and 2E would be fulfilled by descriptive cataloging, and all means except for 3 would be supplied by the same process. However, a subject approach is sometimes made available by descriptive catalogers, e.g., subject content is often revealed by means 2 and by the contents notes of means 6. Also, though Cutter has been described by a twentieth-century commentator as thinking of form entry in means 4 as independent of both subject analysis and descriptive cataloging,[16] form entry as well as language entry headings are today made by subject analysts.

The overarching problems of Cutter's *Rules* were anticipated by the codes of Panizzi and Jewett: (1) the finding list versus collocative bibliographic reference purpose of a library catalog; (2) short versus full records; and (3) subject headings versus classification.

15. Cutter, *Rules for a Dictionary Catalog*, 4th ed., rewritten, 12. This edition was published in 1904 under the same auspices as the earlier ones. Note the dropping of *Printed* in the title.

16. Francis L. Miksa, *The Subject in the Dictionary Catalog from Cutter to the Present* (Chicago: ALA, 1983), 124.

Cutter's objects 1 and 2 show that he was in the camp of Panizzi, who favored a collocative purpose. The British Museum catalog did not attain Panizzi's ideal, but at least Panizzi had stated it unequivocally. The question remains as to whether any catalog can with equal effectiveness achieve both purposes. Experience points to a negative answer. The degree of collocation in our American bibliographic surrogates varies, LC's being the most adequate. The British Museum catalog for much of its existence yielded incomplete collocation. In general, American searchers find that commercially provided catalogs and bibliographies do not measure up to LC standards.

Cutter, following contemporary models like those of Jewett's Boston Public Library catalogs,[17] used main entries for the fullest bibliographic records and added entries for abbreviated detail. The added entries, those under additional access points, could have enough information for retrieval of the work, thus fulfilling the finding list role of the catalog. (One must distinguish "main entry" from "main-entry heading," the latter the element beginning the full bibliographic record, usually with the author's name. Unfortunately, librarians use "entry" for "entry heading"—a confusion this book hopes to avoid.) The purpose of abbreviated entries was to save space in the printed bookform catalogs for which Cutter's original edition of the *Rules* was written. It would have been more convenient, but much more expensive in printing, if the user were to find a complete bibliographic record under every access point. At least one full main entry was available to which abbreviated added entries could direct the user.

In the fourth edition of his *Rules* Cutter noted that LC had been selling sets of identical copies of its printed catalog cards since 1901. Local librarians could type added-entry headings at the top of these unit records and offer a full bibliographic record under every access point chosen from the tracings at the bottom of every card. This growing role of LC in standardizing cataloging prompted Cutter to doubt the future of local original cataloging.[18] Cutter's doubt has been eroded over time, especially by the increasingly complex cataloging codes of the twentieth century and the need for local libraries to make numerous changes even in preparing catalog records from copy.

In codifying subject headings for the dictionary catalog, Cutter tried to distinguish their use from that of a classification scheme and so set the pattern for all later use of subject headings in American libraries. In its simplest sense, as explained by Ernest A. Savage (1877–1966), to

17. For example, Boston, Public Library, *Index to the Catalogue of Books in the Upper Hall of the Public Library of the City of Boston* (Boston: Rand & Avery, 1861).

18. Cutter, *Rules for a Dictionary Catalog*, 4th ed., 5.

classify means to group by some similar characteristic.[19] Grouping already occurs, even in descriptive cataloging, when all the works of an author are entered under last name and subdivided by the author's given names. (Even the entering of a single work by author's last name may be considered a kind of classification, that is, grouping.) Since the subject heading was to be used for more than one book, if Cutter's object 2E was to be satisfied, a grouping or classificatory element was not only sought but inevitable. Cutter yet worked his utmost to keep the verbal subject heading from identification with its classification cousin, though in some ways he fostered the equivalence. He prided himself on what we would consider a classificatory element in his subject-heading relationships, that is, his "syndetic" structure of cross-references: "see" references from unused to used headings, and "see also" references to other used headings. Though he did not theoretically oppose "see also" references to more general or embracing headings, he ruled that, except for rare cases, "see also" references should refer only downwards (subordinate), or to those on the same level of specificity (coordinate). His objection to upwards (superordinate) "see also" references was a practical one. Once we attempt to make upwards "see also" references, the task is endless. For a similar reason, despite the second half of his means 3, he advised against constructing a classified table for subject headings, which would mean an index to the syndetic structure.[20] (The most that traditional subject-heading workers did for their clients was to list alphabetically in the catalog the important "see also" references from the superior or related subject heading.) Cutter believed his syndesis or binding together of subject headings combined the advantages of specificity with hierarchy, at least in relation to other than inclusive or superior headings, and he did not consider this mixture of verbal and classification elements to be a contradiction.

Such syndesis does not separate downwards from coordinate or nonhierarchical "see also" references, besides not carrying hierarchical relationships to their logical conclusion. Building a thesaurus, to be discussed later, is an effort to provide complete syndesis for verbal headings or descriptors.

Though Cutter and some later classificationists seemed to equate the verbal subject heading with the verbal classification term, it is important in this necessarily preliminary account to understand that even when the subject heading and the classification term have exactly the same wording, they serve different functions. The function of the subject heading is to

19. Ernest A. Savage, *Manual of Book Classification and Display for Public Libraries* (London: G. Allen & Unwin, 1949), 10–11.

20. Cutter, *Rules for a Dictionary Catalog*, 4th ed., 80.

indicate a major topic dealt with in a major way by one or more whole works. The classification term, when placed in correct order with other terms, stands in a systematic, usually hierarchic, relationship to them. "Correct" will vary with the classificationists' theories. Any deeper analysis will lead us into an epistemological no-man's-land. For the user, "correct" should be interpreted as helpful or useful. Controversy over the number of subject headings and classification terms that should be assigned a whole work, monograph, or serial article or technical report continues. Analytical access becomes a concern at this point, and the various techniques of indexing (in its most specific sense) become all-important.

Cutter's *Rules* remains the fountainhead of all later American approaches to information, both through descriptive cataloging and subject analysis. His *Rules* was the basis for the *Library of Congress Subject Headings (LCSH)* and for its progeny, the *Sears List of Subject Headings*, designed for public and school libraries.[21] Though not described in the *Rules*, Cutter's EC became the chief model for LCC. His influence was perhaps less permanent on the details of our later descriptive cataloging codes, though his different headings for societies versus institutions had to be reviewed by Seymour Lubetzky (1898–), then at LC, at the request of those designing a new cataloging code.[22] Lubetzky's simplifying recommendations on this and other matters were incorporated in the 1967 first edition of the *Anglo-American Cataloging Rules* (AACR), but for some years only in the British text, not the North American text.[23]

A study of Cutter's *Rules* is a reminder that, like all of us, he could be inconsistent, even contradictory. A specialized part of our library literature consists of criticisms of Cutter's *Rules*. His *Rules* cannot be regarded as sacrosanct, to be applied unchanged to changing conditions, though most of his principles survive. That is not to say that we are not still grappling with the same problems with which he contended. His attitude towards types of users resulted in conflicts with standardization in our period of centralization and networking.

The "average" user of any collection is, of course, an abstraction. Cutter wrote that often the type of collection, e.g., medical literature, is equivalent to its type of user, in this case the medical student or practitioner. Cutter recognized the different vocabularies of the scholarly or

21. Library of Congress, Subject Cataloging Division, *Library of Congress Subject Headings*, 11th ed., 3 vols. (Washington: The Library, 1988); Minnie Earle Sears, *List of Subject Headings for Small Libraries* (New York: Wilson, 1923).

22. Seymour Lubetzky, *Code of Cataloging Rules: Author and Title; an Unfinished Draft . . . with an Explanatory Commentary by Paul Dunkin* (Chicago: ALA, 1960).

23. The gradual disappearance of the differences between the two texts is detailed in the next chapter.

scientific user of a specialized collection and of the layperson using a general popular collection. For the latter, the common, even colloquial, verbal form was preferred; for the former, the scientific or technical term. When both classes of users are involved—and a heterogeneous collection may have both classes of users, depending on their familiarity with any subject in the collection—the library catalog can appropriately use "see" references to the term chosen. We accept a dual terminology outside of the library catalog, such as in general dictionaries, and zoological or horticultural parks, respectively: earache and otalgia, tiger and panthera tigris, honeysuckle and lonicera.

Cutter's emphasis on types of users, which he equated with types of collections, was carried over into his EC, whose several expansions increased in specificity for increasing sizes of subject collections. Unfortunately, EC was not completely expandible, that is, a change from one expansion to another could necessitate changes in previous notations, not just additions to them. (Dewey's scheme now claims complete expansibility).

The year 1876 was an *annus mirabilis* for American librarianship, with its institutionalization as a profession and, as we have seen, the publication of codes and rules governing approaches to recorded knowledge in collections. Cutter's *Rules* was published in 1876 as part of the United States Bureau of Education *Public Libraries in the United States of America*, to which leading American librarians had been invited to contribute. In the report, "public libraries" included academic and special collections. Commemorating the hundreth anniversary of the founding of the United States, the extensive report was presented at the first conference of American librarians, which was held in Philadelphia at the time of the Centennial Exposition. That year also saw publication of the forty-four–page first edition of the Dewey Decimal Classification (DDC).

Thus far, we have been largely concerned with overall access to information in larger formats, e.g., monographs. There is at least an equivalent need for analytical subject and descriptive cataloging access both to information in smaller units within journal articles and technical reports, and to information in monographs that is too specific to be described by traditional subject headings, classification schemes, and descriptive cataloging codes.

Nineteenth-century American librarians recognized the necessity for analytical access and tried to provide for it in their library catalogs. William Eaton Foster (1851–1930) of the Providence, Rhode Island, Public Library described in 1887 the ideal but elusive analytical omnimedia catalog. Such a catalog would give a searcher of information, say on the "Indian question," not only access to monographs but also full detailed access to

> Fiction and poetry concerned with Indian characters, government reports on the subject, works of exploration among the settlements, maps of their allotments, biographies and portraits of prominent Indians, works on their dialects and literature, speeches in Congress on the subject, newspaper and magazine articles about them, addresses on the subject printed in newspapers and pamphlets.[24]

Even if the ideal has remained elusive, the nineteenth-century printed bookform catalogs of major American libraries—Boston Athenaeum, Boston Public, Brooklyn, Peabody Institute in Baltimore—all made the effort. Jewett's 1861 *Index to the Catalogue of Books in the Upper Hall of the Public Library of the City of Boston*, emulating the "alphabetical topical analysis" of the sessional papers of the British Parliament and of U.S. congressional documents, included a separate alphabet of subjects for government documents, unfortunately not incorporated into the main listing.[25] Published between 1874 and 1882, Cutter's Boston Athenaeum catalog listed, in addition to contents notes for book chapters, many analytical references (i.e., entries) in "short style." These included, for example, "Blount, Wm. Corbett, W. Impeachment of B. (*In* Cobbett, W. Porcupine's works. v. 9. 1801.)"[26]

John Shaw Billings (1838–1913) took charge in 1864 of the Library of the Surgeon General's Office, forerunner of the National Library of Medicine, and issued in 1876 the *Specimen Fasciculus of a Catalogue of the National Medical Library*.[27] This work gave authors and subjects for books *and* subjects for journal articles in one alphabet. After Billings became the first director of the New York Public Library in 1896, he established a card "index-catalogue" in April 1898, which listed books and periodical articles in one alphabet.

In his preface to the 1881 edition of the *Analytical and Classed Catalogue of the Brooklyn Library: Authors, Titles, Subjects and Classes*, Stephen Buttrick Noyes (1833–85) cited statistics for the catalog as "very largely analytical and synoptical." Of 12,000 title entries, 1,794 were titles of plays analyzed from collective works. Also:

24. William Eaton Foster, "A Library's Maximum of Usefulness," *Library Notes* 2 (Dec. 1887):203.

25. Boston, Public Library, *Index to the Catalog of Books* . . . , iv: "Prepared by C. C. Jewett, assisted by Frederick Vinton and William E. Jillson."

26. Boston Athenaeum, *Catalogue of the Library of the Boston Athenaeum. 1807–1881* . . . , 5 vols. (1874–82; reprint ed.: Boston: G. K. Hall, 1969), 1:319.

27. U.S. National Medical Library, *Specimen Fasciculus of a Catalogue of the National Medical Library, under the Direction of the Surgeon-General, United States Army, at Washington, D.C.* (Washington: Govt. Print. Off., 1876).

> The subject entries, by analysis of collective works and collections of essays, amount to somewhat more than 13,000, and of articles in the periodical literature of the last twenty-five years, to 11,400, or a total of about 25,000 analytical subject references, bibliographically exact, in addition to 26,000 principal subject entries.[28]

The Brooklyn catalog paid particular attention to analytics for biographical information. Contents of collections and collective and miscellaneous works were given in alphabetical subject order by title keywords. As we have seen, Cutter proposed standardized subject headings to replace such inconsistent title keywords.

The 1883 first volume of the *Catalogue of the Library* of the Peabody Institute of the City of Baltimore reaffirmed the importance of "indexing," that is, creating analytics.[29] In a single alphabet, that catalog had author, title, and subject entries for books and appropriate index entries for periodical articles, bound pamphlets, publications of scholarly and learned groups, historical, antiquarian, and other miscellaneous collections. It also, like the Brooklyn catalog, listed the contents of book chapters alphabetically by title keywords.

In 1867 the Royal Society of London began to publish its *Catalogue of Scientific Papers, 1800–1900*, actually a union catalog.[30] This author index to 1,555 periodicals in different languages was to be supplemented by separate subject index volumes to seventeen sciences, but only three such indexes had been published by 1925, when the project was terminated. This loss of subject analytical access memorializes a classic bibliographic failure.

In the late 1870s, the American librarian William Frederick Poole (1844–1894) enlisted American and British librarian volunteers to index American and British general serials. The resulting *Poole's Index to Periodical Literature, 1802–1906*, including *Supplements*, was the progenitor of many other periodical indexes, often on special subjects, to appear in this country and England.[31] *Poole's Index* was a subject index only and used title-derived catchwords.

28. Stephen Buttrick Noyes, "Preface," in Brooklyn Library, *Analytical and Classed Catalogue of the Brooklyn Library: Authors, Titles, Subjects, and Classes*, new ed. (Brooklyn, N.Y.: The Library, 1881), iii–iv.

29. Peabody Institute, Baltimore, Library, *Catalogue of the Library*, 13 vols. (1883–1905; reprint ed.: Boston: G. K. Hall, 1960?–61), vol. 1.

30. Royal Society of London, *Catalogue of Scientific Papers, 1800–1900*, 19 vols. (London: Clay, 1867–1902; Cambridge: University Press, 1914–25); *Subject Index*, vols. 1–3 in 4 (Cambridge: University Press, 1908–14).

31. *Poole's Index to Periodical Literature*, 1802–81, rev. ed., 2 vols. (1891; reprint ed.: New York: P. Smith, 1938; Gloucester, Mass.: P. Smith, 1963); *Supplements*, Jan. 1882–Jan. 1, 1907, 5 vols. (Boston: Houghton, c1887–1908).

From 1895 to 1940, under varying auspices, Concilium Bibliographicum produced the *Zurich Index*, catalog cards giving descriptive cataloging information chiefly for periodical articles on the life sciences.[32] This index covered literature in many languages.

Classification has been applied to subject-analytical access to other scientific and technical literature. In 1895 two Belgians, Paul Otlet (1868–1944) and Henri-Marie LaFontaine (1854–1943), obtained permission from Dewey to adapt the Dewey Decimal Classification for very detailed analysis in classified catalogs. The 1895 Brussels Classification (also known as the System of the Brussels Institute) resulted, as well as the later Universal Decimal Classification (UDC).[33]

After Cutter's *Rules*, American librarians emphasized subject access through alphabetical subject headings, an emphasis buttressed by the popularity of the dictionary catalog. The first standard listing was the American Library Association (ALA) 1895 *ALA List of Subject Headings* for smaller and medium-size public libraries,[34] but the authority for all libraries was the *LCSH*, whose first edition appeared in 1897 and whose theory and structure stem largely from Cutter's *Rules*. Problems of analytical access to information in monographs continue, but much of the serial literature now has analytical subject access—using verbalized descriptions—through printed indexes and especially databases.

Reflecting on what can be learned from even a fragmentary history of organizing information through surrogates, we realize that those in charge of libraries from ancient times had been aware of the two approaches to recorded information and had tried to make the dual approach possible through access points. Also evident have been the millennial philosophical arguments as to what surrogates should provide and the consequent and sometimes contradictory rules and practices. For the modern searcher the simultaneous existence of many vestiges from these older methodologies in surrogates makes for formidable obstacles to successful retrieval—not to mention the many surrogates that require the user to know a discipline's present and past vocabulary. The rest of this book deals with the practical obstacles described above to aid effective search and retrieval from either printed or computerized records. Starting with the twentieth century, descriptive cataloging codes, classification

32. E.g., Concilium Bibliographicum, Zürich . . . , *Sectio Zoologica Concilii Bibliographici Opibus Complurium Nationum Turici Instituti; Editiones: Anglica, Gallica et Germanica* . . . (Turici: Concilium Bibliographicum, 1897). Commonly known as the *Zurich Index*.

33. For bibliographic detail on various editions of this classification and on related works, see Sheehy, *Guide to Reference Books*, 10th ed., AB237–39.

34. American Library Association, *List of Subject Headings for Use in Dictionary Catalogs*, prepared by a committee of the American Library Association (Boston: Published for ALA Publishing Section by the Library Bureau, 1895).

schemes, and subject-heading authorities were numerous and frequent. They have not always removed but have often increased the practical obstacles to search and retrieval.

In greater detail, these obstacles, as presaged in these historical chapters, are: (1) the grouping of works by the same author, regardless of what name or form of name was employed on the title page; (2) the decision on whether the library catalog will be designed as a reference source or a finding list—that is, whether we can expect to find full bibliographic surrogation or only enough data to locate and retrieve the work; (3) determining the relationship between subject headings and classification schemes, which are both part of subject analysis and thus tempting for practitioners to equate; (4) the constant changing of descriptive cataloging codes, subject-heading authorities, and classification schemes as they keep abreast of developing knowledge; and (5) the questioned need both for recataloging and especially for the newest subject analysis as applied to older works in the collection.

Last but not least, a subject not covered in the previous historical summaries but to which more than one coming chapter are devoted is the effect of current technology on librarianship, particularly the use of mechanized surrogates for search and retrieval.

3 PRINTED DESCRIPTIVE CATALOGING ACCESS

To summarize anew, this book is concerned with searching bibliographic surrogates that exhibit the two approaches to the organization of information—that is, surrogates constructed by descriptive cataloging or by subject analysis. Each approach can provide access to monographs and serials considered as wholes or analytical access to parts of monographs and serials.

The first type of approach—descriptive cataloging—is exemplified by the Library of Congress (LC) *National Union Catalog (NUC)*, which in the past has also given analytical access in a very minor way.[1] A representative source in machine-readable form, largely based on LC records for whole books and serials, is the Online Computer Library Center, Inc. (OCLC) Online Union Catalog (OLUC). (In machine-readable form, both types of bibliographic surrogates are called *databases*.)

Descriptive cataloging analytical access to serial literature is illustrated by the various printed indexes of the H. W. Wilson Company. Lately, Wilson has put parts of its indexes online and has also transferred them to compact discs (CDs). In most descriptive cataloging analytical access to serial literature, articles are identified by author, not by title. Some descriptive cataloging indexes to "periodicals" offer, too, analytical access to books. Access to a group of descriptive cataloging periodical indexes is supplied online by such wholesale vendors as the DIALOG Information Retrieval Service. Individual producers of periodical indexes, like Wilson,

1. For the printed *NUC*, its predecessors, and related publications, see the detailed descriptions in Eugene P. Sheehy, comp., *Guide to Reference Books*, 10th ed. (Chicago: ALA, 1986). (For updatings, see the January and July *College & Research Libraries*.)

have not made use of distributors like DIALOG but have been willing to offer their online services through OCLC, a bibliographic utility.[2]

The second approach, resulting in subject analysis bibliographic surrogates, is again taken for monographs and serials as wholes by LC, which issues records (now in microfiche) under its subject headings of items appearing in the *NUC*. It also issues the printed *Library of Congress Subject Headings (LCSH)*, which is the American authority.[3] All of the major bibliographic utilities subscribe to the LC Machine-Readable Cataloging (MARC) service. The MARC records, based on *LCSH* and the current *Anglo-American Cataloguing Rules*, make up part of the databases of OCLC and the Research Libraries Group (RLG), to name only the two largest utilities.

Subject analytical access to serial literature is given, as is the descriptive cataloging approach, through such indexes as those of the H. W. Wilson Company. (Again some "periodical" indexes also provide analytical access to books.) Distribution of both the subject analytical indexes and the descriptive cataloging analytical indexes is the same as for the above described descriptive cataloging analytical indexes. Most indexes, in fact, combine both approaches in the same publication. Occasionally, as in some of the printed Wilson publications or in the *Public Affairs Information Service (PAIS) Bulletin*, the index will offer only subject access.

This chapter discusses printed descriptive cataloging bibliographic surrogates for access to books and serials as wholes and for analytical access to them. This chapter shows also, not for the last time, that printed and automated bibliographic surrogates may overlap in content.

Despite the ever-increasing presence of computerized surrogates, most libraries of any size or age still resort to manual searches of printed and microform records, not to mention noncomputerized searches of printed indexes in monographs and reference tools. There are interrelated reasons for this continuing reliance on printed surrogates:

1. First, and perhaps foremost, the stock of printed surrogates for whole books and serials is much greater than in machine-readable databases. When the 754-volume *Pre-1956 NUC* was completed in 1981 after more than a decade, its entries were estimated at 11.2 million, about twice the size of the OCLC OLUC, and about 80 percent of the entries were not duplicated

2. "WILSONLINE, VU/TEXT to Become Available via OCLC Intelligent Gateway Service," *OCLC Newsletter*, no. 164 (Aug. 1986):9; "OCLC LINK Service Now Available," ibid., no. 166 (Jan. 1987):8.

3. Library of Congress, Subject Cataloging Division, *Library of Congress Subject Headings*, 11th ed., 3 vols. (Washington: The Library, 1988). Updated by printed *Weekly Lists*, distributed monthly, and by quarterly cumulative editions in microfiche.

by the online network catalogs. About 20 million cards were edited for the *Pre-1956 NUC*.[4] Since then, the margin between *NUC* and online catalog entries has narrowed, caused, among other things, by the retrospective conversion (RETROCON) of bibliographic records to machine-readable format by network subscriber libraries. At the end of 1987, OCLC claimed 17 million records had been entered into OLUC at the annual rate of around two million entries.[5] At the beginning of 1988, RLIN announced it had 25 million book records in its online union catalog, probably including many duplicate entries.[6] Uncontested, however, is that the complete printed or microform *NUC* has more entries than either OCLC or RLIN, and that OCLC has more unduplicated entries for book titles than RLIN.

2. Though computerization of catalogs like the entire *NUC* is underway, LC has acknowledged that the project, under long-term contractual commitment, will not be completed for many years. Henriette D. Avram of LC confirmed this at the 1985 Winter Dinner Meeting of the New York Technical Services Librarians. In this case of machine conversion, as in many others, "computerization" does not mean recataloging to agree with the latest descriptive cataloging codes.

3. Computerization of surrogates for journal literature in databases has been restricted by chronology, original format, and subject matter. Databases cannot now be searched for serial literature surrogates that are older in general than fifteen years. Almost nonexistent is computerized access to information in nonserial literature, e.g., in back-of-the-book indexes and, perhaps less needed, in the indexes to much-used reference books. Also, databases cover mostly technical, scientific, or commercial subjects. They have not given equivalent attention to the journal literatures of the social sciences and humanities. This focus is understandable since databases are generally constructed and made available by profit-making subject-specialized agencies, which tailor the product to the market.

4. John Young Cole, "*National Union Catalog: Pre-1956 Imprints*; a Celebration of Its Completion; a Program Sponsored by the Center for the Book, Library of Congress, January 27–28, 1981," *Library of Congress Information Bulletin* 40 (Feb. 20, 1981):65–68; Arthur Plotnik, "News That Stays News," *American Libraries* 12 (Sept. 1981):453.

5. "Duke University Captures the 17 Millionth Record in the OCLC Database. . . . One Million Records Added to Database in 152 Days," *OCLC Newsletter*, no. 171 (Jan./Feb. 1988):7.

6. "25,000,000th Book Record in RLIN—A Milestone for CSL and RLG," *Operations Update*, no. 46 (Mar. 1988):12.

For all the above reasons, computerized search of surrogates is not always possible or desirable. Although searching effectiveness can be much enhanced by automated access, searches are often ideally undertaken in printed surrogates or sometimes by combining manual and computer techniques. As Ralph R. Shaw pointed out many years ago, some tasks are more easily and accurately accomplished by using mechanical and manual methods at different stages.[7] Almost all libraries still must refer to printed surrogates in searching for information. The appropriate conditions for an exclusively computer search, including the absence of limitations, are discussed in Chapter 6.

The pattern for descriptive cataloging records has been set by LC. When LC began selling its catalog cards to American libraries in 1901, making them available for reference first in depository catalogs, and then in 1942 as reduced copies in book form, it established and strengthened its position as the purveyor of descriptive cataloging records to the nation. (The subject analysis standards of LC are considered in Chapter 4.) This situation represented a de facto reality, since LC was not legally required to perform such a function. The widely purchased LC catalog cards, available also in machine-readable format since the late 1960s, were products of rules and procedures that, if good enough for LC, were surely adequate for other American general libraries acquiring the same items. The present *NUC*, combining the cataloging of LC and cooperating libraries, constitutes the official source of catalog records for this country. All other American catalogs and bibliographies take off from the *NUC*.

Many complications had arisen since Cutter's 1876 *Rules*, and by 1877 Cutter already had begun to help the American Library Association (ALA) construct rules to meet these complications.[8] The need for an official code seemed urgent, though a consensus was not to emerge for another twenty-five years.

The first twentieth-century product of an American committee's work was the 1902 *A. L. A. Rules—Advance Edition*, a draft code submitted for criticism and comments from American librarians.[9] The committee, which

7. Ralph R. Shaw, *Machines and the Bibliographic Problems of the Twentieth Century . . . and Management, Machines and Bibliographic Problems of the Twentieth Century* (Washington: Govt. Print. Off., 1951), 52–53.

8. Charles Ammi Cutter, *Rules for a Printed Dictionary Catalog*, in U.S. Bureau of Education, *Public Libraries in the United States of America; Their History, Condition and Management; Special Report; Part 2*, 2 vols. in 1 (Washington: Govt. Print. Off., 1876).

9. For a short history of the development of most modern descriptive cataloging codes, see Kathryn Luther Henderson, "Treated with a Degree of Uniformity and Common Sense: Descriptive Cataloging in the United States, 1876–1975," *Library Trends* 25 (July 1976):227–61. American Library Association, *A.L.A. Rules—Advance Edition. Condensed Rules for an Author and Title Catalog*, prepared by the Cooperation Committee of the American Library Association, 1883; revised by the Advisory Catalog Committee, 1902; issued by the Library of Congress (Washington: Govt. Print. Off., Library Division, 1902).

began its work in 1901, attempted to reconcile LC procedures with the bibliographic requirements of other libraries and also "to bring about uniformity between its version of the *A. L. A. Rules*, the 4th edition of Cutter's *Rules for a Dictionary Catalog*, then about to be issued, and a new edition of the *Library School Rules*, the issue of which was also under consideration."[10]

Librarianship as a profession, at least in modern times, has striven for international cooperation and standards. It was thus appropriate that our first commonly acceptable twentieth-century descriptive cataloging code was written for the English-speaking world. In 1904 the Americans joined with the British in a joint revision committee. *Catalog Rules, Author and Title Entries (Joint Anglo-American Code)*, prepared by committees of the ALA and the British Library Association (LA) in 1908, though, had to be published in both American and British editions, with the British rule differences noted in the American edition and the American cataloging practices noted in the British edition.[11] Almost immediately, librarians complained that the rules were too complicated and did not cover many troublesome situations.

The next Anglo-American committee effort was interrupted by the Second World War. It was left to the American members to publish their 1941 preliminary edition of the *A.L.A. Catalog Rules, Author and Title Entries*, which included new rules for entry and heading but despite its title included unrevised rules for description proper, e.g., for imprints.[12] As already explained, descriptive cataloging aims not only to give a unique physical description of the information container but also to establish the identity and form of name of the intellectual responsibility. The 1949 *A.L.A. Cataloging Rules for Author and Title Entries* (the *Red Rules*) omitted the physical description part of the preliminary edition.[13] Instead, a sec-

10. Ibid., vi. The codes referred to are: American Library Association, *A. L. A. Rules*, first submitted at the Buffalo conference of ALA in 1883, printed in full in the *Proceedings* of that year in *Library Journal* 8 (Sept.–Oct. 1883):251–54, and reprinted in Cutter, *Rules for a Dictionary Catalog*, 2nd ed., 1889; 3rd ed., 1891 (Washington: Govt. Print. Off.); and 4th ed., rewritten (Washington: Govt. Print. Off., 1904); Melvil Dewey, *Library School Rules*, 3rd ed. (Boston: Library Bureau, 1894); idem, *Simplified Library School Rules* (Boston: Library Bureau, 1898).

11. American Library Association, *Catalog Rules, Author and Title Entries*, compiled by committees of the American Library Association and the (British) Library Association, American ed. (Boston: ALA Publishing Board, 1908).

12. Idem, Catalog Code Revision Committee, *A. L. A. Cataloging Rules, Author and Title Entries*, preliminary American 2nd ed., prepared by the Catalog Code Revision Committee of the American Library Association, with the collaboration of a committee of the (British) Library Association (Chicago: ALA, 1941).

13. Idem, Division of Cataloging and Classification, Clara Beetle, ed., *ALA Cataloging Rules for Author and Title Entries*, 2nd ed. (Chicago: ALA, 1949).

ond volume was accepted by the committee to complement its *Red Rules*. This was the LC *Rules for Descriptive Cataloging* (the *Green Rules*), also published in 1949.[14]

Objections to the 1949 *Red Rules* were again that the rules were too legalistic and that they did not answer many cataloging problems. As usual, committees were appointed to investigate the difficulties and to propose solutions. Postwar cooperation was broadened to include opinions from countries other than America and England. An American, Lubetzky, was commissioned to prepare a research report on problems to be dealt with by a new code, some of which were created by Cutter's 1876 *Rules*![15] Lubetzky's recommendations were accepted at the 1961 Paris International Conference on Cataloguing Principles.[16] The 1967 *Anglo-American Cataloging Rules (AACR)* gave rules for all descriptive cataloging functions, including those in the *Red Rules* and the *Green Rules*. *AACR* was opposed by American library representatives in some respects, especially the internationally accepted Lubetzky suggestions. The Association of Research Libraries (ARL) and LC protested that some of the rule changes were unacceptably expensive for large libraries with established catalogs. As a result, the 1967 *AACR* was published in both North American and British texts. The differences were few but significant.[17] LC even stated that it would not abide with rules appearing in the North American text for entry of serials![18]

LC gradually softened its opposition and announced a sometimes confusing series of policies. First, it proclaimed "superimposition," which meant that some rule changes, though not those for serials, would be applied in the case of first-time entry but not to headings already established.[19] In April 1971, LC announced it would adopt the *AACR* successive cataloging of serials.[20] The *AACR* policy meant that a change in

14. U.S. Library of Congress, Descriptive Cataloging Division, *Rules for Descriptive Cataloging in the Library of Congress (Adopted by the American Library Association)* (Washington: Govt. Print. Off., 1949).

15. Seymour Lubetzky, *Cataloging Rules and Principles: A Critique of the ALA Rules for Entry and a Proposed Design for Their Revision* (Washington: Library of Congress, 1953); idem, *Code of Cataloging Rules, Author and Title; an Unfinished Draft . . . with an Explanatory Commentary by Paul Dunkin* (Chicago: ALA, 1960).

16. International Conference on Cataloguing Principles, Paris, 9–18 October 1961, *Report* (London: International Federation of Library Associations, 1963).

17. *Anglo-American Cataloging Rules, North American Text*, C. Sumner Spalding, general ed. (Chicago: ALA, 1967), 371.

18. Ibid., 22, footnote 12; 238, footnote 4.

19. "Application of the Anglo-American Cataloging Rules at the Library of Congress," Library of Congress, Processing Department, *Cataloging Service*, bulletin 79 (Jan. 1967): 1–2; ibid., bulletin 80 (Apr. 1967): 1–2.

20. "Cataloging of Serials," Library of Congress, Processing Department, *Cataloging Service*, bulletin 99 (Apr. 1971):1.

the main-entry heading of the serial would require a new bibliographic record.

The 1967 *AACR* successor, the 1978 *Anglo-American Cataloguing Rules,* second edition *(AACR2),* was another international committee project, and LC agreed initially to apply it as of 1980. On that date LC would freeze its old catalog and, to comply with *AACR2*, abandon superimposition, the latter change also known as "desuperimposition."[21] Before this implementation date, deferred at the request of large research and academic libraries until 1981, LC had begun to study the optional rules authorized in *AACR2* to decide which of them to adopt.[22] The decisions were announced and published in official organs almost two and one-half years before the postponed implementation date.[23]

However, as a compromise replacement for superimposition, LC initiated a policy of "compatible" or "tolerable headings." After studying a complex list of criteria, a cataloger could supply a heading as long as it did not contradict *AACR2*, even if the heading was not exactly what *AACR2* had legislated.[24] LC finally decided to drop this compromise policy as of September 1, 1982, because it depended on a hopelessly subjective evaluation by catalogers.[25]

Even when LC dropped superimposition and compatible headings, it did not change all pre-1983 *NUC* records to accord with the latest cataloging rules. In general, pre-1983 *NUC* records remained as cataloged originally by LC or as edited by LC for contributed records. Indeed, when LC announced cessation of its policy of compatible headings, it took pains to state that already established compatible headings would not be changed—a reminder that superimposition was still alive in a different form. However, in preparation for its 1981 acceptance of *AACR2*,

21. *Anglo-American Cataloguing Rules*, 2nd ed., Michael Gorman and Paul W. Winkler, eds. (Chicago: ALA, 1978); "LC to Freeze Card Catalog," *Library of Congress Information Bulletin* 36 (Nov. 4, 1977):743–744; "Freezing the Library of Congress Catalog," ibid. 37 (Mar. 3, 1978):152–56; "Information on Freezing the Catalog Updated," ibid. 37 (July 21, 1978):415–19.

22. "AACR 2: Implementation Postponement," *Cataloging Service Bulletin*, no. 2 (Fall 1978):3.

23. "AACR 2 Options to Be Followed by the Library of Congress," *Cataloging Service Bulletin*, no. 2 (Fall 1978):18–29; ibid., no. 8 (Spring 1980):8–14; ibid., no. 16 (Spring 1982):51.

24. "AACR 2 Implementation Plans," *Cataloging Service Bulletin*, no. 3 (Winter 1979):3–7; "Implementation of AACR 2 at the Library of Congress," ibid., no. 6 (Fall 1979):5–8; "Freezing the Library of Congress Catalogs: Descriptive Cataloging Systems," ibid., no. 8 (Spring 1980):3–4.

25. " 'Compatible Headings' Policy Will Cease on September 1st," *Library of Congress Information Bulletin* 41 (May 28, 1982):152; "Compatible Headings," *Cataloging Service Bulletin*, no. 17 (Summer 1982):31; "AACR 2 Compatible Headings," ibid., no. 18 (Fall 1982):49–51.

LC in late 1979 considered a project (BibFlip) for "flipping" monograph and serial headings of its MARC records for items cataloged in machine-readable format since the late 1960s. Only the heading was to be changed to *AACR2* standards; the remainder of the record would be left as cataloged by LC. The project would affect the LC-issued machine-readable records of the pre-1981 era. On the project's completion in March 1986, 238,751 MARC book records headings were changed over a thirty-month period by an outside processor.[26] Libraries with machine-readable catalogs may thus end up with *AACR2* headings for pre-*AACR2* records going back to the 1949 *Rules* or earlier.

Though LC agreed to accept *AACR2* in principle, it reserved the right to take advantage of the *AACR2* rule options and also to interpret the rules as long as the interpretation did not violate the accepted principle. A multitude of LC Rule Interpretations (LCRI) appeared in the LC *Cataloging Service Bulletin*, necessitating frequent cumulative indexes.[27] All these measures, beginning with LC resistance to accepting the first *AACR* even in its North American text, were meant to spare LC and other large libraries from recataloging hundreds of thousands of established records. Fortunately for LC and other huge American libraries, studies showed that *AACR2* conversion would result in a surprisingly manageable labor and cost outlay, although the conclusions of such studies did not at the time appreciably affect LC changes and interpretations.[28]

Like previous international cataloging codes, *AACR2* from its earliest appearance had been subject to many exceptions and variations—principally from LC and gargantuan American collections, and it became increasingly difficult for local American catalogers to keep up with the multitudinous differences. In fact, from the very start of *AACR2*, fears were expressed about an endless chain of new *AACR* editions.[29] To reg-

26. "Bibliographic Flip Project Is Completed," *Library of Congress Information Bulletin* 45 (June 30, 1986):251.

27. For example, "Library of Congress Rule Interpretations (LCRI). Cumulative Index of LCRI That Have Appeared in Issues of *Cataloging Service Bulletin*," *Cataloging Service Bulletin*, no. 41 (Summer 1988):2–11. Commercial indexes to LCRI appear in the bibliography of this book. In 1988, LC announced publication of a loose-leaf collection of all LCRI, to be updated quarterly. ("Cumulative Library of Congress Rule Interpretations," *Cataloging Service Bulletin*, no. 41 (Summer 1988):87–88.)

28. Arlene Taylor Dowell, "Staying Open in 1981," *HCL Cataloging Bulletin*, no. 39 (Mar./Apr. 1979):11–15; Joe A. Hewitt and David E. Gleim, "Adopting AACR 2: The Case for Not Closing the Catalog," *American Libraries* 10 (Mar. 1979):118–21.

29. For example, Phyllis Allen Richmond, "AACR, Second Edition, What Next? [with Discussion]" in *Nature and Future of the Catalog: Proceedings of the ALA's Information Science and Automation Division's 1975 and 1977 Institute on the Catalog*, Maurice J. Freedman and S. Michael Malinconico, eds. (Phoenix, Ariz.: Oryx Press, 1979), 197–200.

ulate these changes officially, at least until the next edition of *AACR*, an international Joint Steering Committee for the Revision of *AACR2* (JSC) began in 1978 to accept or reject changes forwarded by national committees.

A member of the JSC has described its responsibilities and commented that most of the changes sent with copious documentation to the JSC have come from North American libraries, chiefly from the United States. He attributed the comparative paucity of British changes to two possible causes: (1) the British reluctance to change an agreed-on code; and (2) the fact that the two national British cataloging bodies, the Library Association (LA) and the British Library (BL), joined together to submit *AACR2* changes to the JSC, as opposed to the separate agendas and concerns of LC and ALA in the United States.[30]

The latest edition of the *AACR*, published in 1988, is the *Anglo-American Cataloguing Rules*, second edition, revision (*AACR2*, revised), which included all JSC decisions since 1978 (including unpublished revisions authorized by JSC since 1985) as well as the text of *AACR2*.[31] As expected, American practitioners complained about a new code. Richard Smiraglia argued that changes were extensive enough to warrant a retitling to *AACR3*. In an answering article, Michael Gorman, a coeditor of the code, argued there had been no fundamental rethinking of *AACR2* in the 1988 revision, as there had been with *AACR*. He preferred to call the *AACR2*, revised the "daughter of *AACR2*" and claimed that the chief changes were in the chapters for newer library materials like digital recordings and computer software. In describing the hullabaloo over *AACR2*, Gorman used the "felicitous phrase" of Charles Martell: "the war of *AACR2*."[32]

At a program meeting of the ALA Annual Conference in New Orleans, Gorman and Smiraglia met face to face. Gorman repeated his earlier comments but expressed the opinion that the *AACR2*, revised would not wear well because of improved cataloging and because machine searching made the main entry meaningless. He also announced that he was retiring from coeditorship of *AACR* and, perhaps not completely in

30. Eric Joseph Hunter, "*AACR 2*: Revision Mechanisms and Procedures: The Background," *Catalogue & Index*, no. 82 (Autumn 1986):4–7.

31. *Anglo-American Cataloguing Rules*, 2nd ed., revised, Michael Gorman and Paul W. Winkler, eds. (Chicago: ALA, 1988).

32. Richard P. Smiraglia, "The Consolidated Reprinting of *AACR #2*," *Cataloging & Classification Quarterly* 8 (1987):3–6; Michael Gorman, "Daughter of *AACR2*: Call It *AACR2½* or *Après la guerre* or Daughter of a Dynamic Decade," *American Libraries* 19 (May 1988):387–88; Charles Martell, "The War of *AACR2*: Victors or Victims?" *Journal of Academic Librarianship* 7 (Mar. 1981):4–8.

jest, quipped that with his departure, "You won't have Michael Gorman to kick around any more."[33]

Only large American libraries can afford to purchase the entire *NUC* even in microform from LC and commercial vendors, and even as more and more of the *NUC* is put into machine-readable form. Most libraries, though, can consult complete sets in nearby large public and academic libraries. In any case, a knowledge of searching in any chronological section of the *NUC* is vital for all librarians. The brief genealogy in this and the preceding chapters of descriptive cataloging codes from Panizzi to the 1988 *AACR2*, revised has omitted some important developments that are discussed later, e.g., the International Standard Bibliographic Description (ISBD) introduced in 1974 in a separately published revised Chapter 6 of *AACR*.[34] The older codes and LC deviations from them in our catalogs and bibliographies must be kept in mind for effective search and retrieval in the surrogate depository of *NUC*. Works detailing the many rule changes from previous descriptive cataloging codes are listed in the bibliography of this book.

In agreeing to comply with *AACR2* as of January 2, 1981, LC also chose that date to begin a new computerized catalog. The LC announcements used "freeze" rather than "close" to describe what was to be done with its old card catalog, since "freeze" implies that no additions, especially references, would be inserted among the previous records. For 1981 and 1982, between the freezing of its old card catalog and the initiation of the index-register *NUC*, described below, LC in its printed *NUC* made "see" references to real names from pseudonyms, and "search under" references to works cataloged by it before 1981 under non-*AACR2* headings. Since 1983 these references have been omitted. To find out, for example, what names have been used by an author for various cataloged books—since *AACR2* permits main-entry headings for title-page names—the searcher in the post-1982 *NUC* must consult the LC *Name Authorities Cumulative Microform Edition* or standard dictionaries of anonyms and pseudonyms.[35] In fact, consultation of such non-LC reference works is desirable even for searchers of pre-1983 *NUC* who wish to find records of publications appearing in the *NUC* under pseudonyms or anonyms not recognized by catalogers at LC. Searchers after

33. "No More Mr. *AACR2* to Kick Around," *American Libraries* 19 (Sept. 1988):668.

34. *Anglo-American Cataloging Rules, North American Text, Chapter 6 Revised: Separately Published Monographs* (Chicago: ALA, 1974).

35. Library of Congress, *Name Authorities Cumulative Microform Edition*, 1981– (Washington: The Library, 1981–), five issues annually. Supersedes Library of Congress, *Library of Congress Name Headings with References*, 1974–1980 (Washington: The Library, 1974–80), annual cumulations; only source for manual name authority records created by the Library of Congress from 1974 to 1980.

all works by an author, no matter what name appears on the title page, should keep in mind that the *NUC* contains only the records of LC and contributing libraries. Some works by that author may not be recorded in the *NUC*.

Until 1983 the *NUC* was published in print in paperbound monthly issues, quarterly paperbound cumulations, and hard cover annual and multiannual cumulations. From 1969 the *NUC* was also distributed by LC in microfiche. These *NUC* main-entry records were slightly reduced copies of catalog cards back to 1890. After January 1983 the *NUC* was issued only in an index-register format. That format made cumulations of the main-entry records unnecessary. They were now published monthly in random order in the microfiche register, but the cumulative indexes during the calendar year (and multiannual cumulative indexes) led to the register's full main entries. The register entries were identified in the indexes by main-entry and added-entry name headings, monograph titles, series titles and subject headings—all with abbreviated records following. (The added-entry headings, to restate the obvious, are the tracings in the main-entry record.)

The added-entry headings for monograph titles were not previously available in the *NUC*. Monograph titles in a series were usually assigned main entries under their authors or titles in the *NUC*. Only with the 1983 *NUC* was it possible to find in the *NUC* proper all the cataloged items belonging to a series. From 1974 through 1982, searchers for all cataloged series monographs had to resort to a separate LC publication, *Monographic Series*. Before 1974, series listings were not made available by LC.

Only the main entries in the *NUC*, before and after 1983, reproduce the entire bibliographic record, including the tracings. The purpose of the index entries since 1983 is to give enough data to identify the cataloged item and thus to fulfill the finding list function of the catalog. Prior to 1983 the *NUC* also printed expanded references, which were less than full records. (An expanded reference, unlike a "pure" cross-reference, has an abbreviated record.) Searchers might find enough detail in the expanded pre-1983 references or post-1982 index entries (the latter are technically added entries) that they would not need referral to the main entries. The use of expanded references, "pure" cross-references, and shorter added-entry records goes back to the nineteenth century, when saving space in bookform catalogs was economically required. Even when LC introduced the printed unit catalog cards, giving all added-entry cards a full record, abbreviated records and cross-references to full main entries could still be entered under LC-authorized headings in the printed *NUC* as well as in the LC card catalog. So, in the *NUC* from 1981 to 1983, such "search under" references could be found as: "For works cataloged before 1981 search under Clemens, Samuel Langhorne, 1835–1910." Such cross-references did not have abbreviated records, but after 1982 even these cross-references were omitted from the *NUC*.

The name index and the title index of the index-register *NUC* contain records with data through the publication or copyright date—what used to be called the "body of the entry," before *AACR2*. Following these details are the series statement (when available), the LC call number, the LC card number, and, of course, the register number for the full record. Missing are a listing of authors other than the main-entry heading author, the author's name being indexed, the collation—termed by *AACR2* the "Physical Description Area," any notes (including the International Standard Book Number [ISBN], the International Standard Serial Number [ISSN], the Dewey Classification number, and the *Dewey* edition number), and all the tracings. Also omitted in these index entries are the incidental information of the printer's record, an identification for the Annotated Card Series (when necessary), and the cataloging code used, e.g., *AACR2*.

Particularly troublesome to searches that must depend on the name index alone is the omission of any designation of function for added-entry names, e.g., for a joint author or an illustrator. Such information is found only in the text of the main-entry record.

The series index records are similarly abbreviated except that the series statement is omitted. The subject index abbreviated entries exclude the place of publication and the name of the publisher as well as the series statement. Otherwise, the subject index data are the same as in the name and title indexes. Presumably, any added-entry subject heading in the tracings will appear in the subject index, with the exception of special subject headings for juvenile literature in the Annotated Card Series. To find related subject headings not in the subject index, consultation of the *LCSH* would be required.[36] In that current list, for example, as explained in the next chapter, references from broader and narrower subject headings are given and permission is granted to include particular kinds or groups of species entities as subject headings. The inconvenience of switching from an index microfiche to the register index to examine the full record is undeniable. Even looking for the full records of items represented in the index by the same heading means referring to more than one register microfiche. Note taking for index information is ordinarily required. Consultation of the full record in the post-1982 *NUC* register is essential to take thorough advantage of the bibliographic record, for example, when the added-entry headings in the tracings in

36. Library of Congress, Subject Cataloging Division, *Library of Congress Subject Headings*. See note 3.

the full record are needed to explore different aspects of the same work or to collocate related works.

The index-register *NUC* is issued in four editions: *NUC Books*, *NUC U.S. Books*, *NUC Audiovisual Materials*, and *NUC Cartographic Materials*. A companion microfiche publication, valuable for interlibrary loan, is the *NUC Register of Additional Locations*, which is arranged by LC card number and provides location information for monograph titles included in the *NUC*. Other *NUC* catalogs continue to be published in paper editions with the expectation that they will all eventually be converted to microfiche: *National Register of Microform Masters; Music, Books on Music and Sound Recordings*; *Newspapers in Microform*; *New Serial Titles*; and *National Union Catalog of Manuscript Collections*.[37] Although printed monographs are the principal items sought in *NUC* publications, searchers must be aware of these separate catalogs for various media.

Lack of both space and specialized knowledge restricts this book's account of searching to mostly print materials, i.e., books and serials. Although other media may be equally important for certain purposes, very few collections concentrate on nonprint media. Libraries generally have a mix of all formats, with nonprint works in the minority. The principles of access points in bibliographic surrogates discussed in this work may be considered relevant and applicable, with appropriate adjustments, to all media.

Since the chief descriptive cataloging access point for full records in the *NUC* is the main-entry heading, the descriptive cataloging for all *NUC* records should be uniform. Unfortunately, as the editors of the various printed *NUC* sets always preface, many old records remain that were constructed under superseded cataloging codes.

In general, *NUC* entries are searched through descriptive cataloging access points to find a full bibliographic record for a work whose principal authorship is known. (Beginning with the 1983 *NUC*, an indirect search for the full record is possible if an added entry is known, e.g., for a joint author or a contributor or the work's title.)

Sometimes the searcher wants a grouping of books under the same main-entry or added-entry heading. That type of search is made possible by the collocative function of the main-entry heading in the pre-1983 *NUC* and in the post-1982 index entries. If a main-entry record is found, it usually gives the searcher the following bibliographic details:

37. For detailed descriptions and ordering information, consult the latest annual edition (free) of: Library of Congress, Cataloging Distribution Service, *Catalogs and Technical Publications* (The 1988 edition has the added title: *Access '88*) (Washington: The Library). Information is included on which publication is now available in microform or on compact disk-read only memory (CD-ROM).

Full title
The name of any person or body connected with the creation of the work
The number of volumes or pages
Illustrations by kind
Size (height in centimeters for a regular book or dimensions for irregularly shaped books)
Series title (if any)— an index access point in the post-1982 *NUC*
Place of publication
Name of publisher
Date of publication or significant copyright
If necessary, the same data for printer or distributor as for publisher
Price (sometimes)
Contents notes and notes clarifying the publishing history of the work
Standard number, e.g., ISBN or ISSN (sometimes both)
Tracings for descriptive cataloging added-entry headings.

The standardized descriptive cataloging codes have changed with the years. Agreed-on codes have required main-entry (and added-entry) headings either completely different from or in different styles from earlier codes. Unless older records have been changed to conform with the newest code—a practice almost nonexistent in the *NUC*—uniformity is lacking and the retrieval of single, let alone collocated, records is severely hampered. Furthermore, official standardization may be unacceptable to libraries whose readers are accustomed to different phraseologies. Computerization of printed bibliographic records does not necessarily mean that the records have been converted to the latest cataloging rules. As already indicated, the contract awarded by LC for conversion to machine-readable form of all noncomputerized *NUC* records has made only slow progress, and it doesn't involve recataloging according to the latest code, the 1988 *AACR2*, revised. (Searches of computerized older records may meet the same difficulties as searching older printed records.)

The need for a standardized twentieth-century code was obvious long before the 1908 *Joint Anglo-American Code*. Many descriptive cataloging codes were being used in English-language libraries. Confirming the multitude of cataloging codes used by American libraries, Theresa Hitchler of the Brooklyn Public Library published in 1903 *Comparative Cataloguing Rules: Twenty Points in Ten Codes Briefly Compared*.[38] The problems she

38. Theresa Hitchler, *Comparative Cataloguing Rules: Twenty Points in Ten Codes Briefly Compared* (New York: G. G. Peck, 1903).

lists are still with us; the different codes since Hitchler's time have responded differently to these problems.

Hitchler indicates that in all codes "cross-references are understood" for many of her points.[39] Not all reasonable cross-references were then or now always made by the cataloging library. (We shall see again how LC practice has changed over the years.) In any case, a searcher directed by a cross-reference to the form chosen by a library is forced into an indirect search and so loses time—if not patience.

Beginning with the attempted standardization of the 1908 *Joint Code*, many of our access points kept changing. Discussion of twentieth-century cataloging code changes centers on the official national catalog, the *NUC*, because of its pervasive influence on American cataloging. (Never to be forgotten is that the publisher of the *NUC* is not an official "National Library.") Consideration of access points in commercial bibliographies and in indexes to books, reference tools, and periodicals follows.

The following discussion of the changing bibliographic records created by our various superseding twentieth-century codes generally follows the sequence of Hitchler's points. Her codes, though, belong to the nineteenth century and are merely of historical interest to today's searchers.

The 1908 *Code* preferred for a heading the fullest form of the author's name, dutifully adding the clause, "whenever the author uses it regularly."[40] Though the 1949 *Rules* also asked for full form of name and for omission of unused forenames or forename initials, it noted that LC printed in the bottom right corner of the catalog card the author's full legal name even if it was not used on the title page.[41] The 1967 *AACR* stressed using the fullest form of name commonly employed by the author, with forename initials filled out only if necessary for identification.[42] The 1978 *AACR2* and the 1988 *AACR2*, revised heightened this trend by even permitting catalogers to optionally use the differing forms of name appearing on title pages, connecting them with "see also" references.[43]

Filling out forename initials was standard LC practice until LC accepted *AACR2* as of 1981. Searchers in the pre-1981 *NUC* can expect to find these complete forms of names. In the 1981 and 1982 *NUC*, split files for old and new LC headings in the various *NUC* issues are connected

39. Ibid., 7.

40. *Code* (1908), rules 28–29.

41. *A.L.A. Cataloging Rules* (1949), rule 40B.

42. *AACR* (1967), rules 40–41, 43.

43. *AACR2* (1978); *AACR2*, revised (1988), rules 22.1–22.3. (This chapter's citations to rules in *AACR2* and *AACR2*, revised, are the same.)

by "search also under" references. Beginning with the 1983 *NUC*, there are no cross-references to split files.

In the pre-1981 *NUC*, "H. G. Wells" and "D. H. Lawrence" are respectively entered as "Wells, Herbert George" and "Lawrence, David Herbert," with no cross-references from the initials. W. Somerset Maugham, who commonly used his first initial on title pages, was identified by LC as "Maugham, William Somerset." Evidently, Maugham at some time was known by another form of his name, because the pre-1983 *NUC* also offers the unexpected cross-reference: "Maugham, Somerset *see* Maugham, William Somerset." G. B. Shaw, Bernard Shaw, or at times even G. B. S. was recognized by LC as "Shaw, George Bernard," and T. S. Eliot as "Eliot, Thomas Stearns." Sometimes, the research needed by LC to determine the full names lurking behind authors' initials was considerable, though public library users could not care less about such scholarly niceties. This preference of laypersons was acknowledged by *AACR2* (and *AACR2*, revised) when it allowed as an option the use of any name on the title page.

Many corporate names used as headings in the *NUC* begin with personal names containing forename initials. Although codes did not consider filling out these forename initials, since they made up a body's legal signature, all codes from the 1908 *Code* through the 1967 *AACR* placed these forename initials after the family name, the 1967 *AACR* putting the initials in parentheses.[44] The 1978 *AACR2* and 1988 *AACR2*, revised ruled that the corporate name should be entered directly, with any forename initials preceding a family name.[45] This *AACR2* (and *AACR2*, revised) rule, accepted by LC as of January 1981, meant a change in filing order for the entries of the 1981 and 1982 *NUC* and for the indexes of the *NUC* since 1983. A searcher will find in the pre-1981 *NUC* the heading "Wilson, H. W., *firm, publishers*" but in later issues finds "H. W. Wilson Company." The latest *NUC* reference from the older heading is in the 1982 *NUC*.

Entries for compound surnames, surnames with separately written prefixes including an article or preposition or combination of the two, or surnames with prefixes hyphenated or combined with the names have always been a problem for the English-language searcher, occasionally even with an entry for an English-language author. Rule 22.4A in *AACR2* and *AACR2*, revised states: "If a person's name . . . consists of several parts, select as the entry element that part of the name under which the person would normally be listed in authoritative alphabetic lists in his or her language or country." This rule means that searchers, certainly li-

44. *Code* (1908), rule 109; *A.L.A. Cataloging Rules* (1949), rule 104; *AACR*, rule 67.
45. *AACR2* (1978); *AACR2*, revised (1988), rule 24.1.

brarians doing original cataloging, must be fluent enough in the particular language or be able to do linguistic research. A listing of examples of such names in many languages is given by *AACR2* and *AACR2*, revised rule 22.5: Afrikaans, Czech and Slovak, Danish, Dutch, English, Flemish, French, German, Italian, Norwegian, Portuguese, Romanian, Spanish, and Swedish. Most of these entry problems involve the catalogs of only research and academic libraries. However, even public libraries have to catalog English-language authors with exotic names, e.g., Daphne Du Maurier or Mazo de la Roche. Rule 26.1, the *AACR2* and *AACR2*, revised basic rule for making references, would certainly help a searcher for one of these strange names: "Whenever the name of a person or corporate body or the title of a work is, or may reasonably be, known under a form that is not the one used as a name heading or uniform title, refer from that form to the one that has been used." In English, the name "David Lloyd George" should have a reference from "George, David Lloyd," because it is an unhyphenated compound name. The pre-1983 *NUC* does have such a reference. What searcher unversed in Spanish would think of finding the surname "de los Angeles" under "Angeles"? In some instances, references are needed also because the author is better known by a nonofficial name, even by college students and faculty. Thus, the Spanish author known commonly in the United States as Lorca is entered correctly in the *NUC* under his patronymic as "Garcia Lorca, Frederico." The pre-1983 *NUC* refers from "Lorca."

Providing these references becomes the responsibility of local catalogers and the compilers of commercial bibliographers, whether the references are in the *NUC* or not. Beginning with 1974, LC listed all its references in its *Library of Congress Name Headings with References*, superseded in 1981 by the *Name Authorities Cumulative Microform Edition*, also available in machine-readable form. After references disappeared with the 1983 *NUC*, searchers and catalogers had to derive reference information from these sources.

Twentieth-century Anglo-American codes accept nineteenth-century opinion on adding dates when they are not difficult to find or if necessary to establish the author's identity. The latter reason benefits searchers and also seems a matter of common sense. Taking advantage of the option in *AACR2* and *AACR2*, revised rule 22.18, LC continues to add dates even when they are unnecessary.

Searchers encounter a main-entry heading problem in pre-*AACR2* records of the *NUC* when they are looking for compilations and anthologies. Until after the first edition of *AACR*, collections of works with a collective title by more than one author were entered under the name of the editor or compiler. It took many decades for the rule to be changed. Midway between the first and second editions of the *AACR*, a

1975 revision of *AACR* rule 4 was issued, which replaced *AACR* rule 5 and later entered *AACR2* and *AACR2*, revised as rule 21.7B. The revision mandated entry under title for collections with collective titles. For collections without a collective title, the revision kept the older rules to enter under the author of the first selection. For compilations both with and without collective titles, a limited number of name-title added entries was to be made for the other works in the compilation.

Nineteenth-century codes mostly required entry under the highest title acquired by a nobleman unless the author was better known by surname. Interestingly, the British Museum code stipulated entry under surname for those noblemen whose titles did not include the surname or who were subject to higher titles during their lives. The logic of this decision was that the surname was stable, while titles could change. (Using the same logic, the British Museum entered serials under their earliest titles, with title changes referred from and noted on the first record.) It was assumed that the American codes would have "see" references from nobelmen's titles that were not used as main-entry headings. All editions of *AACR* have maintained entry under the highest title—a difference from British tradition—unless a different name or title is better known. Only minor changes in the sequence of elements, other than the entry element, have been introduced by our twentieth-century codes. Thus, the 1949 *A.L.A. Cataloging Rules* entered "Scott, *Sir* Walter, *bart.*, 1771–1832."[46] *AACR2* and *AACR2*, revised dropped "bart." but kept "Sir" in the same position.[47] Before accepting *AACR2* "completely" in 1981, LC, for computerized filing purposes, had put "Sir" after "Walter" and had justified it as a compatible heading.[48] With the 1981 acceptance, LC omitted "bart." but kept "Sir" in compatible heading position so that the *NUC* main-entry heading now read "Scott, Walter, Sir, 1771–1832." (Connecting references to both headings were included in the 1981 and 1982 *NUC*.) Such changes of heading should not much affect search and retrieval in the *NUC*.

Treatment of pseudonyms brings into sharp focus the divergent nature of library patronage and the escalating tension between the scholarly LC and the more popular libraries that used LC cataloging as their source. In the first edition of *Rules for a Dictionary Catalog*, Cutter expressed a preference for entry under real name. In later editions he agreed that choice of main-entry heading should be in accordance with his distinction between types of libraries and their readers.[49] Patrons of

46. *A. L. A. Cataloging Rules* (1949), rule 57.
47. *AACR2* (1978); *AACR2*, revised (1988), rule 22.12B.
48. "Compatible Headings," *Cataloging Service Bulletin*, no. 17 (Summer 1982):31.
49. Cutter, *Rules*, 4th ed., rewritten (1904), 28.

a public library would be seeking books by "Twain, Mark," not by "Clemens, Samuel Langhorne." Cutter had previously stated that the convenience of the public should always be set before the ease of the cataloger, and that in attaining the objects of the dictionary catalog—other things being equal—the entry should be the one "that will probably be first looked under by the class of people who use the library." He still believed that "no code of cataloging could be adopted in all points by everyone, because the libraries for study and the libraries for reading have different objects and those which combine the two do so in different proportions."[50] As a result, he added to his Rule 7 in a later edition: "A large library and a library used mainly by scholars may very properly show a preference for the real name; a town library will do well to freely choose the names by which authors are popularly known."[51] (Cutter's flexibility in both descriptive cataloging and subject analysis may be attributed to his common sense, to the growth of public libraries, and to the fact that his last professional position was as head of the new public library in Northampton, Massachusetts.)

For searchers in the *NUC*, the pre-*AACR2* records are headed by the real name, not pseudonym, even when the pseudonym is the predominant form on the title page. A reference is always made from the pseudonym to the real name in the pre-1983 *NUC*, but this reference does mean more time in indirect search. Thus, "Sholem Aleichem," the Yiddish form of the Hebrew "Shalom Aleichem" ("Peace be with you"), is the pen name of "Rabinowitz, Shalom," to which the pre-*AACR2 NUC* makes a reference and under which all his works will be found. Similar references were made from "Twain, Mark" and "Burgess, Anthony." (The full legal name of the latter is John Anthony Clifford Wilson, who wrote under the names Anthony Burgess and Joseph Kell.) Only when LC decided to follow *AACR2* were works listed in the *NUC* under "Sholem Aleichem," "Burgess, Anthony," and "Twain, Mark." To repeat once more, starting with the 1983 *NUC*, no references are made from the author's real name to a predominant pseudonym.

From the beginning of the century LC had entered some authors under their established pseudonyms, e.g., the author of *Silas Marner* as "Eliot, George, pseud., i.e. Marian Evans, afterwards Cross, 1819–1880," though without a reference from the real name. This kind of entry was not sanctioned by the 1908 *Code* but from the 1949 *Cataloging Rules* through the *AACR2*, revised entry as indicated above was permitted under the pen name if it was the best known to readers and was commonly used by the author. Use of "pseud." in the heading was disallowed by

50. Ibid., 6, 12.
51. Ibid., 28.

AACR rule 42 and *AACR2* and *AACR2*, revised rule 22.2C, a change from the 1908 *Code*, rule 38 and the 1949 *Cataloging Rules for Author and Title Entries*, rule 30. *AACR* and *AACR2*, revised, did ask for a reference from the real name.[52] In the case of "George Eliot," LC had bowed to reality. "D. H. Lawrence" and "T. S. Eliot"—to whom the like principle of best-known name applied—had to wait until 1981 to be entered under their initials, with forenames following in parentheses. Perhaps the parenthetical additions could be justified as a collocative device.

Prior to *AACR2*, if LC printed a record for a pseudonymous work submitted by a cooperating library, the record would be edited by LC to agree with its own policies. Since adopting *AACR2*, LC accepts the record from the cooperating library as cataloged under the title page pseudonym. Again, searchers in the *NUC* who wish to find every work by an author using pseudonyms should first refer to dictionaries of pseudonyms, with the understanding that all works by that author may not be found in the *NUC*. This prior consultation is especially desirable for post-1982 *NUC* search.

The tension between standardized cataloging codes and the preferences of popular libraries has not been reduced by the permissiveness of *AACR2* and *AACR2*, revised, which allow three levels of cataloging (rule 1.0D), reminiscent of Cutter's short-title, medium-title and full-title records. Also, *AACR2* and *AACR2*, revised in rule 22.2A state that authors without a predominant name may, as the last of three options, be entered under the latest name, which is usually the name appearing on the title page of the item being cataloged. In a similar vein, as already mentioned, according to *AACR2* and *AACR2*, revised rule 22.2C3, an author using pseudonyms but with no predominant name may be entered under the name on the title page and all necessary references made. In addition to specific permissive rules, *AACR2* and *AACR2*, revised under the rubric "Alternatives and Options" explains:

> Some rules are designated as *alternative rules* or as *optional additions*, and some other rules or parts of rules are introduced by the word *optionally*. These provisions arise from the recognition that different solutions to a problem and different levels of detail and specificity are appropriate in different contexts.[53]

Conflict is inevitable when libraries of many kinds must rely on the centralized cataloging from any one library applying a "standardized" code, especially a permissive one.

52. *AACR* (1967), rule 42; *AACR2* (1978); *AACR2*, revised (1988), rule 22.2C.
53. *AACR2* (1978); *AACR2*, revised (1988), rule 0.7.

Despite LC willingness to conform to *AACR2* and *AACR2*, revised and to enter under predominant or best-known name, often a pseudonym, many public librarians complain that the *NUC*, since it is created by a research library—though not officially our national library—does not take into account the needs of popular libraries. (The complaints are especially vigorous when subject headings are concerned.) Finally, the Public Library Association in 1985 announced it would prepare its own bibliographic records for use in its own libraries.[54] So much for uniformity!

The 1908 *Code* specified a conjoint main-entry heading for joint authors but added that LC would continue to use only the first author's name as the main-entry heading.[55] (Some of the oldest non-LC records in the pre-1956 *NUC* have these conjoint headings.) Although the 1908 *Code* asked for a reference or an added-entry heading for the other joint authors, if not more than two, all subsequent codes through *AACR2*, revised have prescribed added entries, not references.[56] Pre-1983 *NUC* practice has favored references.

According to all twentieth-century codes, those who contributed in some way to the work without being the sole intellectual agent responsible for the work's existence, e.g., editors of periodicals, translators, and even illustrators, may have added entries or cross-references whenever needed to make the catalog more useful. This code rule is not concerned with how to enter collections of works by more than one author or works produced under editorial direction. The 1975 rule change governing the entry of collections has been mentioned above. Since that change prescribed added entries for compilers and editors, searchers in the post-1982 *NUC* have been given access to collections with collective titles either through titles or compiler's names. In regard to the first cataloging code option mentioned in this paragraph, searchers may also be given local catalog access at the discretion of the library, for example, to all the works in the collection illustrated by Maurice Sendak. *NUC* searchers may be similarly blessed.

Our modern definition of imprint in the catalog record incorporates data on place of publication, name of publisher, and date of publication or copyright. The amount of detail in the bibliographic record, of which the imprint is an important segment, may be significant in matching the surrogate to the work sought. A new "edition," by librarians' definition, justifies a new copyright date for a major part of the text, not just for

54. "Public Library Association Backs Major Cataloging Changes," *Library Journal* 110 (Mar. 1, 1985):14–15.

55. *Code* (1908), rule 2.

56. *A. L. A. Cataloging Rules* (1949); *AACR* (1967), rule 3; *AACR2* 1978; *AACR2*, revised (1988), rule 21.6.

a new preface or introduction. Publishers will sometimes reissue old texts as new editions and include a recent copyright date for a minor part or omit a copyright date if the work is in the public domain. If the text's original pagination (part of our modern physical description area, formerly known as the collation) remains the same for the new edition, a searcher may with some confidence infer no substantial change.

Successive Anglo-American twentieth-century codes have asked for full imprint and paging data, especially *AACR2* and *AACR2*, revised.[57] Other data may be revealing, such as illustrations or translation by a famous name; introduction or editing by an authority; notes on contents, annotations, or bibliographies; and, according to *AACR2* and *AACR2*, revised, a note on indexes. *AACR2* and *AACR2*, revised also call for printer identification when publisher identification is unavailable and when abbreviations indicate no place of publication, name of publisher, or publication date. *AACR2* and *AACR2*, revised also instruct on date approximation.[58]

Although some of the details may be considered anachronistic by today's librarians—e.g., the book's size in the physical description area or collation—some old-timers' opinions deserve a hearing. Isadore Mudge (1875–1957), longtime reference librarian at Columbia University, commented that the catalog record cannot be too full for reference purposes.[59] Unfortunately, LC in 1985 announced a policy of less than full cataloging for less than top-priority materials, a policy reminiscent of its limited cataloging in effect from April 1951 through August 14, 1963, and of its cataloging priorities begun January 1969 and discontinued June 1971.[60] The age-old controversy on the catalog record as a bibliographic reference versus a finding list has again, due to financial pressure, assumed prominence.

Our modern cataloging codes indicate that contents notes may be supplied, particularly when such information would clarify misleading

57. *Code* (1908), rules 150–165; U.S. Library of Congress, Descriptive Cataloging Division, *Rules for Descriptive Cataloging* (1949), rules 3:7–3:15; *AACR* (1967), rules 135–42; *AACR2* (1978); *AACR2*, revised (1988), rules 1.2–1.5, 2.2–2.5.

58. *AACR2* (1978); *AACR2*, revised (1988), rules 1.4, 2.4.

59. Isadore Gilbert Mudge, "Present Day Economies in Cataloging as Seen by the Reference Librarian of a Large University Library," *A. L. A. Bulletin* 28 (Sept. 1934):579–87. See also Constance M. Winchell, "The Catalog: Full, Medium, or Limited," *Journal of Cataloging and Classification* 11 (Oct. 1955):199–206.

60. "Priorities Observed at the Library of Congress in Cataloging," *Cataloging Service Bulletin*, no. 22 (Fall 1983):2–4; "LC to Distribute Minimal Level Cataloging Records," ibid.: 69; "Cataloging Priorities at the Library of Congress," Library of Congress, Processing Department, *Cataloging Service*, bulletin 100 (June 1971):1–2; "Discontinuance of Limited Cataloging," ibid., bulletin 61 (Sept. 1963):1.

titles or reveal unexpected subjects.[61] Catalogers may with impunity list the titles of chapters or appendixes even when their subjects are not unexpected. Partial or full contents notes, a matter of catalogers' judgment, are always helpful to the searcher. As previously stated, such notes—including those explaining the title or other aspects of the work—contribute to subject analysis, even though they are produced according to descriptive cataloging rules. A drawback of the indexes in the post-1982 *NUC* is the absence of contents notes.

Searchers for individual works in series are well served by modern cataloging rules and, as shown above, by LC attention to the problem. The 1908 *Code* stated that the series title should appear in parentheses at the end of the collation, a procedure followed by our codes through *AACR2*, revised.[62] The 1949 *Green Rules* emphasized that titles rather than editors should be relied on for series identification, an emphasis continued by *AACR*, *AACR2*, and *AACR2*, revised.[63] Searchers should be aware that LC lists some series under their editor rather than title. Those seeking all works in a series, whether or not cataloged by LC or cataloged by LC before *Monographic Series*, must resort to commercial bibliographies, e.g., *Titles in Series: A Handbook for Librarians and Students*.[64]

Until the 1967 *AACR*, codes agreed with Cutter in distinguishing societies from institutions, the former entered under name, the latter under city. Only after Lubetzky demonstrated the underlying reason for Cutter's differentiation did code makers enter both societies and institutions under their corporate names.[65] *AACR*, North American text rules 98 and 99 reflected American rejection of the decision that all societies and institutions be entered under their names.[66] Gradually, the differences between the North American text and the British text were removed. Prior to *AACR2*, LC accepted cancellation of Rules 98 and 99.[67]

61. *Code* (1908), rules 167–68; U.S. Library of Congress, Descriptive Cataloging Division, *Rules for Descriptive Cataloging* (1949), rules 3:1b, 3:15A, 3:22; *AACR* (1967), rules 133E, 149; *AACR2* (1978); *AACR2*, revised (1988), rules 1.7B18, 2.7B18.

62. *Code* (1908), rule 166; *AACR2*, revised (1988), rules 1.6A1, 2.6A1.

63. U.S. Library of Congress, Descriptive Cataloging Division, *Rules for Descriptive Cataloging* (1949), rules 3:25, 7:1; *A. L. A. Cataloging Rules* (1949), rule 5F; *AACR* (1967), rules 6A, 6B1; *AACR2* (1978); *AACR2*, revised (1988), rules 1.6E, 2.6B1.

64. U.S. Library of Congress, Catalog Management and Publication Division, *Monographic Series*, 1974–1982 (Washington: The Library, 1974–82), annual cumulations; *Titles in Series: A Handbook for Librarians and Students*, 3rd ed., 4 vols. (Metuchen, N.J.: Scarecrow Press, 1978).

65. *Code* (1908), rules 72–99; *A. L. A. Cataloging Rules* (1949), rules 91–114; *AACR*, British text (1967), rules 1A, 60–98.

66. *AACR*, North American text (1967), rules 1A, 60–99.

67. "Cataloging Rules—Additions and Changes," Library of Congress, Processing Division, *Cataloging Service*, bulletin 109 (May 1974):2–8.

Searchers of bibliographic records in the *NUC*—disregarding the complicated history of LC superimposition and desuperimposition—must expect that older records for institutions have been entered under the city location, though references from the corporate name have been usually made.

Seekers of information in federal government documents usually are aware that the main-entry heading should be the name of the issuing agency. (The same principle applies to all government documents—state, municipal, or local.) Unfortunately, confirmation will not make retrieval any easier for the searchers, since the agencies change frequently as to name, superior body, and even continued existence. For all doubtful cases, the now annual *United States Government Manual* should be examined.[68] The best source for surrogates of federal government documents is the *Monthly Catalog of United States Government Publications* or its predecessors.[69] Since July 1976 the entries, arranged by issuing agency, are in LC printed card format. Indexes access issuing agency, title, and by subject. A few of the documents may be found in the *NUC*, but the *Monthly Catalog* is the comprehensive listing. The *Monthly Catalog* provides for each entry a Superintendent of Documents Classification (SUDOC) notation, which in reality serves more as inventory identification than a subject classification scheme, unless the issuing agency name might indicate the subject scope of the document. Because the SUDOC is based on the very unstable issuing agency name, it presents a major hurdle to searchers, let alone government documents librarians.

Some federal government documents are better known to the public by nonofficial titles. Irregularly, LC publishes *Popular Names of United States Government Reports*, which reproduces catalog cards for reports under the popular names by which they are known.[70] Other major official U.S. government printed catalogs are the *Index Medicus* of the National Library of Medicine, and the *Bibliography of Agriculture* of the United States National Agricultural Library, the latter a catalog of the library's acquisitions.[71] Surrogates and indexing for state and local agency gov-

68. *United States Government Manual* . . . 1935– (Washington, 1935–), Annual, earlier volumes irregular.

69. U.S. Superintendent of Documents, *Monthly Catalog of United States Government Publications*, 1895– (Washington: Govt. Print. Off., 1895–), monthly. For the *Document Catalog*, no longer published, see Sheehy, *Guide*, AG50. For the *Monthly Catalog*, AG51–54.

70. U.S. Library of Congress, Serial Division, *Popular Names of U.S. Government Reports; a Catalog*, 1st ed. 1966 (Washington: The Library), irregularly issued editions.

71. *Index Medicus*, 1960– (Washington: National Library of Medicine, 1960–), monthly; U.S. National Agricultural Library, *Bibliography of Agriculture*, 1942– (Washington, 1942–), monthly with cumulative subject, personal, and organizational indexes.

ernment publications appear in much less comprehensive catalogs and bibliographies.

For searchers, serials entry in the pre-1983 *NUC* is not crucial since most libraries have separate serials catalogs adapted to their needs and prepare their own records in which the holdings are of prime importance. Furthermore, searchers usually are looking for specific articles in serials and are largely dependent on commercial indexes, not on the pre-1983 *NUC*.

A technical distinction has been made between periodical and nonperiodical serials. This distinction has been blurred by time and successive codes as well as by the 1961 International Conference on Cataloguing Principles held in Paris.[72] If the periodical or nonperiodical is clearly the intellectual responsibility of a person or corporate body, all codes permit entry under the name of the responsible entity. The criteria for this principle of intellectual responsibility have not been easy to formulate or apply. Entry under title for all serials has been sought by some catalogers, though *AACR* through *AACR2*, revised have not been completely supportive.[73] Only after accepting *AACR2* did LC agree to enter most serials in the *NUC* under their title, whether or not the title was distinctive. Of perhaps less significance for searchers is that LC also decided to follow *AACR2* (and also *AACR*) and change its serials cataloging style from latest title records to successive title records.[74] Although endlessly complex and fascinating to serials librarians, serials cataloging is not of great practical importance to searchers. Cross-references and added entries ease searching problems.

Analytical access has been defined for this book as having access points to information within encompassing works, i.e., books and serials. (Analysis by subject is not a topic for this chapter, which is concerned only with descriptive cataloging access points.) The definition of analytics is given in *AACR2* and *AACR2*, revised.[75] It omits mention of analytical entries for articles in serials, though earlier catalogers and reference librarians did not hesitate to make them.

Chapter 13 in *AACR2* and *AACR2*, revised provides instructions for analytics of monographic series and multipart monographs. Specific styles

72. International Conference on Cataloguing Principles, Paris, 9–18 October 1961, "Statement of Principles," principle 11.14. "The 'Statement' is contained in the Conference's *Report* (London, International Federation of Library Associations, 1963) p. 91–96; also in *Library Resources and Technical Services*, v. 6 (1962), p. 162–167."—*AACR* (1967), 2, footnote 2.

73. *Code* (1908), rule 121; *A.L.A. Cataloging Rules* (1949), rules 5C–5E; *AACR* (1967), rule 6; *AACR2* (1978); *AACR2*, revised (1988), rules 21.1A–21.1C, 21.2C.

74. "Cataloging of Serials," Library of Congress, Processing Division, *Cataloging Service*, bulletin 99 (Apr. 1971):1.

75. *AACR2* (1978); *AACR2*, revised (1988), rule 13.1.

are designated for analytic added entries, "in" analytics, and multilevel description. Analytics for monographs are by no means as much used in today's library catalogs as in more leisurely times when librarians had the opportunity and inclination.

Analytical access to information within most monographs and collections is not directly available to *NUC* searchers. Descriptive catalogers at LC will sometimes give partial or full contents notes. Occasionally, LC has supplied analytics and, strictly speaking, its *Monographic Series* and post-1982 *NUC* index of series titles have afforded analytical access for individual volumes by series. However, as stated delicately by *AACR2* and *AACR2*, revised: "Cataloguing agencies have their own policies affecting analysis; in particular, a policy predetermining the creation of separate bibliographic records may override any other consideration."[76] In other words, the freedom of libraries to make analytics as they see fit cannot affect the entries in the *NUC*. The problem of access to detailed information in books remains. Much more about this topic is said in the next chapter.

Searchers should remember that in addition to the numerous printed indexes to serials, the contents of many kinds of collections are accessible through standard reference works, like *Granger's Index to Poetry*, *Essay and General Literature Index*, *Ottemiller's Index to Plays in Collections*, and *Short Story Index*.[77] These indexes give access by author, title, and very often, subject. Searchers should not rely on library catalogs like the *NUC* for access to units in collections. Access to smaller units of information in monographs, such as the access that back-of-the-book indexes provide, is not yet possible without recourse to the book's actual index. Back-of-the-book indexes provide access not only to names (the onomastic index) but also to topical subjects.

Successive cataloging codes' major impact has been on the choice and form of main-entry headings, and the myriad changes since the 1908 *Joint Code* need the attention and memory of specialists in searching. Since the main-entry heading is the major access point for retrieval of full descriptive cataloging records, it should become even clearer that an extensive search of surrogates organized in printed sources by descriptive cataloging rules requires a knowledge of catalog code changes over the years. This requirement becomes more urgent as the search extends back in time over older printed sources. The largest segment of the *NUC*, the pre-1956 cumulation, takes LC cataloging of the time as the standard for LC-cataloged works. Thus, an item cataloged by LC in 1908 will usually follow rules in the 1908 *Code*. The 1949 *ALA Cataloging Rules*

76. Ibid.

77. See Sheehy, *Guide*, for these and other useful reference works.

for Author and Title Entries, the latest code for pre-1956 works, was used for some of the pre-1956 records when LC cataloging was not available. Because *NUC* records go back to the last years of the nineteenth century, LC cataloging can have many forms—not to mention the records contributed by non-LC libraries.

On the printed modern unit card popularized by LC, all tracings appear on the bottom of all cards in the printed set. (Modern libraries are not required to make all added-entry headings traced by LC. Libraries usually check those used.) At least the main entries in the *NUC* include all tracings. Locally typed catalog cards may have on the verso of the main entry abbreviated instructions for typing added-entry headings, e.g., "Title, Series, Au.-Ti. Anals." This local practice means that there is no full record on any catalog card of added-entry headings and renders impossible manual coordinate retrieval of descriptive cataloging added-entry headings or subject headings—sometimes both combined.[78]

The codes discussed have chiefly affected entry headings, but they have also influenced the texts of bibliographic surrogates. Sometimes the text changes have been merely typographical; at other times, they are additions to, deductions from, or changes in the wording. Fortunately, searchers—even laypersons—will not be seriously hampered after locating a desired record through its heading.

Probably the most noticeable change in the layout of the bibliographic record resulted from the International Standard Bibliographic Description (ISBD), sponsored by the International Federation of Library Associations and Institutions (IFLA). The first ISBD for monographs, ISBD(M), was codified in the 1974 *Revised Chapter 6* pamphlet of *AACR*. Since then, ISBDs have been designed for various media, e.g., serials, ISBD(S); cartographic materials, ISBD(CM); and the General International Standard Bibliographic Description, ISBD(G), which is the model for all specific ISBDs.[79] The ISBDs incorporated into *AACR2* and *AACR2*, revised, divide the organization of the description into eight areas. Each area is divided into a number of elements, and each area and element are preceded or enclosed by standard punctuation. The only ISBD punctuation mark immediately obvious to searchers is the slash before a state-

78. Richard Joseph Hyman, *From Cutter to MARC: Access to the Unit Record* (Flushing, N.Y.: Queens College Press, 1977), 15–20.

79. *ISBD (G) : General International Standard Bibliographic Description : Annotated Text* / prepared by the Working Group on the General International Standard Bibliographic Description set up by the IFLA Committee on Cataloguing. — London : IFLA International Office for UBC, 1977. This note is copied in ISBD style from *AACR2* (1978) and *AACR2*, revised (1988), 7, where the relationship of ISBD(G) to *AACR2* (1978) and *AACR2*, revised (1988) is explained, and IFLA development of other ISBDs for specific types of material is described.

ment of responsibility. In fact, in their defense of ISBD at its inception, supporters claimed that this slash signaled that a statement of responsibility followed, even to users who were unfamiliar with the language of the work.

The purpose of the ISBD is to facilitate international exchange of bibliographic records by standardizing the contents, sequence, and punctuation of all elements in the descriptive cataloging record, exclusive of headings. Some changes were made in the style of wording, e.g., Latin abbreviations replaced those in English, and imprint abbreviations were expanded as well as Latinized. The ISBD aimed for a self-sufficient bibliographic record and did not concern itself with choice or form of headings. The first level of description, as permitted by *AACR2* and *AACR2*, revised (Rule 1.0D2), seems to violate the principle of self-sufficiency, since omitting the first statement of responsibility violates the independence of the ISBD record. No doubt this compromise was considered necessary by the code makers.

Less consequential changes have been introduced in the bibliographic record, usually at the initiative of LC. In 1970 LC changed the tracing for an added series title heading, from the word "Series" in parentheses at the end of all descriptive cataloging tracings to "Series" without parentheses and preceded by a roman numeral for this last descriptive cataloging tracing. The change was motivated by the LC introduction of new order forms for cards, which meant that machines had to count out the number of cards in each set.

Another LC change was the LC card numbering at the right-hand bottom of the bibliographic record. The year of cataloging had been shown by the first two digits—e.g., "67" meant that the cataloging was done in 1967. After Machine-Readable Cataloging was started in 1968, LC felt it necessary to use the second digit in its seven-series LC card numbers for a computer-check number. The practitioner could not learn the year of cataloging from the digits on records created from December 1968 through the early part of 1972, nor the cataloging code applied by LC. (Since *AACR* was published in 1967 and *AACR2* in 1978, an educated guess could be made.) Early in 1972, LC returned to the old method of catalog card numbering.[80] The cards and records now also have messages that the record is in MARC and the cataloging follows *AACR2* or *AACR2*, revised.

Such changes in *NUC* style have had almost no impact on searching, certainly not when compared with the varying LC policies towards *AACR*

80. "Elimination of Check-Digit in 7-Series LC Card Numbers," Library of Congress, Processing Division, *Cataloging Service*, bulletin 101 (Jan. 1972):1–2.

and *AACR2*: superimposition, desuperimposition, options, compatible headings, and LC rule interpretations.

Because the basic arrangement of *NUC* headings is alphabetical, the filing order has precoordinated all entries. For some voluminous files the order was categorical (including chronological and the canonical groupings for the Bible). Filing rules prior to computerization were extremely complicated. Much depended on the interpretations of the filer, who was expected to choose sense rather than sound ("as if" not "as is"), and to be aware of logical, hierarchical, or classificatory arrangements. Even those who deplore any classificatory element in the filing order have conceded, perhaps unknowingly, that completely alphabetical filing is impractical, since they do not object to the classificatory grouping of authors by surnames subfiled by given names.

Precomputer filing rules had to find ways to file initialisms, abbreviations, acronyms (sometimes the same acronym with different punctuation or capitalization on different title pages), numerals, and headings with similar entry words but different in function among others. The only stable principle in library filing remains word-by-word order (also known as "nothing before something" or "blank to Z"), not letter-by-letter. Word-by-word order places "New York" before "Newark." Some reference works use letter-by-letter filing.

Every library has its own filing rules, though most are adaptations of the filing codes prepared by LC and ALA.[81] Beginning in 1971, LC greatly simplified its filing rules for all computer-generated bibliographic products, and almost simultaneously an ALA computerized filing code was published.[82] Searchers in the *NUC* need to realize that two filing arrangements may be found, depending on the age of the *NUC* set.

The LC computer-oriented filing rules cut a Gordian knot, e.g., by stressing that words be filed as printed and that numerals be filed before letters and strictly in order of magnitude. (Some logical arrangements were, however, retained.) Sometimes the new rules have not protected LC from embarrassing errors. More than once, LC had to acknowledge to *NUC* users that some headings had been filed by their preliminary articles, a major proscription in all filing codes. Machine or human error was blamed.

81. U.S. Library of Congress, *Filing Rules for the Dictionary Catalogs of the Library of Congress* (Washington: Govt. Print. Off., 1956); American Library Association, Subcommittee on the ALA Rules for Filing Catalog Cards, *ALA Rules for Filing Catalog Cards*, 2nd ed. (Chicago: ALA, 1968). "1942 ed. prepared by a special committee of the American Library Association."

82. Library of Congress, *Library of Congress Filing Rules* (Washington: The Library, 1980). "Provisional version by J. C. Rather published in 1971 under title: Filing Arrangement in the Library of Congress Catalogs"; American Library Association, Filing Committee, *ALA Filing Rules*, 3rd ed. (Chicago: ALA, 1980).

The collocative *NUC* filing is helpful in searches for either a single item or a related group. Searching for one item in the *NUC* requires previous knowledge of headings, either main or added. If the searcher knows at least the name of a joint author or of a person or corporate body connected with the work, the work can be found under added-entry headings. With the 1983 *NUC* the item's title became an added access point. Again, the *NUC* includes only the acquisitions of LC and contributing libraries, not the entire publishing output of any country nor all works currently in print.

In the pre-1983 *NUC*, any name traced according to LC descriptive cataloging rules is found as an added entry together with a shortened bibliographic record ending with the imprint, the first paragraph of the traditional catalog card. In the pre-1983 *NUC*, references alone, without abbreviated entries, are also found, e.g., a "see" reference from a pseudonym to the real name used by LC for the main-entry heading, or a "see also" reference to an additional heading. After 1982, as already mentioned, the *NUC* does not include these references.

Beginning with the 1983 *NUC*, the main entries in the register are accessible only through cumulative indexes, but abbreviated entries for descriptive cataloging tracings continue to be supplied. For single item search, both title and series-title added entries give access, the former not available in the pre-1983 *NUC*, though series titles (with full main entries, including tracings) could be found in the separate LC publication, *Monographic Series*. However, since in the post-1982 *NUC*, there are no cross-references, e.g., from a pseudonym or an element of a foreign name to the official LC heading, or from one file to an additional file, a double search may be necessary to find these references. First, the LC-published *Name Authorities Cumulative Microform Edition* (formerly *Library of Congress Name Headings with References*) must be searched and then the post-1982 *NUC*.

The "see also" references connect the split files in recent *NUC* issues when LC has decided to follow *AACR2* but to keep non-*AACR2* entries, exceeding a minimum number set by LC, under the older headings in another file. Thus, entries will be found in the post-1982 *NUC* under both Clemens, Samuel Langhorne, and Twain, Mark, but without "see also" references from one file to the other. To locate all *NUC* entries for the same author, searchers have to consult the above mentioned *Name Authorities Cumulative Microform Edition*.

The precoordination of entries in the *NUC* makes it possible for the searcher of a single item to continue when necessary with manual postcoordinate or Boolean searches—much less tedious in some cases than anticipated. The searcher instinctively applies Boolean logic expressions when scanning the printed catalog for a work that fulfills multiple criteria, like author, title, edition, imprint date, language, educational level, publisher reputation, size, binding, price, illustrations, glossary, index, contents notes, and bibliography. Many of these criteria are met even in the post-1982 *NUC* indexes. Not only has *NUC* filing coordinated the author and title terms in the main entry for a work like Shakespeare's *Hamlet*, but all the other elements can also be searched manually. Even for *Hamlet*, the printed file is not unmanageably long.

The collocative power of the *NUC* printed arrangement is enhanced by use of the uniform title, which can be a main-entry heading. An anonymous classic would have a uniform title in the author position, e.g., *Mother Goose*. The uniform title can also be used as a gathering device for various editions, translations, and versions of a particular work. The uniform title is then placed in brackets on a separate line between the main-entry heading and the rest of the record. This use is especially common in cataloging musical works. For example, for Beethoven's "Moonlight" sonata the uniform title [Sonata. Piano. No. 14. Op. 27, no. 2. E-sharp minor. "Moonlight"] appears below the composer's name.

Chapter 25 in *AACR2* and *AACR2*, revised has rules on uniform titles for individual and collective works; incunabula; legal materials; treaties, etc.; sacred scriptures; liturgical works; and music.

The older *NUC* entries for voluminous authors, e.g., Dante, utilized elaborate classificatory filing schemes. In the *Pre-1956 NUC* cumulation, for example, the Dante entries are arranged in six numbered groups, and the arrangement is explained before the first entry.

Especially valuable to searchers are the *Pre-1956 NUC* volumes for the uniform title "Bible," which LC numerically arranges to provide a ready guide to the Bible or any of its parts. The introductory explanation and alphabetical general index give the entry-group numbers for the *NUC* canonical arrangement. Under the pre-computer filing system, Bible entries began with Genesis, the first book of the Old Testament. Under the computerized alphabetical filing order, the first entry is Acts of the New Testament, and New Testament listed in alphabetical order before Old Testament. A 1980 reprinting in five volumes of the *Pre-1956 NUC* "Bible" entries included an index with many additional access points to the main entries, including editors, translators, and titles of selections, providing "all the 'non-Bible' approaches to the material."[83] Such extensive precoordinated lists, particularly those with classificatory filing, serve as very useful reference tools. Users of the printed *NUC* should be on the lookout for collocative listings, e.g., for entries under the names of countries, like "United States."

83. *The National Union Catalog, Pre-1956 Imprints*, 754 vols. (London: Mansell, 1968–81), vols. 53–56, and vol. 5, Index, [iv].

Those searching *NUC* records for works on a distinctive topic can take advantage of the descriptive cataloging main-entry heading if the topic is a known specialty of a known author, such as James D. Watson on molecular genetic biology, Edward O. Wilson on sociobiology, B. F. Skinner on the conditioned or responsive reaction, Norbert Wiener on cybernetics (a word coined by Wiener), Noam Chomsky on linguistics (among other subjects), Leon Edel on Henry James, and Lionel Trilling on E. M. Forster.

In addition to the *NUC* for printed books and serials, LC issues catalogs for nonprint and audiovisual materials, such as music, sound recordings, motion pictures, and filmstrips. The titles of these catalogs and the access points supplied have varied over the years. Knowing the catalogs is necessary.

After deployment of all the above descriptive cataloging access forces, searchers may succeed in locating bibliographic surrogates and yet be unable to examine the actual works because they are owned by distant libraries or by libraries in which the searchers have no borrowing or reading privileges. Such contretemps often arise, but interlibrary loan service can come to the searchers' aid. The holdings records on the *NUC* entries can be used to discover which libraries own the *NUC*-cataloged items. (Abbreviations for library names are explained in the first volume of the *NUC* set.) The *National Union Catalog, Register of Additional Locations (RAL)*, published by LC, advises on additional locations of *NUC* items as reported to LC. In 1988, LC claimed over forty million *RAL* locations in American and Canadian libraries. About three million new locations are said to be added every year. *RAL* entries are arranged numerically by LC or *NUC* card number printed in the bottom right-hand corner of the *NUC* record. Beginning 1980, *RAL* has been issued in a cumulative microfiche format that contains all reports since 1968. The microfiche edition is now cumulated quarterly.

Searchers in the catalogs of foreign national libraries, like those of the British Museum (BM), now the British Library (BL), and of the Bibliothèque Nationale in Paris (BN), must be ready for as many bibliographic changes as in the *NUC*.[84] The BL has agreed to apply *AACR*, while the BN's country approved the "Statement of Principles" at the 1961 Paris International Conference on Cataloguing Principles, the "Statement" on which *AACR* was based. The catalogs of both the BL and the BN are indispensable for records of items not in the *NUC*, since they include many rare and obscure older works from these collections, as well as recent very specialized volumes published in Britain and France.

84. For the British Museum catalog, see Sheehy, *Guide*, AA132–134; for the Bibliothèque Nationale catalog, AA140–141.

As with our *NUC*, collocative printed precoordinated files can be a searcher's boon. In the BM catalog, official government publications are grouped under country name, and separate volumes are devoted to the Bible, England, liturgies, London, and periodical publications. For the early part of the BM catalog, society publications were entered under "Academies." Individual BM catalogs have also been published, e.g., for manuscripts, Oriental books and manuscripts, incunabula, manuscript, and printed music.

The BN catalog, like those of the BM and BL, is chiefly an alphabetical author catalog and has helpful reference aids, such as alphabetical title indexes that include analytical references for voluminous authors. Catalogs of the BN have been issued for different media (indeed, for different topics), including catalogs for manuscripts, periodicals, dissertations, and works in nonroman alphabets. The printed BN catalog began publication in 1900, and its bibliographical details are consistently fuller than those in the BM catalogs, which include many old records. The BM and BL catalogs have, since *AACR*, expanded their descriptive cataloging entries.

Combining the benefits of a trade and national bibliography, enough data for ordering is given in Great Britain's *British National Bibliography (BNB)*, an official publication of the British Library that merges the functions of the American *NUC* and the *American Book Publishing Record (BPR)*.[85] It accepts *AACR2* for descriptive cataloging and the Dewey Decimal Classification for part of subject analysis and for general arrangement. The *BNB* appears weekly, and in monthly and other cumulations. Indexes in every issue give access by main-entry heading, title, and classification assignment. The latter index, not dissimilar from a subject-heading analysis, was formerly a chain index, originally suggested by Ranganathan, but is now an example of the Preserved Context Index System (PRECIS), created by Austin and his associates.[86] Austin's approach is of special interest for subject analysts and is further discussed in the next chapter. Collocation and bibliographic detail in the *BNB* are equivalent to those in our *NUC*.

Commercial print and microform cataloging services, mostly based on LC records, have supplied access to the *NUC* by book title, LC card number, ISBN, and ISSN. These services frequently go out of business, and they may no longer be effective. Of course, the indexes they supply apply to the records received by subscribers.

85. *British National Bibliography*, 1950– (London, 1950–), weekly with various cumulations.

86. S. R. Ranganathan, *Theory of Library Catalogue* (Madras: Madras Library Assoc., 1938), 77–198, especially 123; Derek Austin, "PRECIS in a Multilingual Context. Part 1; PRECIS, an Overview," *Libri* 26 (Mar. 1976): 1–37.

Many libraries, even those owning the full *NUC*, purchase printed commercial bibliographies, like the *BPR*, the *Cumulative Book Index* (CBI), and, for currently available works, the latest *Books in Print (BIP)*.[87] The *BPR* originates with the *Weekly Record*, which contains copies, whenever possible, of the texts of the LC records, arranged by main-entry heading. There are monthly cumulative indexes by main-entry heading and title to the *Weekly Record*. The *BPR* cumulates the *Weekly Record* monthly (and in various cumulations). It is arranged by the Dewey Decimal Classification and contains main-entry heading and title indexes.

The *CBI* is a monthly dictionary listing (with various cumulations) of English-language works by author, title, and subject heading. The *BIP* gives access by main-entry heading and title to the catalogs of American publishers. Only the *Weekly Record* and the *BPR* follow the *NUC* format; the others may have most of the required data, though not in *NUC* style. Librarians and users are familiar with these sources. Perhaps only librarians fully recognize the unofficial nature of commercially produced records when compared with the *NUC*.

Similar commercial bibliographies of the national book trade are available for many countries, e.g., for Great Britain, *Whitaker's*, and for France, *Bibliographie de la France—Biblio*.[88] Access points and basic arrangements vary from those in American bibliographies, which also have different chronological coverage.

The power of the access points that descriptive cataloging contributes is indisputable, and indeed essential for search and retrieval of known items. For almost-known items, clues may be followed up using descriptive cataloging added entries and references. Larger libraries tend to separate not only copy from original cataloging but also descriptive cataloging from subject analysis. The qualitative and quantitative demands of these specializations in large libraries seem adequate justification. Descriptive catalogers may think of subject analysis as an irredeemably subjective and changeable activity, a belief weakened by the numerous descriptive cataloging codes described above, by their permissiveness and options, and by the varying practices of LC. The difficulties of subject analysis must be granted as well as the continuous need of users to search and retrieve items by topic. The next chapter is concerned with this kind of search in printed sources.

Analytical access to articles in journals is provided by indexes to the serial literature,[89] most of them available in both printed and comput-

87. See Sheehy, *Guide*, for these and related works.

88. For *Whitaker's*, see Sheehy, *Guide*, AA828–31; for *Bibliographie de la France—Biblio*, AA753–54, 758–62, 764.

89. For periodical indexes, see Sheehy, *Guide*, AE215–316.

erized format. Admittedly, subject-analysis access points are more significant in these indexes than access points created by descriptive cataloging. However, almost all these indexes have author headings, either personal or corporate, and some of them even list articles by title. (A few are exclusively by subject.) If one knows the author of an article, the item can be found directly. If one knows the subject heading under which the author's article may be found, the collocative power of the heading can be most useful. The limitations of the computerized versions of these indexes are detailed at the beginning of this chapter. For extensive review of periodical literature through the years, the printed editions of the indexes are essential.

Experienced *NUC* searchers should have little difficulty in utilizing periodical indexes, at least for descriptive cataloging access. Index searchers, though, should be aware that many abbreviations are used in periodical indexes, and the abbreviations usually explained at the beginning of each issue. The index's subject scope and chronological coverage should be ascertained before the searcher attempts to use it. Since many of these indexes specialize in certain subjects, searchers tend to concentrate on a limited number of these bibliographical sources. Knowing when the publication began and when particular journals were first indexed is of prime importance. Although a listing of indexed periodicals usually appears in the preliminary pages, data are not often given as to when the periodicals were first indexed.

Index searchers must remember first that periodical index information is based on surrogation. After identifying an index item, the library may have to obtain a copy of the article from another library if it does not have the journal or the individual issue. Periodical index searches result in a major source of interlibrary loans, though most libraries do not lend serials and will charge for article photocopies.

A second point to remember is that only when the author of the article appears in the main-entry heading is the author's name given in full. Other citations for the same article, such as by subject, give only forename initials for the author. All additional entries and references are abbreviated so that full bibliographical detail can be found just in the main entry under the main-entry heading—an important detail for bibliography or interlibrary loan.

A last point is that these "periodical" indexes can give analytical access to other than periodicals. Almost all of them index chapters or contributions in compilations and anthologies. This point can be especially helpful in searching analyzed reports on technical conferences. A list of these analyzed compilations is frequently found at the back of each index issue.

Even a cursory review of this chapter must convince the reader that changes in our descriptive cataloging codes and LC practices have been numerous and multifarious to the point of bewilderment, especially for a comprehensive search in the *NUC* from its earliest times. Only copious cross-references, when available in the *NUC*, can link the various names or their versions used by an author. The official heading in the *NUC* may be the legal form never used on a title page, such as "David Herbert Lawrence" for "D. H. Lawrence."

The services of a professional librarian who is aware of such changes are required for many searches. Awareness is crucial, not memorization; copies of previous cataloging codes should be at hand for consultation. This awareness is needed by both the technical services and the reader services librarian. As this book proceeds, we see how automation has made this cooperative activity of librarians a staple of today's profession.

Mechanization has hastened this joint relationship without removing the underlying causes. Scanning this chapter shows that a fully retrospective search of bibliographic surrogates, whether using the *NUC* or periodical indexes, cannot rely only on current automated sources. Even if all older bibliographic surrogates were automated and converted to the latest cataloging rules, by the time the chore was completed, other changes—probably another code—would necessitate recataloging once more. Whether or not the *NUC* provides connecting references, dependable reference listings, such as bibliographies and dictionaries of pseudonyms and anonyms, can uncover the names used by a writer on title pages. Some of the author's works, however, may not even have been cataloged for the *NUC*.

Descriptive cataloging analytical access depends on contents notes for book records, and authors' names in periodical indexes. The contents notes practices of LC in its *NUC* are inconsistent, and lack of standardization and stable quality are an expected problem for the descriptive cataloging in periodical indexes.

Since subject access is so important in periodical indexes, a major discussion of using these indexes appears in Chapters 4 and 6 on printed and computerized subject approach to information. The subject search, both for whole works and for parts of works, whether or not mechanized, can be extremely severe because of the very nature of subject analysis. Practical measures to deal with the problem are suggested.

4 Printed Subject Access

Descriptive cataloging tries to answer the question: What is the sought item you can identify usually by author or title? To facilitate retrieval of the item, descriptive cataloging offers a physical description to distinguish that item from all others, no matter how similar. Subject analysis deals with the question: What or whom is the item about? This approach makes author or title less important as access points. Both descriptive cataloging and subject analysis attempt to fulfill the collocative objects of Cutter's catalog by assembling all works in the library by the same author or on the same topic. As we have seen, the oldest libraries in the Western world stressed bibliographic organization based not on author but on topic, or on title if it reflected the contents of the work.

Verbal descriptions of subjects preceded classification schemes, although even classification needs verbal descriptions for its scheme to be practicable. The logical grouping of subject headings led directly to classification, which would rival subject headings in revealing the subjects of the works in a collection. A modern development of subject-heading lists is the thesaurus, which combines verbal and classificatory benefits by identifying and displaying its descriptors or terms in a hierarchical order and by extensive cross-references. Indexing of recorded knowledge, to use a narrow definition, applies subject-heading principles to information within books and articles. In this sense, indexing is subject analysis in depth, the supplying of analytical access points.

Since classification and verbalization are part of subject analysis and label the same materials, many authorities term them complementary aspects of a single process. In most libraries, both methods of subject analysis are the responsibility of the same staff. This rapprochement was championed by S. R. Ranganathan, who believed in the symbiosis of the two elements in the same effort.[1] His ideas were realized in the *British National Bibliography (BNB)* chain index and its successor, the Preserved Context Index System (PRECIS). These two *BNB* indexes are discussed later at greater length. Here we are concerned with the almost total neglect in American libraries of classification as a tool to search and retrieve desired items, whether through printed or computerized surrogates. What are the reasons for this neglect? Are the reasons justifiable?

Classification in American libraries is a respected and even worshipped icon, but even its heartiest partisans acknowledge its theoretical and practical difficulties. Although the scientific weaknesses of library classification may be acknowledged, it is still useful if it is properly applied in organizing the surrogates of recorded knowledge. Classification is most useful when used as part of a classified catalog, conspicuously absent in American libraries. A classified catalog allows as many classification notations as there are subject headings for the same work. The two most common classification schemes in U.S. libraries, the DDC and the LCC, are used almost exclusively for shelf location, a function requiring only a single classification notation per work.

It may be difficult for American librarians to appreciate Georg Leyh's idea that shelf address need not be linked to classification.[2] Shelving may be based on fixed location and thus be independent of the classification symbols, or if open-stack access is the policy, shelving may be based on the first classification symbol given the work. Even fixed location can be used by patrons if they have a classified catalog for guidance. The advantages of the classified or classed catalog have been enumerated by Shera and Egan, but their advocacy has not influenced American practitioners.[3] Why not?

Our librarians tend to think that classification and subject headings perform the same task, and so classification, which is difficult to understand, has been slighted for search and retrieval, except to provide the shelf address. The equating of these two means of subject analysis shows a misunderstanding of the function performed by each in organizing collections. Though the conclusion that subject headings are more effective than classification for search and retrieval may be correct, the

1. S. R. Ranganathan, *Theory of Library Catalogue* (Madras: Madras Library Assoc., 1938), 77–198, especially 123.

2. Georg Leyh, "Das Dogma von der systematischen Aufstellung," *Zeitblatt für Bibliothekswesen* 29 (1912):241–59; 30 (1913):98–136.

3. Jesse H. Shera and Margaret E. Egan, *The Classified Catalog: Basic Principles and Practices* (Chicago: ALA, 1956).

reasoning leading to such a conclusion has robbed classification of its power to fulfill its proper role.[4]

Subject analysis of monographs is different from the depth-analysis in back-of-the-book indexes. Neither classification nor subject headings can encompass the multitude of topics in most monographs. Both methods of subject analysis can only describe the major topics dealt with in a major way in a book. This limitation is especially obvious in the American use of only one classification assignment per item. However, even if as many classification symbols as subject headings were used, the symbols would still have to represent only the principal monographic subjects.

John Metcalfe, father of modern Australian librarianship, criticized any classification system that claimed coextensive treatment by any one symbol of the subjects in a book, even in a journal article. His favorite critical targets were Ranganathan's Colon Classification (CC) and the Universal Decimal Classification (UDC) begun by Otlet and LaFontaine.[5] Aware of the severe restriction of contemporary classification schemes, Ranganathan had promised near the end of his career to create a revised classification scheme to analyze the shorter-than-monograph format.[6] If Dewey had known how the developers of UDC would change his DDC to suit the requirements of scientific article subject analysis, he might not have granted the use of his DDC to Otlet and LaFontaine. Even with multiple subject headings, experts differ on whether those for articles should be the same as for monographs.[7] Yet, subject analysts are instructed to be on the lookout for new subject headings in journal indexes because the Library of Congress (LC) has not yet had to analyze such new information in book form.

4. Grace Osgood Kelley, *The Classification of Books: An Inquiry into Its Usefulness to the Reader* (New York: Wilson, 1937). For discussion of Kelley's conclusions, see Richard Joseph Hyman, *Access to Library Collections: An Inquiry into the Validity of the Direct Shelf Approach, with Special Reference to Browsing* (Metuchen, N.J.: Scarecrow Press, 1972), 58–61.

5. John Metcalfe, *Information Indexing and Subject Cataloguing* (New York: Scarecrow Press, 1957), for example, 116–27.

6. S. R. Ranganathan, "Preface to Edition 6," *Colon Classification*, 6th ed., reprinted with amendments (New York: Asia Publishing House, 1963), 10. For Ranganathan's microthought concept, see his "Colon Classification and Its Approach to Documentation," in University of Chicago, Graduate Library School, Library Conference, *Bibliographic Organization; Papers Presented before the Fifteenth Annual Conference of the Graduate Library School, July 24–29, 1950*, Jesse H. Shera and Margaret E. Egan, eds. (Chicago: University of Chicago Press, 1951), 94–105.

7. Sarita Robinson, "A. Problems in the Production of Subject Indexes"; Dorothy Charles, "B. Problems in the Production of Subject Indexes," in Institute on the Subject Analysis of Library Materials, Columbia University, *The Subject Analysis of Library Materials; Papers Presented at an Institute, June 24–28, 1952*, Maurice F. Tauber, ed. (New York: School of Library Service, Columbia University, 1953), 204–17.

Another built-in limitation of classification is its temporary nature, resulting in frequent changes and the perceived need to reclassify. This need seems greater in the harder sciences. Classical humanities schedules can be thought of as closed-end. Since LCC designated specific slots for the works of ancient Greek dramatists, nobody has discovered a new tragedy by Aeschylus. Many of the older precoordinated schedules of LCC and DDC can be used as reference sources. Keeping up with knowledge in the harder disciplines means changing the various editions of that scheme, and the ensuing quandary of librarians who must decide how to assume the economic and intellectual burdens of reclassification. Changes in DDC have been more obvious, but LCC less overtly has had numerous changes, though reclassification on any major scale has not been practiced by LC or its American library users.

The seed of such changes is in the consensus sought by classificationists when they create their schemes. Bliss, for example, claimed that the correct order of the main classes in his Bibliographic Classification (BC) was determined by the consensus of scholars and specialists, meaning the way scholars and specialists have taught the subjects in educational institutions since medieval times.[8] Certainly, DDC and LCC follow such consensus. Dewey devised his DDC while at the Amherst College library, and most of the persisting difficulties of his scheme, e.g., the very small space given non-Western history, literature, religion, and philosophy, were occasioned by the way these subjects were taught in Dewey's day.

The consensus is far from permanent, a criticism by Kelley in her comments on BC.[9] Bliss evidently believed in the relative permanence of his consensus. (Even during the same period, consensus may differ at educational institutions, such as the priority of factors in economics as taught in college.) In American libraries, DDC or LCC is almost ubiquitous because each has an active editorial board with the financial resources to keep the classification up to date.

We are faced with the irony of the pressure for reclassification felt by librarians who use classification schemes, chiefly DDC, but not for predominantly subject revelatory purposes. The pressure is undoubtedly self-made. Libraries using LCC have usually retained the older symbols, fortified in this practice by LC itself as well as by the great number of already established records.

One reason for confusing library classification with subject headings lies in our misconception of specificity, admittedly a subjective concept, since one person's specificity may be another's generalization. Without

8. Henry Evelyn Bliss, *A System of Bibliographic Classification*, 2nd ed., rev. (New York: Wilson, 1936).

9. Grace Osgood Kelley, "[Review of] *The Organization of Knowledge in Libraries; and the Subject-Approach to Books*, by Henry Evelyn Bliss," *Library Quarterly* 4 (Dec. 1934):665–68.

a classified catalog, it is much easier for the subject-heading worker to apply more than one specific heading to a work, though the number must not violate the unwritten law that a book has a limited quantity of major themes. The editors of the *Sears List of Subject Headings* recommend in their introductory instructions that no more than three headings be chosen for the same work.[10] In his book on *Library of Congress Subject Headings (LCSH)*, Haykin was more permissive:

> If the subject matter of a book represents a systematic treatment of it and can be expressed by a single term, then one subject heading will cover it adequately. When this is not the case, as many subject headings may be used for the book as the distinct topics in it require. A single subject heading may be applied to the collection of monographs, if the collection as a whole represents a comprehensive treatment of a single subject. On the other hand, regardless of the fact that the collection is kept intact on the shelves, as many subject headings may be assigned to it as the individual monographs require.[11]

When in doubt about the number or specificity of headings or classification symbols for any work, the subject analyst follows, perhaps by default, both Haykin's advice on subject headings and the rules of classification schemes and ordinarily chooses a heading or symbol general enough to incorporate the many specific topics accessible only through depth indexing. Haykin's optional permissiveness has not been followed in practice by the *NUC*. Researchers have complained that the average number of subject headings per work in the *NUC* is inadequate. The number varies with researchers' methodologies, but there is no doubt that *LCSH*, as applied in the *NUC*, does not give comprehensive subject analysis.[12]

10. Minnie Earle Sears, "Principles of the Sears List," *Sears List of Subject Headings*, 13th ed., Carmen Rovira and Caroline Reyes, eds. (New York: Wilson, 1986), xiv. This prescription is repeated in earlier editions. Mentioned in the 1986 "Principles," xv, is a much earlier survey by Sears of high-school libraries which found only an average of one-and-a-half *Sears* headings per item.

11. David Haykin, *Subject Headings: A Practical Guide* (Washington: Govt. Print. Off., 1951), 69.

12. Bohdan S. Wynar, *Introduction to Cataloging and Classification*, 7th ed. by Arlene Taylor Dowell (Littleton, Colo.: Libraries Unlimited, 1985), quotes different estimated averages: 2.3 *National Union Catalog (NUC)* "subject entries" per item (p. 453) and 4.09 "distinctive words" per item (pp. 514–15). Pauline Atherton Cochrane, in her *Critical Views of LCSH—the Library of Congress Subject Headings: A Bibliographic and Bibliometric Essay. An Analysis of Vocabulary Control in the Library of Congress List of Subject Headings (LCSH)* (Syracuse, N.Y.: ERIC Clearinghouse on Information Resources, Syracuse University, 1981), cites a 1977 survey, which found in the 1910–73 *NUC* "a stable average of 1.3 subject headings per item" (p. 23). The 13th edition of *Sears*, as in note 10 above, cites an average of one-and-a-half *Sears* subject headings per item, determined by a survey of high-school libraries.

In 1886 Cutter had much common sense to impart on the specificity of monograph classification. He rebutted the arguments of the noted American librarians Perkins and Schwartz who had attacked the specificity of the 1885 second DDC edition—which had all of 314 pages! The two critics had complained:

> This process of division, if carried to its logical result, ends in a *reductio ad absurdum*. If we want to keep *every distinct* subject by itself, we are obliged to provide a separate place in our scheme for every variety of animal . . . every author that has ever written.[13]

Cutter replied:

> Not exactly. There are not books on "every variety of animal," etc. Leaving out of view difficulties of notation, there is no objection to the fifty million heads the Duet calls for, when we have books treating of fifty million subjects. Till then no one is bound to provide so many heads, but only the possibility of so many; and that is afforded by the decimal system.[14]

Cutter's logic was based on his conviction that classification of monographs deals only with major specific topics in the books and is not to be confused with depth indexing. His logic still holds although, since his time, full-length books have appeared on such specific topics as the orange and the chicken.

Another reason the functions of classification and subject headings are confused is the much misunderstood practice of adding classification symbol equivalents for many of the major subject headings in *LCSH* and *Sears*. The introduction to the 1988 eleventh edition of *LCSH* says: "Approximately 40 percent of headings are followed by Library of Congress class numbers which generally represent the most common aspect of a subject."[15] DDC equivalents were omitted from the ninth (1965) and tenth (1972) editions of *Sears*. The editorial explanation was enlightening. Despite the preference of users, it was felt that inclusion of classification symbols would encourage neglect of the scheme and that the printing of these symbols could result in a misunderstanding of the different roles

13. F. B. Perkins and Jacob Schwartz, "The Dui-Decimal Classification and the 'Relative Index'," *Library Journal* 11 (Feb. 1886):38.

14. Charles Ammi Cutter, "Close Classification, with Special Reference to Messrs. Perkins, Schwartz, and Dewey," *Library Journal* 11 (July 1886):183.

15. *Library of Congress Subject Headings*, 11th ed., 3 vols., prepared by the Subject Cataloging Division, Processing Services (Washington: The Library, 1988), ix.

of the two subject analysis methods.[16] This point is worth closer examination once again.

Even when the words are the same for the subject heading and the description of the classification symbol, the function of each is different. At LC, the first subject heading for a work is selected to be as close as possible to the meaning of the classification symbol. If one remembers the different purposes of the two means of subject analysis, a confusion can be removed. The subject heading verbalizes as specifically as possible a major topic of the monograph. The classification symbol indicates where in the order of its scheme that topic is to be placed to show its relationship, usually hierarchical, to other topics of the discipline.

The conventional wisdom on the usefulness of the subject heading method against the classification scheme is that the former, at least since Cutter's *Rules*, is more appropriate for retrieval of works on specific subjects by laypersons while the latter is useful for scholars interested in research and survey of related items in a field of knowledge. The two purposes overlap, but the distinction may still be valid, particularly if one includes the larger number of students in colleges and universities since Cutter's time.

The introduction to the 1988 eleventh edition of *LCSH* stated that 162,750 authority records through September 1987 were included, compared with the 1986 tenth *LCSH*, which held about 145,000 authorities through December 1984. An average of 8,000 LC subject headings, including those with subdivisions, were added annually.[17]

Another introductory comment in the eleventh edition of *LCSH*, which should be noted by those who try to find some logic in subject-heading grammar, is: "Inconsistencies in formulation of headings can usually be explained by the policies in force at the varying dates of their creation."[18]

At the end of 1986, LC adopted for its references in *LCSH* the American National Standards Institute (ANSI) standards for thesaurus cross-indexing:

USE = Use the heading referred to (formerly see)
UF = Used for (formerly x)
BT = Broader Term (formerly xx)
NT = Narrower Term (formerly sa)
RT = Related Term (formerly xx and sa)

16. Sears, *Sears List of Subject Headings*, 11th ed., Barbara M. Westby, ed. (New York: Wilson, 1977), vii–viii.

17. *Library of Congress Subject Headings*, 11th ed., vii.

18. Ibid., ix.

SA = See Also (used to introduce general see also references)
(May Subd Geog) = This phrase replaced the former (Indirect) to indicate that a subject may be subdivided geographically.[19]

Before these changes, users (including librarians) could determine only with difficulty whether, for example, xx meant a subordinate (downwards) or coordinate (equally specific) reference. Following the rules laid down by Cutter, LC avoided superordinate (upwards) references in its subject-heading structure.

The editors of *LCSH 11* were definite about why they had borrowed phrases from thesauri for their subject heading list:

> The symbols x, xx and *sa* had been introduced to represent kinds of references. . . . Although understood by librarians, the symbols were generally considered by users to be unintelligible. . . . The decision was made, with advice from others both inside and outside the Library, to use the coding found in thesauri.[20]

These statements were emphasized in the dedication of *LCSH 11* to "Richard S. Angell, Chief, Library of Congress Cataloging Division, 1957–1966, who advocated creating a hierarchical reference structure and whose proposal to use BT, NT, RT notation is brought to fruition in these volumes." It is unclear whether Angell proposed reorganizing *LCSH* into a full thesaurus, but there is no doubt from the editorial comments that LC's adoption of the new reference nomenclature was meant to help a readership puzzled by arcane symbols.

The explanation as to why LC had changed its cross-reference symbols ended with: "The new symbols need not be used in library card catalogs. Those who wish to continue to make cross-reference cards in the manner in which they have become accustomed should continue to do so."[21] The implication is obvious: American librarians follow the leadership of LC even though LC is not legally a national library.

An automated and abbreviated version of *LCSH*, called the Subject Authority File (SAF), has been criticized by librarians for not being a real thesaurus. This debate is discussed in Chapter 5.

Though Panizzi opposed the use of classification for the British Museum catalog, mainly because of its variability and transitoriness, subject search and retrieval can use classification schemes for individual and groups of works.

19. December 1986 microfiche cumulative edition of *LCSH.*
20. *Library of Congress Subject Headings*, 11th ed., x.
21. Ibid.

A search of the access points supplied by classification schemes is meant to retrieve in the catalog a single or many works on the same or related topics rather than items already known by author, title, or subject heading. It is conceivable that a search may be made for known works that may turn up in a classed array. Whatever the purpose of this subject search, a preliminary question is how and where to enter the library's shelflist or bibliographies arranged by classification symbol, as discussed below. Those who by study or experience are familiar with the scheme can go directly to the relevant part of the schedules. The DDC schedules appear in one volume, but LCC has many fascicles and entry into it is more difficult. For DDC a unified official relative index to the entire scheme exists. With LCC, there is no official single index though each schedule usually has its own index or sometimes a detailed table of contents. In any case, consulting the index—as in actual classing—should be only a step to the scheme itself.

Those starting from scratch can go to the library's catalog for the record of a book known by author, title, or subject heading and find a classification assignment. The classification symbol can then be the starting point for examining the classed records. Another way to determine an entry point is to exploit the availability of classification numbers for subject headings in *Sears* and *LCSH*: DDC in *Sears* and LCC in *LCSH*. After determining what part of the classification scheme would be useful, the searcher can consult the shelflist for an inventory by classification symbol of the library's holdings.

Another source, albeit indirect, of classification numbers is the *National Union Catalog (NUC)* whose main entries can be retrieved by descriptive cataloging access points including the added-title heading after 1982.[22] Since 1983 the *NUC* has incorporated a subject-heading index for all its entries. From 1950 through 1982, the *Subject Catalog* and its pre-1975 predecessor, *Library of Congress Catalog, Books: Subjects,* gave subject-heading access to *NUC* works cataloged by LC.[23] Since these subject guides reproduced LCC and DDC notations, they gave direct information on the classification symbol used with the first subject heading. After finding a classification number in this way, the user can search the

22. *National Union Catalog: A Cumulative Author List Representing Library of Congress Printed Cards and Titles Reported by Other American Libraries*, 1958–1962, 54 vols. (New York: Rowman & Littlefield, 1963). For a detailed description of this work, its predecessors and successors, as well as of related works, see Sheehy, *Guide*, AA123–29. (For updatings to the *Guide*, see the January and July issues of *College & Research Libraries*.)

23. *Library of Congress Catalog, Books: Subjects, A Cumulative List of Works Represented by Library of Congress Printed Cards*, 1950–74. (Various publishers, 1950–74), quinquennial cumulations; Library of Congress, *Library of Congress Catalogs: Subject Catalog*, 1975–82 (Various publishers, 1975–82), quinquennial cumulations.

shelflist as previously described. Because *Library of Congress Catalog, Books: Subjects* omitted the tracings on the *NUC* main-entry records until 1972, searchers who wanted an item's classification numbers given with the other subject headings had to consult the *NUC* main-entry record for a complete list of the subject headings and then return to the pre-1972 *Library of Congress Catalog, Books: Subjects* to follow up. One should remember, though, that the LCC symbol assigned a work would be chosen to match only the first subject heading for the work.

The *LCSH* is usually available as a public tool near the library's catalog. The quarterly cumulative *Library of Congress Subject Headings in Microform*, first issued for 1983, may be substituted and is more current.[24] *Sears* is not often found near the catalogs of the American school and public libraries in which it is generally used. This may be because *Sears* is printed as a potential authority list to be written in by catalogers and because most of the annotations would be reflected in the public catalog. Both *LCSH* and *Sears* are available to the librarian, even if not available to the patron.

The card shelflist may not be always accessible to patrons, but it ordinarily is to librarians. The shelflist identifies the library's holdings not only by classification number but further by author, title, and sometimes by all the descriptive cataloging data on the unit record from LC. Although the library's shelflist does not have the multiple classification and cross-references of a classified catalog, it can adequately identify works in the collection that have been assigned a classification notation for their major topic.

Palmer confirmed that classification is "itself an education."[25] Despite the admitted limitations of classification, following the order of a discipline in a scheme is enlightening and can be of future use in search and retrieval by the classification symbol. Again, classification schedules are available usually only to librarians.

Using the classification scheme for shelf browsing in open-stack libraries is an inveterate predilection of American library patrons.[26] Shelf browsing cannot reveal a library's total acquisitions, however. Items may appear in the shelflist but not on the shelf because they are in circulation, in the bindery, in use at the library, or even mysteriously lost. Although

24. Library of Congress, Subject Cataloging Division, *Library of Congress Subject Headings in Microform*, 1983– (Washington: The Library, 1983–), quarterly cumulations. Since the microform edition, the *LCSH* is also available in a cumulated machine-readable edition.

25. Bernard I. Palmer, *Itself an Education: Six Lectures on Classification*, second edition, containing a continuation by Derek Austin entitled "Two Steps Forward . . . " (London: Library Assoc., 1971). Palmer quotes in his title from Alexander Bain. The quotation is on the verso of the title page.

26. Hyman, *Access to Library Collections*, 355–82.

shelf browsing is not a scholarly method of determining the subject strengths of any collection, it can be helpful in showing the range of library acquisitions in a subject and even reveal unsuspected related works. Shelf browsing most helps the patron for whom the shelflist is not available. As Ranganathan stated:

> The shelf arrangement should display the full field of a reader's interest, unexpressed as well as expressed. . . . Indeed, it is only then that he will be able to realise exactly what it is he wants.[27]

Practitioners also benefit from familiarity with the books themselves, especially the noncirculating reference works, so regular shelf examination is highly desirable for librarians. Librarians have long extolled the value to students and other users of direct contact with the books as shelved. Mid–nineteenth-century librarians considered it a powerful aid to learning and wisdom. Cutter was definite on shelf access: "The best catalog is the books themselves."[28] We may politely differ that in search and retrieval by classification symbol, nothing is better than a classified catalog or the shelflist. Yet, patrons—one hopes not librarians—who find the shelf address of an item in the catalog may use the classification notation solely to obtain the item, not to study the relation of that item's subject to those of the adjacent shelved works.

Browsing in the shelflist or stacks is most helpful when the works themselves are focused on, not the notation. After all, the purpose of library classification is to establish not notation but the subject relationships of the book represented by the notation. Classificationists have always downplayed the significance of notation, an attitude expressed by Bliss when he likened the DDC notation to the wagging tail of a friendly dog and claimed it was a major reason for DDC's popularity.[29] The expressiveness and mnemonics of DDC notation are attractive to users, but they are fully comprehensible only to those familiar with DDC techniques.

One reason for the apparent readability of DDC notation is that additions are made to a base number like railroad cars hooked on to a locomotive. This type of agglutinative notation allows the DDC to be truncated at logical points, which decreases its specificity. The DDC numbers on *NUC* records are divided, whenever possible, into three segments for use by libraries of increasing subject collection size. This division creates an intellectual contradiction. It implies that, as with Cutter's Ex-

27. S. R. Ranganathan, *Elements of Library Classification*, 3rd ed. (New York: Asia Publishing House, 1962), 82.

28. Cutter, "Close Classification," 180.

29. Bliss, *The Organization of Knowledge and the System of the Sciences* (New York: H. Holt, 1929), 104.

pansive Classification (EC), the specificity of the classification may be governed not by the subject of the work but by the quantity of works the library has on that subject. On the whole, the more specific the DDC scheme, the longer its notation. Some libraries have a policy of not using DDC notation longer than a set number of digits following the decimal point, though this seems more Procrustean-bed logic than theoretical reasoning. The potential length of DDC notation remains a problem.

The LCC methods of adding to a base include agglutination of other schedule parts, as with DDC, and also arithmetic addition of numbers from tables, such as totaling 2 and 2 to make 4. This latter renders the notation harder to read for those not thoroughly familiar with that part of the scheme and caused one committee to call browsing in an LCC collection "impossible."[30] Because of its structure, the LCC notation cannot be cut back unless the LC-supplied symbol is completely reclassified. However, one reason academic libraries shifted from DDC to LCC in the sixties is that the LCC notation on publicly distributed *NUC* records is a complete call number, including main-entry heading cuttering, while the DDC notation, also appearing on some *NUC* records, lacks the main-entry cuttering of LCC.

After cuttering the DDC number, its length does not seem greater than the average LCC notation. Earlier experience in DDC public libraries reinforces the browsability of DDC compared to college students' later use of LCC. The combination of letters and numerals in the LCC notation should mean shorter base numbers than in the pure numerical DDC notation, and some psychologists feel that staggering letters and numbers in longer notations makes more memorable symbols. It does not appear that classification browsers—either patrons or nonspecialist librarians—have studied DDC and LCC enough to justify any claims of superior browsability. Concentrating on the notated works instead of the notation should reduce browsers' need for technical understanding of any scheme's notational system.

The American Book Publishing Record (BPR) is a commercial bibliography of American publications arranged by DDC and subfiled by main-entry heading. It is a monthly, annual, and multiyear cumulation of the *Weekly Record (WR)*, which lists the *BPR* items in main-entry order.[31] Whenever possible, the catalog records are as supplied by LC and con-

30. American Library Association, Classification Committee, "Report, May 15, 1964: Statement on Types of Classification Available to New Academic Libraries," *Library Resources & Technical Services* 9 (Winter 1965):104–11.

31. *American Book Publishing Record*, 1960– (New York: Bowker, 1960–), monthly with annual and multiannual cumulations; *Weekly Record*, 1974– (New York: Bowker, 1974–). The *Weekly Record* previously was bound with *Publishers' Weekly, the Book Industry Journal.*

stitute complete *NUC* entries. Indexes to the *BPR* are for main-entry headings, titles, and major DDC terms. Available space in the term index often truncates the DDC notation. Entry to the *BPR* is facilitated by its own indexes and by the above-described method for deriving classification numbers from *Sears*. Searching the *BPR* is limited by its chronological division of records (the same difficulty in *NUC* searches); by the fact that *BPR* selects only domestic books; and, of course, by its use of DDC, which is a handicap for LCC libraries. Once a record in *BPR* is located by author, title, or DDC symbol, however, it is possible to note its LCC assignment and then scan an LCC-organized catalog, such as a shelflist. The *BPR* is used most effectively by collection development officers who can examine segments for acquisitions in their DDC libraries. It can also be used to locate works by author or title and to obtain the official LC bibliographic records. The *BPR* may appear almost six months after the *WR*, and its multiyear cumulations can include entries omitted from the monthly *BPR*, for whatever reason.

An intriguing feature of *BPR* is that it includes, with minor exceptions, records for all LC-cataloged domestic publications, even though American DDC libraries usually do not acquire many of the highly specialized or scholarly *BPR* works. Because the *BPR* assigns DDC numbers when they are lacking from *NUC* records, it meets, at least for domestic works, the complaints from DDC libraries that only a selection of domestic works has been assigned DDC numbers on LC records. Those responsible at LC for assigning DDC notations have claimed in the past that they chose only works likely to be in DDC libraries, a claim supported at that time by sales records for LC printed cards. Since then, the *NUC* records have included many more DDC numbers.

A bibliography that is similar in many respects to the *BPR* is the *British National Bibliography (BNB)*,[32] which also arranges its entries by DDC and includes, with some exceptions, all current British publications. It appears weekly and in monthly, annual, and multiyear cumulations. Its records are on a par with those in our *NUC* and can be used in the same way as models for libraries' catalog records. Indexes for each issue include main-entry headings, titles, and subjects. Enough detail is given in *BNB* records for ordering as well as for search and retrieval by classification number.

The subject indexes to the *BNB* take us closer to another concern of this book, the use of subject headings for search and retrieval of surrogates for monographs. From 1950 to 1970, the alphabetical subject

32. *British National Bibliography*, 1950–   (London, 1950–   ), weekly with varying cumulations. (Originally published by the Council of the British National Bibliography, British Museum, the name of the latter sponsoring agency changed in 1973 as the reorganized British Library.)

index to the *BNB* was in the form of a chain index, based on ideas of Ranganathan.[33] Chain indexing aims to construct a complete alphabetical subject index to a classified file or catalog. It identifies and indexes each link in the hierarchical chain of classes represented by the classification notation, beginning with the full notation with its most specific subdivision. Each digit of a DDC number should be separately indexed within the context of the notation. For example, a DDC number with nine digits would ideally have nine chain-index entries, but only the index entry for the number including the last subdivision would reveal the full meaning of the notation for the item. As each other link is indexed, progressively less of the full context is shown. Chain procedure can be traced back to the relative index of DDC, which can also be described as a technique to collocate those distributed relatives scattered by the classification scheme.

A simple example of chain indexing would be for DDC 821, English, that is, British, poetry. All three of the digits can be indexed:

Poetry ; English literature 821
English literature 82
Literature 8

Chain indexing has been described as a series of upwards cross-references, since it directs the searcher to the next higher step in the hierarchy, beginning with the first full notation entry. It has been promoted as economical; once a digit is indexed, it need not be indexed again for any work assigned a DDC notation in which that digit keeps the same meaning. Unfortunately, many problems prevent complete chain indexing, at least of DDC as used in the *BNB*. The chief problem, apparently endemic with chain indexes and admitted even by their champions, is that the context of the element being indexed is shown fully only once. Application problems include hidden links, false links, unsought links, indexing of digits that only duplicate previous meanings, indexers' inconsistency, and—probably the root of most of these ills—hierarchically imperfect classification schemes. For example, a DDC number worked out by Wilson was 364.135, "International crimes, including piracy."[34] The correct chain-index entries for this six-digit DDC number—after eliminating unsought, false, and repetitious links—boiled down to three:

33. Ranganathan, *Theory of Library Catalogue*, 77–198.

34. T. D. Wilson, *An Introduction to Chain Indexing* (London: C. Bingley; Hamden, Conn.: Linnet Books, 1971), frames 71, 68. (Numerous other texts teach techniques of chain indexing.)

Piracy : Criminology 364.135

.

.

.

Offenses : Criminology 364.1

.

.

.

Criminology 364

Dissatisfaction with the *BNB* chain index resulted in its being supplanted in 1971 by PRECIS. Users of the 1950–1970 *BNB* should be aware of the structure of chain indexing to successfully search and retrieve through classification notation. Chain indexing was most popular during the time of its *BNB* application. It was recommended by its British supporters as suitable for all hierarchical classification schemes, including LCC, and was used by the British classificationist Coates in his construction of subject-heading references for nonclassified catalogs.[35]

Applying Ranaganthan's faceted classification analysis in chain indexing appears more appropriate to a description of classified scientific books and articles in specific disciplines, where a comprehensive account in a single statement might more easily be made of the item's subject. Perhaps for this reason, Coates, who did not favor classified catalogs for general collections, created faceted classification schemes for special subject libraries. To what extent the Coates schemes were applied also to journal articles remains a question.

Even closer as a rival to our subject-heading methods is PRECIS indexing, introduced along with 18 DDC in the 1971 *BNB*.[36] PRECIS has garnered even more support than chain indexing has from British and American librarians, who have published at least two guides for its use.[37] In 1977 LC was persuaded to test PRECIS as a replacement for

35. Eric James Coates, *Subject Catalogues; Headings and Structure* (London: Library Assoc., 1960), 135–48.

36. Derek Austin, "Two Steps Forward . . . ," in Palmer, *Itself an Education*, 100–105; idem, "Commentary; PRECIS: An Analysis," *Canadian Library Journal* 29 (Nov.–Dec. 1972):469–73; idem, *PRECIS: A Manual of Concept Analysis and Subject Indexing*, with assistance from Mary Dykstra, 2nd ed. (London: British Library, Bibliographic Services Division, 1984); Austin, "PRECIS in a Multilingual Context. Part 1: PRECIS, an Overview," *Libri* 26 (Mar. 1976):1–37; idem and Jeremy A. Digger, "PRECIS: The Preserved Context Index System," *Library Resources & Technical Services* 21 (Winter 1977):13–30.

37. Mary Dykstra, *PRECIS: A Primer* (London: British Library Bibliographic Services Division, 1985, slightly revised reprint, 1988); Phyllis A. Richmond, *Introduction to PRECIS for North American Usage* (Littleton, Colo.: Libraries Unlimited, 1981).

its *LCSH*. The reported decision of a brief experiment was negative, though PRECIS advocates still urge its use.[38]

PRECIS design has been influenced by Ranganathan's concept of facet analysis and chain procedure and also by Farradane's relational system.[39] PRECIS has been described by Austin as a highly precoordinated index system, meaning that once an entry has been prepared, its elements become parts of an authority list or controlled vocabulary.[40] All succeeding entries are checked against this vocabulary. Though not apparent to its users, the printed index entries are rotated by a computer, which has been fed "an input string containing the terms which are the components of index entries, plus certain codes which would serve as computer instructions during entry generation."[41] The computer also provides previously established cross-references.

Examples of PRECIS indexing may be more instructive than a detailed explanation of its technicalities. The top line of its two-line entry consists of the "lead," or the filing element, followed, if necessary, by a "qualifier" which gives a broader context for the lead. The "display" of the second line shows hierarchy in contrary direction. Sometimes the qualifier and the display are omitted because they are not needed. A. C. Foskett pointed out that a two-line entry may be rotated until the second display line is vacant, at which point the top line reproduces the natural language order, omitting prepositions, of the complete topic.[42]

The following PRECIS examples illustrate most of these points:

Great Britain
  Docks industry. Strikes, Intervention by Government.

.
.
.

38. "Subject Heading System," *Library of Congress Information Bulletin* 37 (Mar. 3, 1978): 154. A rebuttal of LC test conclusions is: Mary Dykstra, "The Lion That Squeaked: A Plea to the Library of Congress to Adopt the British PRECIS System, and to Reconsider the Decision to Overhaul the LC Subject Headings," *Library Journal* 103 (Sept. 1978):1570–72.

39. J. E. L. Farradane, "A Scientific Theory of Classification and Indexing," *Journal of Documentation* 6 (1950):83–90; idem, "Psychology of Classification," *Journal of Documentation* 11 (Dec. 1955):187–201; idem, "Relational Indexing," *Indexer* 2 (1961):127–33; idem, "Relational Indexing and Classification in the Light of Recent Experimental Work in Psychology," *Information Storage and Retrieval* 1 (Jan.–Mar. 1963):3–11.

40. Austin, "Two Steps Forward . . . ," in Palmer, *Itself an Education*, 81.

41. Idem, "PRECIS in a Multilingual Context," 3.

42. Anthony C. Foskett, *The Subject Approach to Information*, 2nd ed. rev. and enl. (London: C. Bingley; Hamden, Conn.: Linnet Books, 1972), 71. The statement does not appear in later editions.

Docks industry. Great Britain
  Strikes. Intervention by Government

.

.

.

Strikes. Docks industry. Great Britain
  Intervention by Government

.

.

.

Government. Intervention in strikes. Docks industry
  Great Britain

France
  Universities, Teachers. Remuneration

.

.

.

Universities. France
  Teachers. Remuneration

.

.

.

Teachers. Universities. France
  Remuneration

.

.

.

Remuneration. Teachers. Universities. France

These examples make some implications of PRECIS immediately clear. Regardless of qualitative considerations, the entries occupy much space. Each entry may have two lines rotated by entry words that, because they indicate important parts of the book's contents, are considered searchable. The relationships of the various elements, e.g., active or passive as in "The Conquest of France," are carefully designated, though this age-old semantic problem of English has been dealt with in the past by measures like roles and links in verbal indexing and in the grammatical phrasings of subject headings.

A criticism of PRECIS in the *BNB* is once again the assumed claim for coextensive coverage in one statement of the major topics in a monograph. The use of the phrase "index system" is perhaps consciously ambiguous. It implies a complete reference to all the topics of consequence considered in a major way by the monograph, a difficulty responded to by the multiple application of subject headings to the same work. It is doubtful that any single PRECIS primary statement can incorporate this possible multitude of subjects. Certainly, a traditional subject-heading system cannot. A conclusion from this criticism is that PRECIS should be interpreted in its narrowest sense as primarily suitable for less than full-length books, for which one-statement coverage is more feasible by narrowly limited subjects. The various examples in PRECIS descriptions and handbooks, in fact, seem to cover topics we would expect would be written about not in monographs but in serials. The suggestion to limit PRECIS to depth indexing is no more radical than Coates's suggested replacement of the DDC by Ranganathan's CC in the *BNB*![43]

As with chain indexing, expanded application has been recommended for PRECIS. Austin and his associates early stated that PRECIS is relevant to all languages and classification schemes. A chief advantage of PRECIS is that each of its entries for a work gives the full context. This context is a goal of more than one PRECIS predecessor in verbal subject indication, that is, Keyword in Context (KWIC) indexing. The use of PRECIS in the *BNB* emphasizes classification as a locational device, not as a method to show the ordered relationships of topics in the corpus of recorded knowledge. Understanding the principles underlying PRECIS would undoubtedly help searchers in the post-1970 *BNB*, but even more it would bring into sharp focus the differences between classified and verbal approaches to surrogates organized by subject content. Some of today's classificationists have blurred or tried to eliminate these differences.

Classification for analytical access, i.e., for journal articles and information within books, has existed for many years, though its influence on modern American practitioners has been very minor. After Otlet and LaFontaine requested Dewey to allow them to adapt DDC for subject analysis of scientific journal articles, the outcome was the UDC, much different in its latest versions from its forebear.[44] Many nondomestic bibliographies, indexes, and reference tools are principally arranged by classification symbol. Because these publications usually include many indexes by title, author, and subject, American librarians need not know the classification scheme used in order to search for and retrieve any of the items. The classification schemes applied have been varied: DDC, UDC, and special faceted classifications designed for the publications.

Walford's Guide to Reference Material, the British multivolume equivalent of Sheehy's *Guide*, is arranged by DDC.[45] (Sheehy's *Guide* has a

43. Coates, *Subject Catalogues*, 91, 130.

44. For bibliographic detail on various editions of this classification and on related works, see Sheehy, *Guide*, AB237–39.

45. Albert John Walford, ed., *Walford's Guide to Reference Material*, 4th ed., 3 vols. (London: Library Assoc., 1980–86).

letter code for its sections, the code having changed in successive editions. The code is apparently based on LCC main-class notation, in turn heavily influenced at the start by Cutter's EC letter symbols.) Reference librarians know that to find a source that will answer a patron's query, that query must first be categorized in the librarian's mind, and then reference tools chosen to respond to that type of question. Classed arrangement by subject and reference tool type in *Walford's* and Sheehy's *Guide* locates and groups the available reference materials accordingly. Subject and typological collocation are essential to the reference librarian's success.

Thompson's *Vocabularium Bibliothecarii*, a multilingual glossary in English, French, German, Spanish and Russian, is organized by UDC.[46] The work is sponsored by the United Nations Educational, Scientific and Cultural Organization (UNESCO or Unesco). In his introduction, Thompson gives an interesting explanation for choosing the classification scheme: when items in a nonroman alphabet are to be accommodated, a classification with a pure numerical notation like DDC or UDC must be used. Unesco has also published works, including *Bibliography of Interlingual Scientific and Technical Dictionaries* and *List of Annual Reviews of Progress in Science and Technology*, both classified by UDC.[47]

Various annual bibliographies have been issued in the *Unesco Documentation in the Social Sciences* series.[48] These bibliographies employ faceted classification schemes created by the British classificationist Kyle and based on her differentiation among people, things, and activities.[49] The British *Library & Information Science Abstracts* (*LISA*) successor to *Library*

46. Anthony Thompson, *Vocabularium Bibliothecarii: English, French, German, Spanish, Russian*, 2nd ed. (Paris: Unesco, 1962).

47. United Nations Educational, Scientific and Cultural Organization, *Bibliography of Interlingual Scientific and Technical Dictionaries . . . Bibliographie de Vocabulaires et Techniques Multilingues. Bibliografía de Diccionarios Ciëntificos y Tecnicos Plurilingües*, 5th ed. (Paris: Unesco, 1969); idem; *List of Annual Reviews of Progress in Science and Technology. Liste de "Mises au Point" Annuelles sur les Progrès de la Science et de la Technique*, 2nd ed. (Paris: Unesco, 1969).

48. The series, United Nations Educational, Scientific and Cultural Organization, *Unesco Documentation in the Social Sciences*, includes: *International Bibliography of Economics. Bibliographie Internationale de Science Économique*, v. 1– , 1952– (Publishers vary, 1955–), annual; *International Bibliography of Social and Cultural Anthropology. Bibliographie Internationale d'Anthropologie Sociale et Culturelle*, v. 1– , 1955– (Publishers vary, 1958–), annual; *International Bibliography of Sociology. Bibliographie Internationale de Sociologie*, v. 1– , 1951– (Publishers vary, 1952–), annual; *International Bibliography of Political Science. Bibliographie Internationale de Science Politique*, v. 1– , 1953– (Publishers vary, 1953–), annual.

49. Barbara Ruth Fuessli Kyle, "Lesson Learned from Experience in Drafting the Kyle Classification," in Library Association, Library Research Committee, *Some Problems of a General Classification Scheme; Report of a Conference Held in London, June 1963* (London: The Assoc., 1964), 21–31.

Science Abstracts, orders its abstracts in accordance with a 1971 faceted classification for the discipline as created by the British Classification Research Group (CRG) and has a chain index for subjects.[50]

To summarize how classification notation can be used for search and retrieval in printed bibliographic surrogates, although classification by nature militates against retrieval of specific items, such retrieval is possible with difficulty in American bibliographic surrogates. Until the classified catalog becomes common in American libraries (its poor cousin the shelf-list at least is available to practitioners) our use of classification will continue to violate its real goal. For analytical access, classification is generally unused in American indexes, though classified reference tools can be helpful in finding a number of items fulfilling the searcher's purpose.

Verbalization of subject matter is the method most American libraries use for search and retrieval in printed and computerized bibliographic surrogates.

Verbalization of subject matter may be defined as that part of subject analysis that attempts to describe and order the topical contents of recorded knowledge in words, not classification. This definition leaves room for many types of verbal subject analysis: subject headings, thesaurus descriptors, index terms, and title-derivative entries including Schlagwort and Stichwort headings. When full-length monographs are not analyzed as wholes, we apply analytical subject-access methods for search and retrieval of the smaller pieces of information within them. (Subject analysis of printed journal articles is considered later.)

Subject headings are the preferred subject analysis method in American libraries for subject search and retrieval of monographs represented by bibliographic surrogates. In his 1876 *Rules*, Cutter codified the application of subject headings in American library catalogs. The basic codification has not since changed nor have the difficulties in its use. Because we are dealing with words, we are faced with many linguistic problems, including meaning, synonymy, transitoriness, bias, entry words for phrases, and lay versus scholarly usage—all the semantic uncertainties of living, changing language. The overall problem is matching the subject heading with the words chosen by the searcher for the subject description. One way out of this dilemma is to use different subject headings for different classes of searchers.

Cutter seized this expedient by constructing his rules for different kinds of libraries: those for study and those for reading. He did not

50. *Library & Information Science Abstracts*, no. 1– , Jan./Feb. 1969– (London: Library Assoc., 1969–), bimonthly; supersedes *Library Science Abstracts*, 1950–1968 (London: Library Assoc., 1950–68), quarterly. Information on the classification scheme used is on the inside back cover of *LISA*.

believe that any one descriptive cataloging or subject analysis code could satisfy the needs of the users of various types of libraries. He was also aware that there could be different groups of users within any one library, and he called for a children's catalog in public libraries.[51]

The conditions of Cutter's day are even more pronounced now. The standards for subject headings in today's American libraries are set by LC with *LCSH* and its frequent updatings: realizations of Cutter's code. The LC collections and legal service responsibilities incline its subject-heading methodology to the scholar and researcher more than to younger readers or public library patrons. The unusefulness of *LCSH* for the popular or school library is often criticized, especially when the cataloged work is acquired by both scholarly and popular libraries. These problems are perhaps insoluble if LC is to avoid the extraordinary intellectual and financial expense of preparing subject headings—in fact, complete bibliographic records—for more than one kind of library. Already, LC is committed (shades of Cutter!) to juvenile literature records in two styles, one for its research collection and the other for school libraries and children's collections. The latter style is the Annotated Card Series with summaries and different subject headings.[52] It is probably an unsatisfactory compromise that the two styles are on the same record.

The periodic editions of *Sears*, though based on *LCSH*, are an effort to satisfy the demands of school and public libraries for subject headings relevant to their patrons. (The popularity of DDC in American public libraries continues because, among other things, the notation can be shortened for less scholarly needs.) The complaints against LC subject headings and descriptive cataloging persist among public librarians. As noted, the Public Library Association plans to prepare its own catalog records. In the meantime, the expansion of networks for all kinds of libraries and the extent to which LC contributes its own catalog records to these networks have made the standard set by LC even more inescapable.

Without denying the reality or seriousness of the situation described, and obviously without trying to solve the ensuing problems, this book fulfills its purpose by assuming that verbal subject search and retrieval for monographs will employ *LCSH* as used for the *NUC*, and also that public librarians will turn to other measures consistent with the LC level of bibliographic surrogation.

51. Charles Ammi Cutter, *Rules for a Dictionary Catalog*, 4th ed., rewritten (Washington: Govt. Print. Off., 1904), 11, 6.

52. "Annotated Cards for Children's Literature," Library of Congress, Processing Department, *Cataloging Service*, bulletin 74 (Apr. 1966):1; "Annotated Card Program. AC Subject Headings," Library of Congress, Subject Cataloging Division, *Library of Congress Subject Headings*, 11th ed., 3 vols. (Washington: The Library, 1988), 1:xxi–xxiv.

A book may have more than one subject heading assigned to it because most books deal in a major way with more than one major subject. The tracings at the surrogate's bottom record all subject headings assigned to the book and are preceded by Arabic numerals. The subject headings are grouped before the record of the descriptive cataloging added-entry headings, which are preceded by roman numerals. Librarians' attitudes about revealing the tracings to the public border on embarrassment. Attempts at concealment have been common. Librarians have felt that subject headings other than the one selected for the heading are not related to the work itself but are clues for "someone" unknown to other works on similar topics. As a result, practitioners and LC have for many years omitted tracings whenever possible. The following instruction for typing catalog cards is typical:

> Since tracing is a record for the cataloger's use, not the public's, there is no reason for putting it on the face of the card unless to save printing costs. There is frequently insufficient room on the face of the card for tracing and nothing is gained in calling a reader's attention to information which does not concern him. . . . It is certainly easier to type it *only* on the back of the main entry card.[53]

The compilation of *NUC* entries by subject heading for LC-acquired items is, as already noted, its *Subject Catalog* and predecessor *Library of Congress Catalog. Books: Subjects*. In May 1972 it was decided to incorporate previously excluded pre-1945 imprints.[54] As of 1983 this compilation was superseded by the subject index for the index-register *NUC*. Through 1971 all tracings were omitted. From 1972 until 1983 the tracings were reproduced. From 1983 the *NUC* subject index omits the tracings again.

The omission of tracings makes it difficult but not impossible to determine all the subject headings given a work, since it means a double search: locating an item under a subject heading in the LC subject guides, and then finding the full tracing for the item under its main-entry heading in the *NUC* or its register edition. A full tracing enables the searcher to see all the major topics of one work as expressed by the subject headings. Thus, in the 1975 *Subject Catalog*, which reproduces the tracings, are two entries under the subject heading "Compressed air—Physiological effect," with the other subject headings indicated:

53. Russell E. Bidlack, *Typewritten Catalog Cards: A Manual of Procedure and Form with 125 Sample Cards* (Ann Arbor, Mich.: Ann Arbor Publishers, c1959), 27.

54. "*Library of Congress Catalog—Books: Subjects*," *Library of Congress Information Bulletin* 33 (Jan. 11, 1974):A–9.

Entry I
1. Compressed air—Physiological effect.
2. Stimulants.
3. Sedatives.
4. Pharmacology, Experimental.

Entry II
1. Underwater physiology.
2. Compressed air—Physiological effect.
3. Diving, Submarine—Physiological aspects.

These two entries under one subject heading produced five related topics. "The subject tracings make up—within the limits of traditional subject heading application—an analytical summary of the principal topics to be found in the book."[55] The searcher can then choose the works that meet the search requirements or suggest other topics worth examining. Such headings as "Stimulants," "Sedatives" and "Pharmacology, Experimental" are quite general. Presumably, if Cutter's axioms are followed, they are also considered within the context of the physiological effect of compressed air and can be studied, too, in relation to underwater physiology and the physiological effects of submarine diving.

As the LC subject guides multiplied, such suggestive contexts were easily recognizable until 1983, when the full tracing record was no longer reproduced in the *NUC* subject index.

The tracing for any item may reveal even more unexpected aspects of the major topic than the first subject heading. In the 1980 *Subject Catalog* is an entry for *Death and Society: A Book of Readings and Sources*, with this tracing reproduced:

1. Death—Social aspects—United States—Addresses, essays, lectures.
2. Abortion—United States—Addresses, essays, lectures.
3. Suicide—United States—Addresses, essays, lectures.
4. Terminal care—United States—Addresses, essays, lectures.

Who would suspect that a general book on the social aspects of death in the United States would also discuss in a major way the subjects of abortion, suicide, and terminal care? Yet, it must be admitted that the foregoing are connected with death. The free-floating subdivision of "Addresses, essays, lectures" is a somewhat old-fashioned *LCSH* subdivision

55. Richard Joseph Hyman, *From Cutter to MARC: Access to the Unit Record* (Flushing, N.Y.: Queens College Press, 1977), 18.

meaning "collected miscellaneous papers or essays . . . or for one paper or essay dealing with a topic as a whole in general terms."[56] In this case the former is meant, as inspection of the book will confirm.

Understanding the subdivision points to how specialized knowledge helps to exploit *LCSH* fully. A book has been devoted entirely to the detailed ways in which LC applies its subject headings. The author of that book complains that although *LCSH* approaches the synthesis and facet analysis of classification schemes in its use of subdivisions, it has no stated or perceivable policy in the sequence chosen for most of the subdivisions.[57] Fortunately for searchers, these refinements of *LCSH* techniques do not significantly affect ordinary subject search, since most LC subject headings start off with a topic to which subdivisions are appended in some sort of order. Matching one's words for a topic with the verbalization of the subject heading remains a serious problem, but it can be alleviated by using *LCSH* with its numerous cross-references and, just as important, by locating a known analogous work's subject heading.

The collocative power of subdivisions is affected by their direct or indirect form. A decision has been made—and kept—by LC to use indirect geographic subdivision.[58] In a classic example, "Banks and banking" is subdivided by state and then by city, rather than directly by city. All the cities are first collocated by state name. Otherwise, the city names would be scattered alphabetically and very difficult to assemble in search.

The sequence of added entries, but not of all subdivisions, has been set by LC and may be valuable for computerized searching. The most extensively treated major topic in the work is given the first subject heading, which is expected to agree as closely as possible with the classification assignment. The other subject headings follow in descending order of relevance. As with making the tracings public, practitioners have been admonished against following LC practice in the order of subject headings:

> Unwritten rules and practices would be subject to the same pragmatic scrutiny. Some catalogers, for example, think that the sequence of subject headings in the tracing should follow certain requirements. Attention to such detail is completely valueless

56. Library of Congress, Subject Cataloging Division, *Library of Congress Subject Headings*, 8th ed., 1:xix.

57. Lois Mai Chan, *Library of Congress Subject Headings: Principles and Applications*, 2nd ed. (Littleton, Colo.: Libraries Unlimited, 1986), 86.

58. "Subject Headings," Library of Congress, Processing Department, *Cataloging Service*, bulletin 114 (Summer 1975):7; 121 (Spring 1977):14; "Indirect versus Direct Subdivision," *RTSD Newsletter* 13 (Winter 1988):3.

> except where printed or mimeographed cards are concerned and even there its value is doubtful.[59]

It is easy to exercise hindsight. The value of weighting subject headings has become perhaps surprisingly important in current computerized search. A moral to be drawn is that most decisions, especially in subject analysis, are time-bound. Intellectual stagnation would result if fear of changes forestalled decisions made in light of contemporary realities.

The full tracing can be used in manual coordinate retrieval of works through surrogates that contain subject cataloging data.[60] Strictly speaking, the traditional subject heading is not the same as the coordinate indexing term or descriptor. Objections to precoordinated controlled vocabularies produced postcoordinate or coordinate indexing. Here, the coordinating process is suggested for manual search and retrieval in non-computerized files.

The coordinating process can be used in two ways. First, as in the above examples of the physiological effect of compressed air, one or more items may be selected under a subject heading if the other headings in the tracing provide a relevant context for the searcher. The collocative function of the subject heading benefits the searcher by grouping works on the same subject. The tracings on the records for these works fill out the context or give related topics. A second way is to follow up on the indicated added-subject headings, find out what other works are listed under these added-entry headings, and decide which of the items are described as combining the topics sought. This second way comes close to the instructions posted in libraries telling how readers can use the tracings to consult related topics, though coordinate search is not mentioned.

Undoubtedly, manual coordinate search can be a tiresome procedure, especially in comparison with automated searching, but it can be done and sometimes is the only procedure available. Many of the steps are instinctive and take longer to describe than to perform.

Coordinate search may merge descriptive cataloging added entries with subject headings.[61] The searcher may want works on a subject that is related to a person or body whose names are given in the descriptive cataloging tracings. Such merging of search requirements is particularly important for determining reliability or authoritativeness. The search may begin from the opposite end, when works are sought by main-entry or

59. Andrew D. Osborn, "The Crisis in Cataloging," *Library Quarterly* 16 (Oct. 1941): 404. Cf. Bidlack, note 53.

60. Hyman, *From Cutter to MARC*, 16–20.

61. Ibid., 19–20.

added-entry descriptive cataloging headings associated with certain subjects.

The subject heading, at least in general American usage, can be manifold compared with the classification symbol or its description. In both LCC and DDC, the biography of one or more persons connected with a particular subject, such as Einstein with atomic physics or relativity, can be placed in different parts of the scheme. Voluminous authors may have classification locations of their own for biography and criticism, like Shakespeare in DDC. The subject heading can use the name of any biographee as well as the subject of the biographee's claim to fame. However—to keep repeating—the classification symbol and the subject heading must be general enough to collocate all the topical works in the collection but specific enough to distinguish what is being collocated.

The *Cumulative Book Index (CBI)* is a commercial bibliography. With its supplements to the older *United States Catalog*, it attempts to cover English-language publications since 1898.[62] In its current editions, published eleven times a year and variously cumulated, it gives in one dictionary listing author, title, and subject entries. Each of the main *CBI* entries contains full descriptive cataloging data, including price, but omits tracings and both DDC and LCC symbols. Its publishers claim coverage of some 50,000 to 60,000 hardcover and paperback English-language books each year. The International Standard Book Number (ISBN) and the LC card number are included so that obtaining the *NUC* record becomes easier with later issues. Its value is especially appreciated in searching for older books for which the author, title, or subject is known, but the date of publication may be only estimated. The subjects are verbalizations modeled on *LCSH* and with numerous subdivisions.

In general, the *CBI* assigns only one subject heading per work; if necessary, more may be assigned. For example, in the March 1984 *CBI* appears the title, *Using SCRIPSIT with the TRS-80 Microcomputer Model III and Model I.* This book is entered under its author, title, and two subject headings, "Scripsit (Computer program)" and "TRS-80 (Computer)—Programming." Though the average number of *LC* subject headings per item in the *NUC* is calculated at less than two, the modal number is two, so *CBI* does not give as full subject coverage as the *NUC*. The subject headings in *CBI*, especially in cumulated editions, do collocate English-language publications during known or estimated periods, but lack of tracings and multiple subject headings restricts coordinate subject search.

62. *Cumulative Book Index, a World List of Books in the English Language*, 1928/32– (New York: Wilson, 1933–), varying cumulations; *Cumulative Book Index* (New York: Wilson, 1898–), monthly except August; *United States Catalog; Books in Print, Jan. 1, 1928*, 4th ed. (New York: Wilson, 1928).

Though the British do not have exact equivalents of U.S. official and commercial bibliographies, *Whitaker's Cumulative Book List* is similar to our *CBI*. Its subtitle is: *Alphabetical List under Author and Title, and, in Many Cases, under Subject. Whitaker's* appears quarterly and in annual and multiannual cumulations. It merges the weekly listings of *The Bookseller: The Organ of the Book Trade*.[63] Like our *CBI*, it tries for a complete listing of English-language publications, at least from its own country, but its subject headings are of the Schlagwort or title-derivative kind. Its introduction explains that the subject word is used when it forms part of the title. Like our *BPR*, it uses a form heading for nontopical works, e.g., "Fiction." Cutter in his *Rules* defines Schlagwort and Stichwort entry with the phrases "Subject-word-entry" and "Important-word or catch-word entry," respectively. (One should not define Schlagwort entry as catch-word entry.)

> *Subject-word-entry*, entry made under a word of the title which indicates the subject of the book. *Important-word* or *catch-word-entry*, entry made from some word of the title other than the first word and not indicative of the subject, but likely to be remembered and used by borrowers in asking for the book. (Not recommended in these Rules)[64]

Cutter's rules for subject headings were established to promote uniformity or standardization that was impossible with Schlagwort and Stichwort entry. His purpose was to codify construction of a controlled vocabulary of subject heads. A subject word (a derived term) could, if appropriate, be accepted as a subject heading (an assigned term). Cutter's definition of "subject-entry" was for the assigned heading: "registry under the name selected by the cataloger to indicate the subject."[65]

Subject word entry (Schlagwort entry), as shown by *Whitaker's*, is not uncommon in European bibliographies. Even LC in the United States has not always resisted the temptation; Lubetzky, as late as 1941, was complaining about LC substitution of subject word entry for an authentic subject heading.[66] In 1958 Luhn, in this country, revived Schlagwort

63. *Whitaker's Cumulative Book List . . . ; a Classified List of Publications . . .* , 1924– (London: Whitaker, 1924–), quarterly, cumulating throughout year, with multiannual cumulations; *The Bookseller: The Organ of the Book Trade*, 1858– (London: Whitaker, 1858–), weekly since 1909.

64. Cutter, *Rules*, 4th ed., 19.

65. Ibid.

66. Seymour Lubetzky, "Titles: Fifth Column of the Catalog," *Library Quarterly* 11 (Oct. 1941):412–30.

entry with his Keyword in Context indexing, a means of his selective dissemination of information (SDI), as described below.[67]

Another subtitle for *Whitaker's* is "a classified list of publications." *Whitaker's* classification groups its subject word entries under some forty-six rubrics, from Aeronautics through Wireless and Television. This kind of grouping reminds one of Cutter's classed subject-table, one of the means to attain the objects of a dictionary catalog as listed in his *Rules*.[68] The subject word entry–group name in *Whitaker's* is printed in abbreviated form at the end of each entry, e.g., Pol for Political Science. *Whitaker's* applies its classification, for example, to tabulate the number of its books for each of these groups. *Whitaker's* subject approach, even more than the *CBI*, restricts subject collocation and coordinate search.

Nineteenth-century American library catalogs used analytics mainly for volumes in series and sets and for parts of composite works.[69] This tradition continues in printed indexes and bibliographies. Analysis of noncomposite books poses a much more difficult problem, which is discussed later in this chapter.

In 1901 the *A. L. A. Index to General Literature*, a subject index for books of essays and general literature that tried to do for books what *Poole's Index* had done for periodicals, was published.[70] Through 1910, the *A. L. A. Index* and *Supplements* analyzed books; they were superseded with some overlapping by Wilson's *Essay and General Literature Index*, still being published in semiannual and annual cumulations.[71] Like *Poole's*, the *A.L.A. Index* did not have author or title access. The *Essay and General Literature Index* added access points for authors and some titles.

The Wilson *Public Library Catalog*, formerly the *Standard Catalog for Public Libraries*, has since 1934 included, besides some noncomposite books, entries for analyzed subject material in hundreds of books of a

67. Hans Peter Luhn, *Keyword-in-Context Index for Technical Literature (KWIC Index)* (Yorktown Heights, N.Y.: International Business Machines Corporation, Advanced Systems Development Division, 1959); idem, "Selective Dissemination of New Scientific Information with the Aid of Electronic Processing Equipment," *American Documentation* 12 (1961):131–38.

68. Cutter, *Rules*, 4th ed., 12.

69. Richard Joseph Hyman, *Analytical Access: History, Resources, Needs* (Flushing, N.Y.: Queens College Press, 1978), 16–18.

70. American Library Association, *A. L. A. Index . . . to General Literature*, 2nd ed., enl. (Boston, Chicago: ALA Publishing Board, 1901–1914); *Poole's Index to Periodical Literature*, 1802–1881, rev. ed., 2 vols. (1891; reprint ed.: New York; P. Smith, 1938; Gloucester, Mass.: P. Smith, 1963); *Supplements*, Jan. 1882–Jan. 1, 1907, 5 vols. (Boston: Houghton, c1887–1908).

71. *Essay and General Literature Index, 1900–1933; an Index to About 40,000 Essays and Miscellaneous Works*, ed. by Minnie Earle Sears and Marian Shaw (New York: Wilson, 1934), semiannual, annual and multiannual cumulations since basic volume.

composite character.[72] It has three parts: a classified catalog, arranged by DDC; an author, title, subject, and analytical catalog index; and a directory of publishers and distributors. Annotations are given for the main entries, constituting a buying guide for public librarians. All of the aforementioned indexes and bibliographies afford analytical subject access to nonfiction works and, though not giving the depth-analysis found in back-of-the-book indexes for monographs, are most useful in analytical subject search of collections of essays and separate contributions.

The above kinds of indexes and bibliographies prompted the comment by a recognized authority in cataloging that such analytical reference works provide a usable substitute for a large amount of analysis, the cost of which would be prohibitive in the average catalog.[73] When the same techniques are extended to collections of belles lettres, the analysis is more useful—and sought—for its descriptive cataloging access points, that is, for identification by author and title of the included work rather than for its subject approaches.

An example of an index to belles lettres is the Wilson *Short Story Index*, which gives access by subject as well as by author and title.[74] The subject headings, as in all Wilson bibliographies and indexes, are modeled as far as possible on the *LCSH*, though many have had to be adapted to fit the work described, particularly true for the Wilson indexes of belles lettres.

A major problem in assigning useful subject headings in these indexes is that the themes are often vague, overly general, or even overly specific. The *Short Story Index*, for example, has subject headings for Fantasies, Farm life, Godmothers, Paintings, Romans in Judaea, and Trucks. Only Farm life and Trucks appear in the *LCSH*. The others either have references to LC accepted headings or are absent. A saving grace is that searchers are looking more for identification by author and title, and subsequent location in a collection, than for the subject content of a particular work. For those searchers keen on subject identification, another saving grace is that the subject heading in the index can be identified by its closeness to the *LCSH* entry.

Ottemiller's Index to Plays in Collections should be distinguished from the Wilson *Play Index*.[75] The former excludes separately published plays

72. H. W. Wilson, *firm, publishers*, *Public Library Catalog*, 8th ed., 1983 (New York: Wilson, 1984), plus 4 annual paperbound supplements.

73. Margaret Mann, "Elimination of Subject Analyticals," *Introduction to Cataloging and the Classification of Books*, 2nd ed. (Chicago: ALA, 1943), 154.

74. H. W. Wilson, *Short Story Index* (New York: Wilson, 1953–), annual and multiannual cumulations.

75. John Henry Ottemiller, *Ottemiller's Index to Plays in Collections: An Author and Title Index to Plays Appearing in Collections Published between 1900 and Early 1975*, by John M. Connor and Billie M. Connor, 6th ed., rev. and enl. (Metuchen, N.J.: Scarecrow Press, 1976); *Play Index*, 1949/52–1978/82 (New York: Wilson, 1953–83).

and lacks the subject access of the latter, which has also an index to the plays' casts by gender and number. The most useful headings for searchers are either those derived from descriptive cataloging, that is, author and title, or form headings, which are considered a species of subject heading. The form headings identify the item by genre or type of literature, e.g., farce or fantasy or science fiction.

Other analytical indexes like *Granger's Index to Poetry* and the *Sears Song Index*, as well as those already mentioned, are described in works like Sheehy's *Guide*.

Subject analytical access to journal (periodical or serial) literature is more practical and rewarding for searchers. Analytical access to journal articles through subject verbalization began at least two centuries ago, as shown in the historical chapters. Today numerous printed serials indexes give such access. Most also have headings for authors, though not usually for titles. Most, too, include access to noncomposite and composite books, though not with depth indexing.

The indexes are ordinarily specialized by discipline. A typical group is that published by the H. W. Wilson Company. Subject headings follow *LCSH* to the extent possible, with adjustments for new or very specific article subjects. The Wilson indexes, except the general *Readers' Guide to Periodical Literature*, cover such special genres or disciplines as: applied science and technology, art, bibliography, biography, biology and agriculture, book reviews, business, education, general science, humanities, law, library science, and social science.[76]

Except in rare cases, the Wilson periodical indexes assign only one subject heading per article. Cross-references and subheadings are numerous, but unless one's verbalization of the subject matches the chosen heading or its reference, the subject search may be fruitless. Complaints from users on lack of multiple subject headings do not seem numerous. This strengthens a belief that topics of journal articles are narrow enough to be encompassed by one coextensive heading known to the searcher. Under each subject heading the articles are arranged alphabetically by title. As in title-derivative indexing, the titles may have to be enriched to fill in the context, but in Wilson indexes the enrichments serve also as content summaries. For example, in the 1984–85 cumulation of the *Readers' Guide*, under "Football. Italy," the article, "A new kick on the boot," appears, followed by the bracketed "jag" or enhancement, "American A. Primavera coaching football and making violins." In the same cumulation "The year the Heisman Trophy went to a pro," followed by the bracketed "1983 winner M. Rozier," appears under "Football players.

76. *Readers' Guide to Periodical Literature*, 1900– (New York: Wilson, 1905–), semimonthly, annual and multiannual cumulations.

Awards." Both Primavera and Rozier are also listed as subjects under their names. (These are rare exceptions to the policy of one subject heading per item.)

A comparison of "Football" subject headings in this Wilson index with those in *LCSH* is somewhat surprising—not because, as expected, the periodicals index lists more, but because some in *LCSH* are so specific that it is almost difficult to believe that entire books were written on the topics. Both the Wilson index and *LCSH* have "Kicking (Football)." Some of the *LCSH* headings are even more specific than those in the *Readers' Guide*, e.g., "Line play (Football)" and "Passing (Football)," neither of which appears in the Wilson index. Evidently the subjects of monographs can be just as specific, sometimes more so, than those of periodical articles, at least from the evidence in *LCSH* and this Wilson index cumulation. Since the Wilson subject headings try to follow *LCSH*, consulting the latter can help refine a search in the former.

Other indexes for journals (and some monographs) do not employ the traditional Cutter subject-heading approach, but use a thesaurus to list its vocabulary of terms or descriptors as members of a classified hierarchical order. The Educational Research Information Center (ERIC) thesaurus shows for each descriptor its Broader Term (BT), Narrower Term (NT), and Related Term (RT), the last a nonhierarchical relationship.[77] It also gives numerous cross-references from unused to chosen terms. Cutter in his *Rules* had advised against upwards "see also" references, not on theoretical grounds but because he felt that this practice, once begun, would be endless.[78] (Even in pre-1986 *LCSH* there have been exceptions to Cutter's admonition.) The thesaurus makers ignore Cutter completely by merging the two faces of subject analysis: subject headings and classification. The *ERIC Thesaurus* is an excellent example of the thesaurus concept as it has been applied to the ERIC publications, *Current Index to Journals in Education (CIJE)* and *Resources in Education (RIE)*, formerly *Research in Education*, which indexes monographs, reports and other nonperiodical literature.[79]

Studying the *ERIC Thesaurus* and its application to *CIJE* and *RIE* can be most beneficial to subject searchers for depth indexing in any field. Complications abound in the structure of this thesaurus, but some salient differences from traditional subject-heading work are unmistakable. First,

77. Educational Research Information Center, *Thesaurus of ERIC Descriptors*, 11th ed., ed. James E. Houston (Phoenix, Ariz.: Oryx Press, 1986).

78. Cutter, *Rules*, 4th ed., 79–80.

79. *Current Index to Journals in Education*, vol. no. 1/2– , Jan./Feb. 1969– (Various publishers, 1969–), monthly with semiannual and annual cumulative indexes; *Resources in Education* (title: *Research in Education* through vol. 9, 1974) (Washington: various publishers, 1966–), monthly with semiannual and annual cumulated indexes.

as in chain indexing, browsing among broader terms is emphasized. Reciprocally, going down the chain of clearly delineated narrower terms makes browsing in this direction easy, not to mention pursuing the leads given by the listed related terms.

An even more significant distinction between the conventional subject headings and the thesaurus terms or descriptors lies in the number of each which can be assigned to the same work. *Computer-Readable Databases: A Directory and Data Sourcebook*, sponsored by the American Society for Information Science (ASIS), is valuable for its criteria for identification of the various databases.[80] One criterion is the average number of thesaurus descriptors and uncontrolled keywords applied to the database entries. (As with the *ERIC Thesaurus*, descriptors and keywords can be assigned to both printed and automated formats.) *CIJE* was credited with an average of seven controlled thesaurus descriptors or terms and 1.3 uncontrolled keywords per document. (In the *ERIC Thesaurus*, uncontrolled keywords are called identifiers and are assigned as needed to individual items, but they are not in the official thesaurus-controlled vocabulary.) For *RIE*, *Computer-Readable Data Bases* reported an average eleven thesaurus-controlled terms and 1.5 uncontrolled keywords per document.

Furthermore, the ERIC vocabulary is applied in *CIJE* and *RIE* to summaries or abstracts of the document's contents. The summary, an example of additional surrogation, boils down to essentials of the subject matter of the item and, like the catalog added entry, can make consulting the original unnecessary. These ERIC terms and keywords are assigned mostly to nonmonographic items, typically much shorter than books. Even *RIE*, according to *Computer-Readable Databases*, contained monographs making up only some 14 percent of all its coverage. The greater specificity possible with a thesaurus, in comparison with an average of about two subject headings per *NUC* entry, confirms the usefulness of the thesaurus concept in depth indexing but also points up the accepted role of the subject heading—exemplified by *LCSH*—in the analysis of unsummarized monographs.

The summaries or abstracts of articles, even the enrichments or enhancements of titles, in journal indexes are invaluable in searching for and retrieving records of items relevant to a subject. One must be aware, however, that most printed indexes and automated databases yield only the abstracts or summaries, not the original documents. In other words, search of bibliographic surrogates in printed or automated files ends in

80. *Computer-Readable Databases: A Directory and Data Sourcebook*, 4th ed., 2 vols., comp. and ed. Martha E. Williams (Chicago: ALA, 1985). A 5th ed. with other editors and publisher came out in 1989.

the retrieval of other, if fuller, surrogates. Perhaps this result is the ultimate possible in bibliographic surrogation, though a search can be pursued until the original is retrieved. A summary may fulfill the searcher's needs. Some commercial services provide copies of indexed articles on request. The Institute for Scientific Information in Philadelphia, publisher of citation indexes, maintains a tearsheet service. Full-text displays coupled with free-text search capability have recently been promoted by some distributors of machine-readable databases. This approach, designed among other things to make abstracts unnecessary, presents its own theoretical and practical problems, which are discussed in Chapter 6.

A most useful criterion of *Computer-Readable Databases* for searchers in printed surrogates is the "Other aids" on the availability of paper copies of the computer-readable database. Many of the hundreds of databases in *Computer-Readable Databases* began as printed indexes. Some database producers have automated their entire index, as has ERIC, but have also maintained the original printed version. Fortunately for searchers in automated databases, *Computer-Readable Databases* cites for all databases their starting automation date. Retroactive conversion to automated format has sometimes been done, but rarely for the entire time span of the printed index.

Descriptive cataloging and subject analysis have been merged in KWIC indexing, a title-derivative indexing technique created by Luhn in 1959 to facilitate his selective dissemination of information (SDI).[81] Although processed by computer, the resultant KWIC index appears in print form and rotates the words of article (and some monograph) titles so that each significant word appears in alphabetical sequence, excluding articles and many common prepositions. Because the remainder of the title is grouped around the alphabetized word, the indexing is said to give the context of that word. Slightly different forms of KWIC indexing are Keyword Out of Context (KWOC) and Keyword Alongside of Context (KWAC) indexing. Luhn sought a "quick and dirty" computerized sorting of title words to apprise patrons as soon as possible of publications of subject interest. No specialized knowledge of the subject is claimed of the computer processors.

Title entry is formally part of descriptive cataloging, but KWIC and earlier Schlagwort practices exploited the subject value of titles, especially for technical works. Objections to KWIC are easily raised, e.g., dependence on unreliable subject content words, and semantic perplexities if they are unsolved by title enrichments or enhancements. Yet, KWIC indexing remains popular for technical specialists concerned with current

81. Luhn, *Keyword-in-Context Index*; idem, "Selective Dissemination."

publications in their field. Subject expertise enters, of course, into the selection of the items to be indexed. KWIC indexing is not designed for permanent cumulation, though the products of computer-rotated terms appear in the indexes of thesauruses, like ERIC, and in the citation indexes prepared by the Institute for Scientific Information.

The citation indexes just mentioned can be used to identify and retrieve cited works in articles and books on specific subjects. As for KWIC indexing, computer processors of citation indexing are not expected to know the subject. The computer processing is strictly mechanical. Citation indexes are of principal value to those in search of previous works on a subject and also to collection development or acquisition personnel. It must also be remembered that an item may be frequently cited for rebuttal, not for authoritative status.

The *Science Citation Index* (SCI) is published quarterly and in annual cumulations by the Institute for Scientific Information.[82] Both descriptive and subject approaches to bibliographic organization are utilized for access points to the surrogates. Descriptive cataloging access points are given by the *SCI* and its Source Index. The *SCI* order is alphabetical by cited author, or by title for anonymous works. One section of the *SCI* is the Patent Citation Index, which lists all cited patents (foreign and domestic) in numerical order by patent number. The Source Index is arranged alphabetically by source item author, that is, by author of the citing work. For each source item there is a code letter indicating the type of source item, e.g., *M* for abstracts from meetings and *R* for reviews and bibliographies. Within the Source Index is a separate section, the Corporate Index, where all source items are listed alphabetically by author under the name of the organization where the work was performed. Bibliographic detail in these indexes is full enough to identify the item or locate it in a main-entry listing. Subject access is provided by the *SCI* Permuterm Subject Index (PSI), described as follows:

> Permuterm is a contraction of the phrase "permuted terms." In the *PSI*, the term "permuted" is used in its correct mathematical sense. This is to be distinguished from a Key-Word-In-Context (KWIC) index which rotates the words in an article title rather than fully permuting them. . . .
>
> To produce the *PSI*, a computer is used to permute all significant words within each title and subtitle of any item included in the *Source Index*. All possible pairs of terms are formed. Thus, for a title containing n significant words, there will be $n\ (n-1)$

82. *Science Citation Index*, 1961– (Philadelphia: Institute for Scientific Information, 1961–), quarterly with annual cumulations.

> pairs. With this system, every significant word takes a turn at being the primary term *as well as* being a co-term.[83]

Though most newspapers appear more frequently than journals or periodicals or magazines or other types of serials, they are given separate bibliographical treatment, e.g., Gregory's *American Newspapers, 1821–1936*, Brigham's *History and Bibliography of American Newspapers, 1690–1820*, and LC publications, all of them union lists dedicated to one genre. *Ulrich's International Periodicals Directory*, our most comprehensive English-language bibliography, excludes newspapers.

Analytical access is available in indexes to leading American newspapers, probably the outstanding one being the *New York Times*.[84] Like most newspaper indexes, that of the *New York Times* is generally a subject index, the headings created by its compilers. Including reprinting and some reworking of its "Prior Series," it dates back to September 1851. Varying over the years in frequency and structure, it is now published in semimonthly and annual cumulations. (The newspaper itself appears in microfilm some weeks after the print version.) Within the index is a page, "How to Use the New York Times Index," which should be read by all users.

The *New York Times Index* tries to enter all stories under the most specific subject heading, e.g., Steel rather than Metal. Since people are commonly the focus of news events, personal name subject headings are numerous. Under the subject heading the stories are grouped in order of appearance in the paper, each story having a synopsis in its full main entry. Often the same story with its synopsis is repeated under a subject heading, connected by a "see also" reference. Sometimes the "see also" reference is general, referring not to the location of a particular story but to a related topic where other stories can be found. The synopsis frequently can substitute for the actual story. The *New York Times Index* is based on the paper's late city edition, and stories that appear only in other editions are not indexed.

Other American newspapers have useful indexes that pay special attention to stories of local interest. Unlike periodicals indexes, there is not a printed newspaper index that covers numerous newspapers. Combined printed indexes for newspapers have been attempted but have generally not succeeded commercially, perhaps because they have not offered fully retroactive coverage.

83. Marvin Weinstock, "Citation Indexes," *Encyclopedia of Library and Information Science* (New York: M. Dekker, 1968–83), 5:27.

84. For details on the bibliographies and indexes in this and the preceding paragraph, consult Sheehy, *Guide*, under Newspapers and Periodicals.

The British equivalent of the *New York Times Index* is the index to the London *Times*, which can be traced to 1790.[85] Like the *New York Times Index*, it has undergone many changes of frequency, coverage, and format. Only familiarity in its use can clarify its many intricacies. Indexes for newspapers of other countries are much more fragmentary in both time span and subject coverage than those for the *New York Times* and the London *Times*.[86]

Analytical subject access to noncomposite books remains a stubborn problem. Even thesaurus application to abstracts of books in *RIE* does not equal the depth indexing of a good back-of-the-book index. Previously described surrogates may lead the searcher to an undesired option: reading the book itself to find out what the author has to say about all the topics encompassed. At least a back-of-the-book index makes selectivity possible.

Books may not be so important to those who wish records of the latest progress in the harder sciences. Such information usually appears first in nonmonographic publications. Information in books may be outdated even before publication. Luhn's Selective Dissemination of Information might better be called immediate or introductory dissemination of information, while his KWIC obviously implies speed both in processing and distribution.

Some searchers are concerned with book summaries of scientific developments, extensive treatments of literary figures and themes, or ancient problems in philosophy and other humanities. For searchers after detailed information in books, only the books' indexes or precise tables of contents can give the depth indexing required. Not surprisingly, a recent investigation of how to improve subject access in surrogates for monographs recommended more subject headings as well as excerpts from tables of contents and back-of-the-book indexes.[87]

This author proposed in 1978 that an abstract be printed in every book and included in its surrogates.[88] The abstract, at least for technical subjects, could be prepared by the author and edited for clarity, specificity, and significant subject words by the publisher. Depth indexing of monographs could take advantage of the techniques used for surrogates of nonmonographic items in journal or periodical indexes. Book abstracts in computerized databases would also benefit nonautomated libraries because printed card, bookform, and microform catalogs as well as

85. London *Times Index to the Times*, 1906– (London: *Times*, 1907–), varying frequency; *Palmer's Index to the Times Newspaper*, 1790–June 1941 (1868–1943; reprint ed.; New York: Kraus, 1965),

86. See Sheehy, *Guide*, under Newspapers.

87. Cochrane, *Critical Views of LCSH*.

88. Hyman, *Analytical Access*, 29–31.

printed bibliographies and indexes are increasingly produced from machine-readable sources.

An interesting and underestimated expansion of depth indexing of monographs was Kilgour's 1976 printed *The Library and Information Science CumIndex*,[89] an interfiled cumulation of back-of-the-book indexes of ninety-six library and information science items with an average publication date of 1966. Though the work was criticized for inadequate editing and lack of currency, its underlying purpose merits attention, especially now when computerization advances can make the effort easier. Kilgour's cumulation was specialized by discipline, a lesson worth taking also from many periodicals indexes.

The problems of subject search in printed bibliographic surrogates, problems that also occur in automated search, are many. A principal one is the transitory quality of subject analysis, whether the results be subject headings or classification notations. Another difficulty is obviously the frequent inability to match the standardized heading in an authority list, like the *LCSH*, to the searcher's chosen verbalization of the topic or topics of the item sought. This difficulty is of major significance in American libraries, where subject headings, not classification schemes, are the primary tools of bibliographic organization for subject access.

In suggesting a way to deal with the problem of the transitoriness of subject analysis, the librarian must, reluctantly or not, accept the fact that subject analysis is a time-bound procedure. Recognizing the temporary nature of subject analysis should sharply reduce the craving of practitioners to recatalog a collection in accordance with the latest subject headings and classification schemes. If the truth be told, most catalogers in large collections allow the subject-heading entries of their older acquisitions to remain whenever possible, for lack of time and money. Intellectual considerations have little to do with that decision.

The time problem in subject analysis is most serious in giving access to whole books. It is somehow expected that subject analysis in periodical indexes will change more rapidly to accommodate newer concepts and verbiage. A possible reason is that subject search in periodicals ordinarily emphasizes state-of-the-art information, so subject analysis of the literature is assumed to be up-to-date in its language. Fortunately, most periodical indexes meet the expectation. Back-of-the-book indexes are not at all standardized in their subject access. Many noncomposite works, in fact, lack indexes, and indexes for books, furthermore, are usually the responsibility of the author.

89. Frederick G. Kilgour, *The Library and Information Science CumIndex* (Los Altos, Calif.: R & D Press, 1976).

Indexes to reference tools, like Sheehy's *Guide to Reference Books*, favor descriptive cataloging access over subject analysis. If a librarian can remember the author or title of only one reference source, the grouping in the text of similar works justifies an indirect subject or form search in such a work as the *Guide*. (Incidentally, the *Guide* has a detailed and categorized table of contents.)

There are definite advantages to keeping older books under former subject headings or classification assignments. This earlier subject analysis can identify the attitude of an author to the subject. Older subject headings and classed arrangements are subject to semantic and social changes. Respectable previous headings and terms can later become offensive to various groups. A good example of such a change is the Afro-American subject heading, which in *LCSH* has replaced older headings, like Negro. Because of the growing popularity of the term Black, LC consulted experts on its use in *LCSH*, including the Black Caucus of the American Library Association. Responses were surprising. "Black" was considered appropriate for subject headings for ethnic groups outside of the United States, such as Blacks in Nigeria, while Afro-American was recommended to describe the ethnic group in this country, evidently to agree with other *LCSH* headings like Italian Americans and Jewish Americans. (Even dropping the hyphen when grammatically possible was taken by observers to be a liberalizing trend.) Although LC accordingly changed its subject heading, the *Sears List of Subject Headings* uses Black instead of Afro-American. Neither the National Association for the Advancement of Colored People (NAACP) nor the ALA's Black Caucus has changed its name.

In classification schemes, homosexuality ceased to be treated as an ailment or disease and became a sociological choice of gender partner—another effect of changing mores on subject analysis.

Librarians could exploit this transitoriness of subject analysis by deliberately retaining the older forms on bibliographic surrogates. Ideally, an older work being cataloged now should be assigned the subject headings and classification symbols that are contemporary with its publication date. Such cases are not numerous, so newer codes can be used without an excessive number of distracting anachronisms. Notes should be inserted in catalogs to the effect that works cataloged before or after a certain date may be found under the indicated subject heading. For classification changes, perhaps cross-references or dummies on the shelves could alert the user. The information on classification changes, though, is best conveyed by the librarian directly to the shelf-searcher or browser.

The second major problem in subject analysis is the frequent inability of a searcher, practitioner, or end user to match the individual's wording of a subject with the official heading. Solving this problem would involve many cross-references, including "See," "Used for," and "See also." The printed *LCSH* has many cross-references of this kind. The varying characteristics of libraries and their patrons can add more linguistic confusions. Thesauruses, even those designed for automated surrogates, can help guide the searcher even when the searcher is trying to match a heading in printed surrogates.

The problem in matching printed subject headings is probably insoluble, though standardization is both made known and helped by authority lists and thesauruses. Here, experience can be of great aid, experience most likely to be gained by the professional librarian.

Automation has greatly increased the ease of searching bibliographic surrogates organized by descriptive cataloging and subject analysis. Librarians, though they can be proud of librarianship's early adoption of computerization, must be constantly aware that the access points provided by newer systems have not, in principle, changed in origin or practical application. The chronological limitations of databases must be acknowledged. Some searches will be, as noted much earlier, more suited to a manual search of printed surrogates. Boolean algebra, free-text search, the use of keywords, and uncontrolled vocabulary—all have strengthened the capability for search and retrieval of automated analytical surrogates. Full-text display, joined to free-text search, has also increased the usefulness of searching automated sources. These newer functions are discussed in Chapter 6. We are left here with the melancholy consideration that search and retrieval of all records, printed or machine-readable, confront similar problems.

5 Automated Catalog Access

Carrying through the aims of this book, these next chapters emphasize the enduring principles of bibliographic organization, even when they are used for new computerized sources. Although the French saying, "Plus ça change, plus c'est la même chose," may not be true in all situations, it applies with considerable force to computerized searching. Apparently modern accessing methodologies are actually time-tested ways of retrieving traditional data. Over the centuries, the two approaches to the bibliographic organization of recorded information have remained largely intact: describing in surrogates and providing access points for (1) the physical nature of the text and (2) its topical content.

Because of different equipment, bibliographic format, computer commands, and Machine Readable Cataloging (MARC), online searching of bibliographic surrogates has been divided into trying to find information for (1) cataloging and affiliated library functions, such as interlibrary loan, as well as identifying and retrieving holdings shown in the Online Public Access Catalog (OPAC); and (2) answering questions, mostly about the identification and contents of journal articles. As pointed out in this chapter, some of this distinction is becoming unclear as the bibliographic utilities responsible for the first function are willing to incorporate the second in their activities. The present chapter deals with cataloging and affiliated functions; the following one with answering questions on analytical access.

Automation of bibliographic organization started in 1963 when the Library of Congress began studying the possibility of computerizing bibliographic surrogates.[1] In 1966 LC instituted its MARC I Pilot Project,

1. Henriette D. Avram, *MARC: Its History and Implications* (Washington: Library of

which lasted until June 1968. MARC is a communications format that standardizes the structure, content, and coding of bibliographic records for various media so that libraries can exchange information among themselves for computer application. The products of this communication do not have to be machine-readable, including the card and Computer Output Microform (COM) catalogs.

The operational distribution service, MARC II, began in 1969, when LC sent subscribers computer tapes of cataloging data for English-language monographs. The first LC-published *MARC II Format* was for books. Expansion of the LC MARC program has since been rapid and continuous: extensive printed documentation, including formats for nonbook media, and widening the MARC chronological and language scope. *USMARC Format for Bibliographic Data (USMFBD)* has annual *Updates* and contains specifications in tabular form for seven USMARC communications formats: books, visual materials, archival and manuscripts control, maps, music, serials, and machine-readable data files. Also, LC has published its 1987 looseleaf *USMARC Format for Authority Data* for name, subject and/or series.[2]

MARC formats have been accepted internationally. Now there are numerous national MARC formats, e.g., UKMARC for the United Kingdom and INTERMARC for France. The practical impact of MARC can be seen in the closing or freezing by many libraries of their printed card and bookform catalogs—especially the delayed closing of the LC public card catalog in 1981—to be replaced by COM catalogs or OPACs. Hardly an American library has remained uninfluenced, directly or indirectly, by this fast growth of standardized computerized bibliographic organization made possible by MARC.

The LC MARC may appear to duplicate in many ways the International Standard Bibliographic Description (ISBD), described in Chapter 3, sponsored by the International Federation of Library Associations and Institutions (IFLA) as vital to its Universal Bibliographic Control (UBC) program, leading to Universal Availability of Publications (UAP). ISBD was made part of *Anglo-American Cataloging Rules (AACR)* in 1974, *Anglo-*

Congress, 1975)—"Based on an article entitled 'Machine-Readable Cataloging (MARC) Program,' which appears in the *Encyclopedia of Library and Information Science*, Volume 17"; Lucia J. Rather, "Exchange of Bibliographic Information in Machine-Readable Form," *Library Trends* 25 (Jan. 1977):625–643. For later developments, see the publications of the Library of Congress and particularly its *Annual Report of the Librarian of Congress for the Fiscal Year Ending September 30* (Washington: The Library).

2. For details on currently available LC publications, see the annual issue of Library of Congress, Cataloging Distribution Service, *Catalogs and Technical Publications* and its *MARC Distribution Services*, both free on request. (The 1989 edition of the former has added *Access '89 . . . for 1989.*)

American Cataloguing Rules, second edition (*AACR2*) in 1978, and *Anglo-American Cataloguing Rules*, second edition, 1988 revision (*AACR2*, revised) in 1988. MARC preceded ISBD by some years. Indeed, LC and IFLA had agreed on the ISBD. Both MARC and ISBD are designed to regulate the contents and sequence of the bibliographic surrogate. They share the desire for standardization in international communication of bibliographic data and have followed similar paths in development: ISBDs and MARC formats for different media, national ISBDs and MARCs, general versions for intercountry use, and switching, that is, ISBD (General) and SUPERMARC. ISBD punctuation has been made part of the MARC record so that many of the elements of all *AACR2* bibliographic surrogates are labeled for visual examination. MARC and ISBD are not duplicative but complementary. MARC analyzes and tags more elements than ISBD, supplying a detailed breakdown for computerized input and retrieval of bibliographic record units, in addition to supplying in its fixed and variable fields information about the work not shown by the ISBD format. ISBD was designed to be a self-sufficient description of only part of the catalog record, what was called before *AACR2* the body of the entry. ISBD is not concerned with the main-entry heading, tracings, or subject analysis of the surrogate. A far-off hope is that, publishers willing, every title page will have ISBD punctuation so that descriptive cataloging of the item may be accomplished by machine.

Critics of MARC I objected that the format served up old wine in new bottles; the card-catalog surrogate was retained for contents and sequence, despite the opportunity to create a completely new kind of bibliographic record appropriate for the machine age. Chapters 1 and 2 traced the emergence of this traditional bibliographic surrogate and explained its rationale. It is difficult to imagine, with due respect to the critics, a more significant record, at least for descriptive cataloging. None of the critics has come up with satisfactory suggestions for different contents and sequence. In fact, MARC has added data not previously on our surrogates, such as tags for the cataloging source and languages from which and into which a work is translated, a potentially murky matter when either of the languages is unidentified.

MARC also contributed the labeling of every searchable element in the traditional catalog-card format. The following examples will be familiar to many practitioners. Imprint data have been analyzed for place of publication, name of publisher, and date of publication, and each element in this tagged field is identified by a subfield code. Indicators show various aspects of a field, such as for a personal-name main-entry heading (tag 100), the first indicator telling whether the main entry is also a subject. All tracings are labeled. The head of the MARC record, the fixed field paragraph, explains characteristics like its bibliographical level (monograph, serial, etc.), intellectual level (adult or juvenile), language, and existence of index for the cataloged item.

This description of MARC content designators shows that all labels apply to all cases, and that retrieval of the codes themselves cannot individualize a searcher's choices. For search purposes, the coded information must be retrieved, such as the language of the work, its publication period and at least its first subject heading, for example, books in English published since 1983 on atomic physics. Controlled vocabularies and authority files may be consulted for such elements as main-entry headings, and subject headings may be found in the list of *Library of Congress Subject Headings (LCSH)*. Otherwise, free-text search of the encoded data is necessary. The Boolean operators AND, OR, and NOT are used to combine fields, subfields, tracings, and fixed-field information, such as monographs in French on Molière published before 1985. Of course, Boolean search is possible also with free-text search. Much time can be saved if the searcher checks strategies against controlled vocabularies and authority files and resorts to free-text search only when necessary.

Progress in searching bibliographic surrogates has resulted, however belatedly, from exploiting more of the full potential of the MARC record. Extricating the data remained an unresolved difficulty until recently for one of the first and still the largest American bibliographic utility, Online Computer Library Center, Inc. (OCLC), which is considered in detail below.

As the MARC distribution service developed, in a way perhaps not unwelcome to LC, LC sold its MARC tapes mostly to hundreds of wholesalers who in turn serviced thousands of customers. If the number of its MARC subscribers were a decisive economic factor for LC, MARC distribution business might soon go bankrupt. The wholesalers were chiefly national or regional network operators, and their customers were the thousands of libraries that belonged to the networks.

It is easier to identify a bibliographic utility than to define one. The Matthews definition is not sufficiently distinguishing: "An organization that maintains large online bibliographic data bases and provides products and services related to these bases to its customers/members."[3] This definition would include more than the four utilities Matthews is actually defining: OCLC, Research Libraries Information Network (RLIN), University of Toronto Library Automation Systems (UTLAS), and Western Library Network (WLN), formerly the Washington Library Network. When Matthews defines the catalog subsystem, he comes closer to a distinction: "the one function or service that is common to all four util-

3. Joseph R. Matthews, "A Utility User's Glossary," *American Libraries* 11 (May 1980): 266.

ities."[4] The four major bibliographic utilities listed above are described here according to this distinction. Although the major utilities have provided gateway access for their members to analytical databases, described in detail below, these utilities still merit separate attention because they remain the principal suppliers of automated cataloging records for whole books and serials.

Matthews begins his 1980 treatment of the four utilities with this statement: "During the 1970s, perhaps the single most significant impact in the area of library automation has been the emergence of the online bibliographic utility."[5] The rise of OCLC is a leading example.

OCLC (originally Ohio College Library Center), now in Dublin, Ohio, began in 1967 with fifty-four member libraries in Ohio.[6] It has since grown into the largest U.S. bibliographic utility, an international organization with over 7,900 members and users in the United States and at least ten other countries. Its name was changed in 1981 to Online Computer Library Center, Inc., to represent its current geographical and corporate status. Beginning with LC as its supplier of MARC tapes, OCLC later stated that well over 50 percent of its records were supplied in MARC format by participating libraries. In 1988, OCLC claimed well over 17 million entries in its Online Union Catalog (OLUC).[7] Member libraries of OCLC may contribute new bibliographic records for their archival tapes, and these records are also added to the OLUC. Additional acquisitions of books already recorded in the OLUC are entered in the holdings sections of OLUC records and are essential for interlibrary loan (ILL) and resource sharing.

The size of the OCLC database is reflected in the utility's institutional strength: almost 9,000 subscribers worldwide and the stability of its extensive financial assets. The OCLC President reported in 1986 that "OCLC is committing significant resources—a major part of a $40-million, three-year capital expenditure program—to the redesign and reimplementation of its system, which is already the largest and most efficient

4. Ibid.

5. Idem, "Understanding the Utilities: An Introduction to the Birth and Development of the Major Online Bibliographic Utilities," *American Libraries* 11 (May 1980): 262.

6. The history and search strategies of OCLC are from: Matthews, "Understanding the Utilities," 262, 264; Jean Slemmons Stratford, "OCLC and RLIN: The Comparisons Studied," *College & Research Libraries* 45 (Mar. 1984): 123–27; Susan K. Martin, "OCLC and RLG: Living Together," *American Libraries* 11 (May 1980):270–71; Arthur Plotnik, "OCLC: Diversification at the Nation's Largest Library Utility," ibid., 274–75; *1989 Encyclopedia of Information Systems and Services*, 9th ed., Amy Lucas and Nan Soper, eds. 3 vols. (Detroit: Gale, 1989), entry 1699; OCLC, *Searching the Online Union Catalog*, loose-leaf (Dublin, Ohio: OCLC, Inc., c1983–).

7. "One Million Records Added to Database in 152 Days," *OCLC Newsletter*, no. 171 (Jan./Feb. 1988):7.

bibliographic network in the world."[8] Regional administration, resulting in local maintenance and assistance, has also made OCLC the bibliographic utility of choice for the majority of American libraries.

Many subscribers have complained about the duplication of entries from other libraries and with later records from LC. These complaints center not only on the quantity of bibliographic records for the same item, but also on the frequently inadequate cataloging by local libraries. Though OCLC has issued instructions for cataloging quality control, there was evidently no extensive monitoring. In January of 1980, OCLC incorporated an unlinked LC name authority file into its database, and in December of 1980, ran its records against the file and converted the headings to *AACR2* standards, at least as interpreted by LC.[9] OCLC has also announced expansion of an enhanced quality control program, a volunteer monitoring activity by subscriber libraries.[10]

From the start, a stated aim of OCLC was to reduce the processing costs of member libraries by supplying centralized cataloging products—an automated version of the long-held ideal that a work, once cataloged, need never be cataloged again by another library. Emphasis was on retrieval of records for individual items, not reference search strategy. Access to the OLUC includes title, author/title, personal author, corporate author and conference name, ISBN, Library of Congress card number (LCCN), ISSN, CODEN (for serial titles), OCLC control number, government document number, and music publisher number.

OCLC gives more descriptive-cataloging access points for its OLUC than LC does for its printed or microfiche *National Union Catalog*. Unfortunately, previously known descriptive cataloging data about the sought item is required, as they are for searches of this type in any union catalog. The OCLC search key for the personal author's name is, as of now, the first four letters of the last name followed by the first three letters of the first name and the initial of the middle name if used (4, 3, 1); the commas are mandatory between the groups of letters. The searcher cannot formulate the personal author's name more precisely. Accordingly, the search key—which has inevitably been lengthened as the database increased—may retrieve also names of other authors. Since there are no cross-references in the OLUC, collocation becomes difficult.

Doubts have been expressed about the importance of the main-entry heading for automated bibliographic surrogates since it would be possible

8. Rowland C. W. Brown, "A Special Report: The New OCLC System," *OCLC Newsletter*, no. 161 (Feb. 1986):1.

9. "OCLC Installs LC Name-Authority File," *OCLC Newsletter*, no. 127 (Feb. 6, 1980):1; "OCLC Converts Data Base to *AACR2* Form," ibid., no. 134 (Jan. 16, 1981):4.

10. For recent developments in the quality control program of OCLC, see Tom Storey, "New Enhance Libraries Chosen," ibid., no. 173 (May/June 1988):6.

in theory to retrieve the surrogate by any part of its contents. OCLC search keys are most useful for locating single items. The abundant data in a MARC bibliographic record, once found, prompts the searcher to decide if the record satisfies as to edition, pagination, publication date, language, and so forth.

Arguments in favor of the continuing value of the main-entry heading revolve around the collocative function of an online catalog. If one searches for all the works by the same person or corporate body, no matter what form of the name on the title page, authority control is essential. Lack of an automated authority control linked to the OCLC database has meant serious problems for researchers. Such automated authority control is an advantage claimed by rival utilities, such as RLIN, described later. In a linked situation, the established form is automatically assigned when the suggested heading matches either the authorized form or its cross-references. If no match is achieved, the suggested heading is rejected. A completely automated and linked authority file can make global or wholesale changes, that is, alter all older headings at one time to the latest authorized form. A moral to be drawn again is that an automated file is only as good as its human input. (We have become too prone to blame personal errors on the computer.) It is assumed for all complete union catalog collocation that all the works of an author have been entered, a frequently dubious assumption.

The lack of subject access to the OLUC is another failing of OCLC that has been often noted by its members as well as by other utilities. In 1986 OCLC announced it was making available, through BRS Information Technologies (formerly known as the Bibliographic Retrieval Services), searching of the OCLC Electronic Access to Subject Information (EASI) Reference database. This database is a subset of approximately 1 million bibliographic records from the OLUC for works published during the last four years.[11] Other BRS search options announced included author, title, bibliographic control number (e.g., LCCN, ISBN, ISSN, standard technical report number, and music publisher's number), keywords, and controlled vocabulary search keys. Subject access with BRS was to include: free-text searching of words contained in subject headings, corporate or conference names, titles, and series statements; classification numbers; phrase (controlled vocabulary) searching of subject headings—*LCSH* or *Medical Subject Headings (MeSH)*. BRS search inquiries could be refined by Boolean operators AND, OR, NOT, and XOR (either one

11. In 1986 the OCLC intelligent gateway service, which would make access to the EASI Reference database possible from OCLC terminals, had its name changed from UNISON Service to LINK (not to be confused with the LC Linked Systems Project [LSP], discussed below). See "OCLC LINK Service: New Name for Intelligent Gateway System," ibid., no. 165 (Nov. 1986):19.

term or the other, but not both); positional operators SAME, WITH, and ADJ to link terms in the same sentence or paragraph or to signify juxtaposition of terms in order of entry; truncation of terms; and qualification by data elements, such as language, date, and country of publication. The EASI Reference database continued to grow.[12]

OCLC also announced in 1986 that its subscribers could access WILSONLINE and its some twenty Wilson indexes using Boolean operators, free-text, and controlled vocabulary. Searching the Wilson and BRS databases was to be accomplished through the OCLC intelligent gateway service. This gateway was to make feasible OCLC-member access from any OCLC terminal to non-OCLC databases.[13]

In January 1987 at the American Library Association (ALA) Midwinter Meeting in Chicago, OCLC and RLIN both announced they would provide gateway access to DIALOG, discussed in Chapter 6.[14] The accelerated merging through new technology of all computerized information as well as the library's technical and readers' services could be easily foreseen.

In December 1987, OCLC made available to its members online access, though unlinked, to currently created LC subject authority records, the so-called Subject Authority File (SAF).[15] Henceforth, OCLC members could access unlinked LC authorities for both names and subjects. As discussed below, catalogers complained that in any format, the *LCSH* had not been converted into a true thesaurus.

Early in 1988, OCLC stated that effective April 30, 1988, it would discontinue its intelligent gateway service, introduced in November 1986, because of low use.[16] According to OCLC, technology had changed; almost all member libraries now had microcomputers that afforded them dial-access to databases, or they were consulting compact-disc versions of the same databases. When OCLC had begun its gateway service, very few of its library members owned microcomputers. As an inducement, OCLC discounted the cost of using the gateway for non-OCLC database

12. "OCLC EASI Reference Database Is Expanded," ibid., 170 (Oct./Nov. 1987):29; *1989 Encyclopedia of Information Systems and Services*, entry 1701.

13. "WILSONLINE to Be Available via OCLC Service," *Wilson Library Bulletin* 61 (Sept. 1986):12; "WILSONLINE, VU/TEXT to Become Available via OCLC Intelligent Gateway Service," *OCLC Newsletter*, no. 164 (Aug. 1986):9; "OCLC LINK Service Now Available," ibid., no. 166 (Jan. 1987):8.

14. "DIALOG and BRS to Be Available through OCLC LINK Service," *OCLC Newsletter*, no. 167 (Mar./Apr. 1987):27; "DIALOG Now Available through RLIN Terminals," *Operations Update*, no. 40 (Mar. 1987):4–5.

15. "OCLC to Provide Online Access to LC Subject Authority Records," *OCLC Newsletter*, no. 171 (Jan./Feb. 1988):24–25.

16. "OCLC Discontinues Gateway Service," *Information Today: The Newspaper for Users and Producers of Electronic Information Services* 5 (Apr. 1988):6.

access, but this discount was evidently not effective. The OCLC algorithms for searching and retrieval were different from those of the general DIALOG commands, for example, or the specialized commands for the individual DIALOG databases. Also, special playback equipment was required for compact discs.

The gateway service of RLIN has not, at this writing, been discontinued, though the extent of RLIN-members' use of the service has not been documented. The EASI Reference database apparently is still available, not through the OCLC gateway service but directly from BRS.

Besides the OCLC cataloging subsystem, still its most heavily used facility, OCLC has added subsystems over the years for interlibrary loan (a sophisticated and successful facility), acquisitions, and serials control. The subsystems were all planned for input or search of individual items. The question must be raised as to which subsystems are best relegated to locally distributed processing and access. Circulation systems were wisely left to local application. It would be an economic and intellectual waste for all library functions to be operated centrally by every OCLC-participant library. With the serials control subsystem, doubts have been expressed about the practicality of invoices and claim notices being handled from one computerized center. It is only to be expected that every proposed subsystem is not appropriate for centralized processing. Eventual termination of its serials and acquisitions subsystems was announced by OCLC in 1986. Final dates for these subsystems have been postponed, for the Serials Subsystem to December 31, 1988, and for the Acquisitions Subsystem, about a year later. These subsystems are to be replaced by microcomputer-based programs supplied by OCLC that will be applied locally by OCLC members.[17]

The OCLC database was copyrighted in 1982. The purpose of copyright was to prevent non-OCLC members from downloading or transferring OLUC records. Subscribing libraries immediately grumbled about restrictions placed on them by a cooperative, not-for-profit organization. A series of statements issued by OCLC did not silence complaints. Finally in 1987, the OCLC Board of Trustees published a new "Guidelines for the Use and Transfer of OCLC-Derived Records. Revision of November 16, 1987," which removed all restrictions on transfer of OCLC members' local records.[18]

The claimed disadvantages of OCLC chiefly have to do with search capabilities: often imprecise rigid search keys that lead to false drops,

17. "New OCLC Micro-Based Acquisitions System Now in Field Test," *OCLC Newsletter*, no. 168 (May/June 1987):25; *1989 Encyclopedia of Information Systems and Services*, entry 1700.

18. Marilyn Gell Mason, "Copyright in Context: The OCLC Database," *Library Journal* 113 (July 1988):31–34. (A copy of the "Guidelines" is included.)

lack of subject access, and linked automated authority control (the latter two are highly touted by RLIN). The 1980 addition of the LC name authority file, which in 1988 contained over 2 million records for personal, corporate, conference, and geographic names and uniform titles, and the 1987 incorporation of the LC Subject Authority File into the OCLC database go some distance in remedying authority deficiencies, though both are unlinked.[19] The OCLC EASI Reference database was an effort to give subject access to at least part of the OLUC.

Scheduled for early 1987 and since postponed to 1989 was a new OCLC system that would provide subject access to the entire OLUC, new search qualifiers, Boolean operations, exact text searching, and a save file for searches.[20] These projects and promises support the conclusions that (1) OCLC is now trying to use more fully as access points the MARC-formatted data, identified by content designators; (2) its efforts to expand into services heretofore offered by database vendors, like BRS Information Technologies and WILSONLINE, have been stymied by technological developments; and (3) perhaps most important, OCLC has taken to heart the differing requirements of centralized and distributed automation. As for this last conclusion, OCLC has proceeded to supply programs and hardware for local libraries' microcomputer operations. It has also supplied bibliographic surrogates on compact discs.

In his special report of February 17, 1986, the president and chief executive officer of OCLC had made some predictions that have been realized in unexpected ways. (One must admire OCLC's entrepreneurial flexibility in dealing with some of these outcomes.) The president in his report foresaw there would be unpredictable changes in how OCLC was to be used by its subscribers, but he stressed a new system design, the Oxford project, for an environment to allow microcomputers to process at all levels as needed: local, regional, national, and international. He also prognosticated a growing trend to communications links and common databases.[21]

The details of the OCLC system have been given first, not only because OCLC is the largest of the American bibliographic utilities and is continuously redesigning its structure, but also because the other bibliographic utilities were created with the rationale that they could offer services or search capabilities unavailable in OCLC. The other leading American bibliographic utilities can now be compared with OCLC.

19. "OCLC to Provide Online Access to LC Subject Authority Records," 24.

20. Brown, "A Special Report"; "Update on New System Development from OCLC President Rowland Brown," *OCLC Newsletter*, no. 167 (Mar./Apr. 1987):3; Nita Dean, "New System Redesign and Implementation—A Progress Report," ibid., no. 168 (May/June 1987): 16.

21. Brown, "A Special Report."

The Research Libraries Information Network (RLIN) in Stanford, California, is second to OCLC in database size and is owned and operated by the Research Libraries Group (RLG).[22] OCLC's chief rival for academic libraries, RLIN has had an uneasy career, faced with a complete computer breakdown in 1982. RLIN began in 1978 for research libraries that felt that authority control and subject search capability, both lacking in OCLC, were essential for their own bibliographic tasks. Stanford University's Bibliographic Automation of Large Library Operations Using a Time-Sharing System (BALLOTS) was adopted by RLIN. RLG wanted a union catalog focusing on entries for works normally acquired only by research libraries, whereas OCLC serviced all types of libraries. The small size of RLIN membership—administrators once said that a membership of some thirty to sixty research libraries would be ideal—has elicited charges of elitism.[23]

The literature comparing OCLC and RLIN did not, in Stratford's 1984 opinion, offer adequate evidence for libraries to choose between the two. Stratford hedged. She did not believe that OCLC and RLIN were strictly comparable because OCLC relied chiefly on its database, whereas RLIN had additional tools for cooperation, preservation, and collection development. However, because of the ability of the two to perform similar functions, an evaluative comparison was necessary for informed library planning and decision making. The points mentioned by Stratford all concern the size and accessibility of the respective databases.[24]

Because RLIN began more than a decade after OCLC and was created to serve research collections exclusively, it was only to be expected that the RLIN database would be noticeably smaller than that of OCLC. Some years ago, in fact, the RLIN database was estimated at only about one-half the size of OCLC's. It came as a surprise, after OCLC announced that as of 1988 the OCLC OLUC had added its 17th million record, when RLIN issued a press release that the 25th million "book record"

22. The history and search strategies of RLIN are from: Matthews, "Understanding the Utilities"; Stratford, "OCLC and RLIN"; Martin, "OCLC and RLG"; Arthur Plotnik, "RLIN: The Bibliographic Utility in Cap and Gown Nears Graduation," *American Libraries* 11 (May 1980): 273–74; *1989 Encyclopedia of Information Systems and Services*, entry 1932; Research Libraries Information Network, *Searching in RLIN II: User's Manual*, loose-leaf (Stanford, Calif.: Research Libraries Group, 1984–).

23. David H. Stam, "Networks and the Common Cause," *American Libraries* 11 (May 1980):278; Amar K. Lahiri, "Toward a Bibliographic Republic," ibid., 279; Jo Chanaud, "One for the Record," ibid.; Michael Gorman, "Comments with Rejoinder," ibid., 278–79. These four articles appear under the overall heading: "On Utilities, Elitism and Democracy. Three Readers Respond to a Portrait of OCLC as a 'Bibliographic Democracy' and RLG as an 'Exclusionary Group'."

24. Stratford, "OCLC and RLIN," 126–27.

was then held in its automated union catalog.[25] This wide discrepancy means that RLIN "book records" represent total holdings, not separate titles. In any case, the common belief is that the OCLC OLUC is much larger in discrete item records than the database of RLIN, and that a major advantage of OCLC over RLIN lies in the OCLC's greater database size.

The number of hits against the OCLC database is said to be considerably greater for OCLC libraries than for RLIN members searching the RLIN database. Many OCLC libraries, of course, do not collect in advanced specialized areas. The inevitable overlap of the two databases has not been great enough to prevent OCLC libraries from using the RLIN union catalog in a search-only mode, a service not available with the OCLC database.

An RLIN source-specific search will produce titles of all works in the database that are written by a particular author. The question, "What titles do you have by Ralph Nader?" can be answered by formulating the search command "fin pe nader, ralph," with translates into "find all titles with the personal name entry, Ralph Nader." This collocative search in the RLIN database is aided by the automatic authority file and by the full form of the searched name, though somewhat limited by database size. It is surely easier and less time-consuming than using the OCLC "4, 3, 1" search key and the unlinked LC name authority file. False drops in using OCLC may be numerous.

A search in RLIN for an LC subject heading can produce hits either for the entire subject heading or for its subdivisions which are labeled by MARC. The search request

fin sp "medical laws and legislation—united states"

will retrieve RLIN records with this subject heading, complete with the desired subdivision. Without the quotation marks, the search request will retrieve only those records with the two separate subject headings: "medical laws" and "legislation—united states."

The search request

fin sd canada

will retrieve RLIN records with "canada" as a subdivision (≠z value), but not those with "canada" as a main heading (≠a value).

25. "25,000,000th Book Record in RLIN—A Milestone for CSL and RLG," *Operations Update*, no. 46 (Mar. 1988):12.

A user preparing a bibliography on "surgery" could benefit from the search request

fin sp surgery # or sd surgery

which would retrieve all items with "surgery" as a principal subject heading or as a subdivision. Combining SP (principal subject heading) values with a second SD (subject-heading subdivision) or SP value would be particularly valuable in a geographical search.

The search request

fin (sd fisheries or sp fisheries #) and (sp Greenland # or sd Greenland)

will retrieve all items with the following MARC-formatted subject headings and subdivisions:

650 0 Fisheries ≠z Greenland
650 0 Greenland ≠x Fisheries (x = topical subdivision)
650 0 Treaties ≠z Greenland ≠x Fisheries

RLIN has used Boolean operators applied to the MARC record similarly to DIALOG or other computerized information suppliers. RLIN search strategies have been much more sophisticated than those of the pre-1986 OCLC.

In advertising, general publicity, and public relations and in visibility at library conferences, OCLC expansion has been much more noticeable than RLIN activity, to which skeptics might respond that OCLC, for many years almost exclusively an online union catalog designed for copy cataloging, has had to change to meet the demands of competition and its own subscribers.

WLN (Western Library Network, formerly Washington Library Network) is the third major bibliographic utilities discussed here. WLN has about one-half the membership of RLIN.[26] Like OCLC, its original name indicated a state limitation. Wholly owned and operated by the Washington State Library at Olympia, Washington, it has crossed state boundaries and sells its services and products nationally, though it has retained

26. The history and search strategies of WLN are from: Matthews, "Understanding the Utilities"; Arthur Plotnik, "WLN: The Better Mousetrap Looks toward Bigger Game," *American Libraries* 11 (May 1980):275–76; *1989 Encyclopedia of Information Systems and Services*, entry 2787; Washington Library Network, *Inquiry Reference Manual*, 2nd ed. (Olympia: Washington State Library, 1983).

a geographic orientation in its 1985 change of name. Unlike OCLC and RLIN, it encourages replication of its system through purchase of its software by other state libraries, networks, or library groups. Its market has become international; in 1985 its software was installed by the British Library. Its union catalog can be accessed online by full members who are sought in the western states.

From its start in 1972 with nine pilot libraries entering their holdings into the computerized database, WLN has offered sophisticated search capabilities. Its excellent access facilities were recognized by RLG, which in 1979 agreed to join WLN in developing joint programs leading to a multinetwork database. The agreement led first to linking bibliographic records and sharing authority files. In 1983 WLN joined RLG as a member of the LC-sponsored Linked Systems Project (LSP), designed to coordinate searching by the major bibliographic utilities whose computers had incompatible protocols. In 1984 OCLC also agreed to participate. As Avram explained, LSP users searched the LC database not through direct terminals to LC, but through terminals to their own networks.[27]

The WLN Inquiry Facility can retrieve entries in the database of its bibliographic subsystem through traditional catalog card access points labeled by MARC. In addition, keywords may be used to retrieve title words, corporate or conference name headings, subject, and series headings in bibliographic and authority records. The key file contains unique keywords from titles and corporate or conference names, and from subfields (or logical portions of a heading) for author, series, and subject. The number of hits resulting from the use of keywords is shown in the key visual display of the key file. Similar to the identifiers in the *ERIC Thesaurus*, keywords in WLN are, nevertheless, kept track of as if they were units of a controlled vocabulary.

The WLN authority file has author, subject, and traced series headings with cross-references and scope, reference, verification, and catalog use notes. This file uses forms sanctioned by *AACR2* and by LC practice. Authority file headings are linked to the records in the bibliographic file so that all bibliographic records linked to that heading can be displayed for the user. All bibliographic records with an authority heading that is changed or canceled will automatically alter that heading with a global change—a great time-saving advantage of a computerized file. Consulting the authority file or the key file can save much search effort. A subject search in the authority file is a better way of identifying subject headings—mostly from *LCSH*—than guessing at them in the bibliographic file.

27. Henriette D. Avram, "The Linked Systems Project: Its Implications for Resource Sharing," *Library Resources & Technical Services* 30 (Jan./Mar. 1986):37.

Searchable access points for records in the bibliographic file include: WLN record identifier, ISBN, ISSN, title keywords, author (including main entry, author added entries, and author or title series added entries), corporate or conference keywords (including main entry, author added entries, and author or title series added entries), subject, corporate or conference subject keywords, series title. The data in these searchable fields have MARC tags and subfield indicators.

Alphabetical mnemonic abbreviations are used as the key identifiers to categorize the kind of WLN search of fields and subfields, for example, A or AUTH for author names, and S or SUBJ for subjects. Such search codes are much used, as we shall see, by information networks like DIALOG.

A truncated search statement for author records in the Bibliographic File

f a heyer george #

will produce a summary display of more than 150 bibliographic items, because the search would reveal both "Heyer, George S" and "Heyer, Georgette."

A search for works by Georgette Heyer

f a heyer georgette

will yield a display only of works by the author with that name.

A sample search in the authority file for a subject heading complete with a geographical subdivision

t st hiking—british columbia
(*t*erm search for the following *s*ubject *t*opical)

will extract

1. Hiking—British Columbia

WLN subsystems include acquisitions, circulation, periodicals, co-operative storage, and interlibrary loan. The searcher of the WLN bibliographic file has many more search options than for the pre-1986 OCLC. WLN has taken advantage of the MARC format and has also added a linked authority file, unlike the unlinked OCLC LC name authority file and the later subject authority file (SAF). Clearly, the WLN search and retrieval arrangements were superior to those of the contemporary OCLC.

Last of the four major bibliographic utilities to be described, Utlas (formerly known as UTLAS, the University of Toronto Library Automation Systems) has been supplying database services and products online since 1978.[28] Its history may be said to begin in 1963 when the University of Toronto Library began studying computerization. In 1967 the University Library established a separate systems department, and in 1971 the department became UTLAS. Like OCLC and WLN, its name denoted a geographical area of concern—the Province of Ontario and, by extension, the bilingual English-French libraries of Canada. It has since expanded internationally, a development intensified by its 1985 sale to International Thomson, Limited. Since its sale to International Thomson, Limited, the acronym is spelled "Utlas" in its public communications. Utlas International Canada, a division of International Thomson, Limited, has offices or representatives in Canada, Japan, the United Kingdom, Australia, and Europe. In 1985 Utlas gained access for its users to Japan/MARC. Utlas International U.S. Inc. is incorporated in the United States where it advertises four offices.

Company advertisements have claimed that:

> Over 500 institutions, members of consortia and government agencies, representing over 2,000 libraries, maintain user-owned databases through Utlas' facilities. Utlas also provides local library systems based on state-of-the-art computer technology. . . . The Utlas international database has over 55 million MARC records and over 5 million REMARC (retrospective conversion of LC cataloging prior to 1971) records including records from the Library of Congress, British Library, National Library of Canada, Government Printing Office, National Library of Medicine, Utlas customers and many other sources.

Utlas states that it generates annually more than 10 million catalog cards and other products for over 1,800 catalogs in some 600 libraries on six continents. If its statistics are reliable, Utlas ranks second in size internationally only to OCLC. What distinguishes it from OCLC and RLIN and brings it closer to WLN is that Utlas client libraries own their own records and maintain their own files so they can not only edit records as they choose, but also add local holdings codes and other necessary information. A no-copyright policy applies to all Utlas files, including

28. The history and search strategies of Utlas are from: Matthews, "Understanding the Utilities"; Arthur Plotnik, "UTLAS: A Canadian Contender for the U.S. Market," *American Libraries* 11 (May 1980):276–77; Wyley Powell and Norville Webb, "UTLAS—A High Tech Success Story," *Technicalities* 4 (Oct. 1984): 7–9; *1989 Encyclopedia of Information Systems and Services*, entry 4238; Utlas, *Utlas System Manual: Guide to Using REFCATSS Conversational*, loose-leaf (Toronto: Utlas International Canada, 1986–).

REMARC (LC Machine-Readable Cataloging before 1979). Records retrospectively converted for clients by Utlas become the property of the local library and may be downloaded by others. Like WLN and unlike OCLC, Utlas has not become embroiled in copyright problems.

An estimated 85 percent of all cataloging in Canada is supplied by Utlas. In 1980 the Rochester Institute of Technology became Utlas's first online customer in the United States, a clientele to be increased by other American libraries, such as the Westchester Library System in Elmsford, New York, whose 38 public libraries make it Utlas's largest U.S. client.

Utlas has recognized that centralized processing is inappropriate to every library function, and therefore offers distributed processing for some local library activities.

The Utlas Catalogue Support System (CATSS) is of primary concern in this book. CATSS supports both copy and original cataloging, and like the OCLC OLUC, remains the central Utlas operation. CATSS II is a result of Utlas conversion from Honeywell Sigma to Tandem Non-Stop computers, completed in 1984. New documentation and training became necessary for CATSS II.

Original cataloging by Utlas users is input into CATSS, but each institution also has its own database permanently stored in the central Utlas computers, a departure from the much criticized OCLC practice. Subsystems or modules of CATSS include authority facility, REFCATSS for public service librarians, interlibrary loan, acquisitions, and retrospective conversion.

The 1986 *Utlas System Manual: Guide to Using REFCATSS II Conversational* (that is, interactive as in editing catalog records online) "is directed to public service and interlibrary loan personnel who want to search for, verify, or locate bibliographic items represented by the records in the database." The database can be either the local library's or the Utlas union catalog. The *Manual* instructs on a variety of search options: help facility, online authority system searching, and both imprecise (browsable or textual) and precise searching.

> The bibliographic record is based on the CATSS II MARC record, but the display is less complex. Tag numbers have been replaced by mnemonics, and indicators, occurrence numbers, subfield codes, and other details required by technical services personnel have been deleted.[29]

Utlas displays MARC tags mnemonically as "author, title, note, subject." The author mnemonic, for example, stands for MARC tags 100,

29. Utlas, *Utlas System Manual*, 1–1.

110, 111, 700, 709, 710, 711. For browsable searching, all entries are arranged alphabetically in a browsable index similar to a card catalog. The entries are retrievable by author, title, series, and subject heading. Browsing of the index can be pursued by searching specific MARC tags, such as the tag 245 (title); one type of entry, such as subject; or by general searching covering author, title, series and subject entries. Boolean operations can be used in browsable searching, though the first Boolean term must be an indexed one. Free-text search is accordingly available in Boolean operations after the first indexed term is employed.

Precise searching is performed through the use of control numbers, that is, RSN (the unique Utlas number for each bibliographic entry), ASN (the unique Utlas number for each authority record), ISBN, ISSN, and LCCN. Precise searching can retrieve only one item.

An example of a browsable author search

au/crane s?

includes the question mark as truncation symbol.

For a browsable title search, the statement

245/Fantastic pomp and circumstance

uses the MARC title tag as its access key, though the alphabetical mnemonic TI or ti can also be used. A browsable subject search could begin with SU/ or 6/, either followed by the sought subject. The "6" represents MARC subject tags beginning with 600.

The Utlas authority files can be searched, as for the bibliographic file, either by control number or by browsable catalog-record elements in the entry text. These authority files include LC Names, LC Subject Authority File, National Library of Canada Names (English and French), a translation of *LC Subject Headings* into the French *Répertoire des Vedettes Matières (RVM),* and a variety of private files in the University of Toronto, University of Alberta, and so on. Once a match or hit is obtained, a link is automatically created between the bibliographic record and the authority entry. Changes in the authority file are made globally, as described above.

Utlas offers Boolean searching for either the bibliographic or the authority file. The Boolean operators, AND, OR, and NOT are represented, respectively, in Utlas search statements by a period (full stop), vertical bar, and asterisk. Examples of a browsable Boolean subject search could be the entries

1. (SU/London | SU/Paris) · SU/travel and leisure
2. SU/London | SU/Paris · SU/travel and leisure

for which the parentheses change the meaning. The first entry is a Boolean search for works with subjects ("London" and "travel and leisure") or "Paris" and "travel and leisure." The second would retrieve works with the subjects "London" or ("Paris" and "travel and leisure").

Many more examples of Utlas accessing techniques could be cited. Utlas as well as RLIN and WLN offer searching possibilities and linked authority files unavailable with the original OCLC, a pioneer in online centralized and shared cataloging. Later utilities benefited from OCLC's experience, and they were small and agile enough to add the search and retrieval possibilities, already used by the online database information vendors described in the next chapter, that were desired by bibliographic utility clients. Only recently did OCLC begin to break out of its monolithic rigidity to give its users more flexible access to its own and other databases. This overlapping of the bibliographic utilities and the online database analytical information vendors has been commented on. The implications of such changes are yet to be seen, not to mention those of unforeseen advances in computer technology. The intelligent gateway service terminated by OCLC may be resurrected under a different name than LINK, and there is as yet no official word from RLIN that it will end its gateway service.

As the four bibliographic utilities—OCLC, RLIN, WLN and Utlas—developed, their services expanded beyond offering online cataloging access to utility databases. Other services of the different utilities were retrospective conversion of a library's bibliographic records to machine-readable form; computer modules for acquisitions and serials; interlibrary loan (ILL); authority control; distributed processing; computer consultation; gateway services to analytical information databases like those of DIALOG and BRS Information Technologies; and, in the cases of WLN and Utlas, computer software that allowed any library to mount an online public access catalog (OPAC) using machine-readable surrogates prepared either locally or by utility networks.

The access points of author, title, or subject needed by catalogers to search and retrieve records in the utilities' union catalogs were, with slight variations, the same for library users dependent on OPACs. As this book has emphasized, a knowledge of bibliographic organization, comprising the principles of descriptive cataloging and subject analysis, is essential for all professional librarians. Ideally, this knowledge and its application should be the same for librarians in the readers' and the technical services. OPACs hastened the merging of the functions of all librarians. The spring dinner meeting of the New York Technical Services Librarians, held on May 6, 1988, had as its program title, "The Online Catalog: Merging Responsibilities of Technical and Public Services Librarians." Representatives from libraries with online catalogs—Princeton

University, New York Public Library, Columbia University—stressed the importance of cooperation. The speakers' message, however, had less to do with continuing cooperation after installation of the computerized public catalog than with the required joint efforts of all librarians in planning for the OPAC. Questions had to be answered as to which parts of the bibliographic surrogate should be indexed and retrievable for readers. Advancing technology had imposed on the library a need for cooperation, at least for the drafting stages of the OPAC.

The search strategies of the four bibliographic utilities have been detailed to show that although they aim for the same results, they differ confusingly in their related methodologies. The outcome is a lack of standardization for readers who use more than one library, with the possibility that catalog consultation will be impeded by different systems. (The speakers at the above-mentioned dinner meeting all used different systems for their OPACs.) This lack of standardization becomes even more troublesome in databases that give analytical access to serials and other items, as noted in Chapter 6. The Library of Congress was well aware of such problems, and at least for the bibliographic utilities, it succeeded in having its linked systems project (LSP) accepted to coordinate the provision and searching of utility databases containing MARC records.

One promised benefit of LSP is that catalogers will be able to perform intersystem searching—an activity also to be performed by reference librarians—that is, to consult the union catalogs of RLIN, WLN, LC or OCLC when the first utility does not yield the desired surrogate.[30] When LSP is fully implemented for the utilities, this switching from one system to another is claimed to be almost effortless. Something like this ability has already been accomplished without LSP, though admittedly with more physical effort, when a library becomes a limited user of another system, such as when an OCLC subscriber uses RLIN on a search-only basis and, as explained later, the "target" individual system's unstandardized commands must be used.

OCLC success in providing cataloging data to thousands of libraries is undoubtedly a reason for the rise of the online computer catalog, treated next, but the increase is due also to the increasing access demands by its users. Some years ago, the then-head of OCLC boasted that centralized online cataloging allowed libraries to tailor the format and contents of their catalog records, thus preserving the advantages of local

30. Avram, "The Linked Systems Project"; Gary McCone, "The Linked Systems Project: Impact on Bibliographic Networks and Systems," *LITA Newsletter*, no. 26 (Fall 1986): 1–2; Richard W. McCoy, "The Linked Systems Project: Progress, Promise, Realities," *Library Journal* 111 (Oct. 1, 1986):36–38.

adaptation.[31] All the bibliographic utilities already discussed claim this advantage. Unfortunately, many libraries about to shift to computer catalogs have found that their earlier records fell below an acceptable standard. The advantage of local adaptation has also produced a lack of standardization in online computer catalog technology.

The growing movement of American libraries to the OPAC from other types, including the COM catalog, is attributable not only to the bibliographic utilities but also to vendors of computerized circulation systems. More likely, the utilities could supply bibliographic records better suited to OPAC use since, in most cases, MARC surrogates for the library's collection were available. American libraries that first computerized their circulation operations—a logical distributed processing decision—learned that the bibliographic records for circulation control were too abbreviated for OPAC. Only bar or zebra coding (with short records) was necessary in computerized circulation for unique identification of library items (and patrons). Libraries had to convert circulation surrogates to MARC format if they were to make a usable OPAC.

It did not take American librarians long to realize that they had the makings of an OPAC once their bibliographic records were in machine-readable form, either because their catalog card data were already on computer tapes or because a rudimentary machine-readable catalog was present in their computerized circulation system. For very large collections with card catalogs constructed prior to computerization, a judgment had to be made on automated catalog size. Usually the decision was to freeze the old catalog and to photograph its cards for a bookform catalog. The OPAC would contain bibliographic records prepared after those in the frozen catalog.

This decision meant that searchers would have to consult at least two catalogs of the library's holdings. Pre-OPAC bookform catalogs often entailed many printed supplements as well as the old card catalog. Large American libraries, like LC and the New York Public Library Research Libraries, photographed their enormous card catalogs and continued with OPAC. Small to medium-size libraries, however, could convert their entire printed card catalog to machine-readable format. Retrospective conversion conforming to MARC and *AACR2* standards is a service offered by bibliographic utilities, such as OCLC and Utlas, as well as by LC and vendors previously known for their computerized circulation systems, such as CLSI (formerly C L Systems, Inc.) through Utlas. The lesson, hard-learned and echoing the opinions of public service librarians

31. Frederick G. Kilgour, "Computer-Based Systems, a New Dimension to Library Cooperation," *College & Research Libraries* 34 (Mar. 1973):137–43.

like Mudge and Winchell, was that in the long run it is cheaper not to create an abbreviated bibliographic record.[32]

The advantage of OPAC is considerable (not necessarily including that of keeping up with the times for a machine-oriented clientele): retrieving through a computer terminal of up-to-date bibliographic records by author, title, subject, or other access points, all without having to move from the terminal! The trend now is to load additional information into OPAC beyond the bibliographic surrogates, such as self-teaching help screens, library hours, histories of the libraries, and size and scope of collections.

The OPAC is usually menu-driven, that is, a choice of search options is displayed in words on the terminal screen, and the user chooses among them. Though screen-sensitive (or touch-sensitive) OPAC terminals, instead of those with keyboards, have been used in smaller public libraries, their installation in large academic collections is doubtful. The fear of radiation, however ill-founded, militates against their proliferation.

The various OPACs in different libraries show a complexity and lack of standardization in display and search commands.[33] Most users will not be able to use even their own library's OPAC without instruction, not to mention the OPACs in other libraries, which is one more reason for trained professionals. An equally important recognition is that machine-readable bibliographic surrogates should follow the full MARC format; increasing the power of OPAC searching entails increasing the use of the complete MARC record and its content designators.

A survey by Douglass and Leung of the use of the full MARC record in academic OPACs confirms this conclusion: "The full MARC record is still both desirable and a reality as the best bibliographic description for an item." The surveyors discovered, however, that many academic libraries often omitted the subject headings in a brief catalog form for their OPAC.[34] This omission might support the findings of Markey that

32. Isadore Gilbert Mudge, "Present Day Economies in Cataloging as Seen by the Reference Librarian of a Large University Library," *A.L.A. Bulletin* 28 (Sept. 1934):579–87; Wyllis E. Wright, "Full, Medium and Short," *Journal of Cataloging and Classification* 11 (Oct. 1955):196–99; Constance M. Winchell, "The Catalog: Full, Medium, or Limited," ibid., 199–206.

33. Stephen R. Salmon, "Characteristics of Online Public Catalogs," *Library Resources & Technical Services* 27 (Jan./Mar. 1983):36–67; Walt Crawford and others, *Bibliographic Displays in the Online Catalog* (White Plains, N.Y.: Knowledge Industry Publications, 1986); Walt Crawford, "Testing Bibliographic Displays for Online Catalogs," *Information Technology and Libraries* 6 (Mar. 1987):20–33.

34. Nancy E. Douglass and Shirley Leung, "Use of the Full MARC Record: Myth and Reality," in *Academic Libraries: Myth and Realities: Proceedings of the Third National Conference of the Association of College and Research Libraries, April 4–7, 1984, Seattle, Washington* (Chicago: Assoc. of College & Research Libraries, 1984), 177–82.

subject search was, surprisingly, strongly desired by OPAC users, who often mentioned indexes and tables of contents as worthy OPAC enhancements for subject search.[35] A frequent defense by librarians of subject headings omission was that sophisticated Boolean search in online catalogs would overcome lack of subject access. Other librarians countered that no amount of Boolean search can retrieve headings that are not present. The fact that most academic libraries eventually upgrade their briefer bibliographic records to full MARC format attests that reality wins out in the long run over the beginning myth that some other library will spend the time and money to construct a full MARC record.

In 1985, after many mechanical and technical delays, Columbia University Libraries (CUL) introduced its OPAC, the Columbia Libraries Information Online (CLIO), a menu-driven computer catalog with seven search options: author, title, author and title, subject, on order/in process material, item location/call number browse.[36] Six standard choices at the foot of each screen aid the searcher in navigating CLIO: start, help (information and advice, fully explaining the seven search options), back (restores the previous screen), up (moves back to the start of the search), quit (ends the session), and tutorial (provides a step-by-step introduction to the CLIO system). Once a search option is selected, search statements are input in natural language, which can be truncated using a truncation symbol and sometimes without it.

Because of their smaller databases and greater need to give clear instructions to users, OPACs employ natural language instead of the more complicated and unnatural search keys of a bibliographic utility, such as OCLC's 4, 3, 1 author search algorithm. Subject search in CLIO is based on *LCSH*, which should be used as an authority file before searching. A printer is placed next to most CLIO terminals. OPACs have been installed in the Columbia Butler Library's General Reference Department. Many others are being placed throughout the various Columbia libraries, at least one per library. Eventual access to CLIO OPACs will be available from faculty offices, dormitories, and even private residences.

CLIO is a good OPAC example because it is still transitional. A "generic" case, its problems will be or already have been confronted by other libraries. CLIO contains records for CUL materials cataloged since January 1, 1983. Items cataloged before that date are in a huge card

35. Karen Markey, "Thus Spake the OPAC User," *Information Technology and Libraries* 2 (Dec. 1983): 381–87; idem, "Subject-searching Experiences and Needs of Online Catalog Users: Implications for Library Classification," *Library Resources & Technical Services* 29 (Jan./Mar. 1985):34–51.

36. Information on CLIO is from interviews, personal experience, and the "Easy Access Pocket Card," published by Columbia University Libraries and placed at each OPAC as well as distributed to users.

catalog, divided into (1) names and titles and (2) topical subjects. CLIO records are, depending on search type, more or less abbreviated versions of the full MARC surrogate. Accordingly, the CLIO catalog is more a finding list than a bibliographical reference source.

Even the single record display, CLIO's equivalent of the traditional main entry, does not have all the details of the MARC record. Such a record, retrieved by author search (not all searches produce the single record display), includes: personal author; names (added author entries); title; publication facts (formerly called the imprint); series title; physical description (pagination, illustrative matter, size); subject tracings (*LCSH*); library; item location code (call number); and holdings. A typical display is: GEOLOGY TN871.35 .A778 1982).

Missing from this rather full main entry are the descriptive-cataloging tracings and *AACR2*-mandated notes, for example, noting the presence of bibliography and index. (Information from the MARC Fixed Field and MARC indicators is not expected on MARC-derived main entries.) The record is even more abbreviated when it is retrieved through the searches for on order/in process, or item location/call number browse. In the latter, for example, only a listing of titles is given with the same Library of Congress Classification (LCC) symbol as the beginning part of the Columbia University Libraries' call number. (The browse, if continued, goes on to the next LCC beginning symbol.) The listed items are numbered so that records can be selected for fuller bibliographic detail.

Almost all CLIO search options are present in the pre-CLIO card catalog or in the post-1982 *NUC*. Sometimes, CLIO makes access easier to files. Prior to CLIO, for example, CUL maintained a separate microfiche catalog for its on order/in process works. CLIO browsing by item location code/call number, though, makes the CUL shelflist newly open to the public.

The search options of the typical OPAC confirm a belief that the access points of traditional bibliographic organization have not changed but, indeed, been reduced in number. As with all library catalogs, a complete listing of an author's books might be available in a union catalog of many libraries, such as the *NUC*, or in a printed bibliography of all documentable titles by that writer. Cross-references are not given by CLIO for different forms of the author's name—Twain, Mark and Clemens, Samuel Langhorne, for example. Collocation is not a CLIO strong point, nor does the lack of Boolean search foster coordinate retrieval.

The full MARC records and the authority file for CLIO are based on those of WLN, but the overlay imposed on CLIO for public viewing omits some of the MARC record, as already shown, and all of the WLN authority file. These full records and WLN's authority file cross-references are at present available to the library staff, though not the public, with the direct command mode in CLIO. Here is one more reason for trained practitioners in libraries; client self-help may be admirable and desirable, but not for advanced searching methodology.

An example of the simple-mindedness of computers is the CLIO item location/call number browse. In browsing the LCC as assigned to CUL holdings, the search can become puzzling in its outcome. If both the user and computer take the search command literally, such as "barnard (an affiliated Columbia library) ps3515.e37 s9 1977," CLIO will display CUL call numbers after the "ba" of "barnard," i.e., the LCC sequence for BC, quite far in LCC from PS! A better search statement in this case would have been "ps3515" or "ps3515.e37." (The shorter first statement would have produced an unwieldy quantity of citations.) When the LCC symbol is close mnemonically to the Columbia library location designation, such as "geology tn871.35 .a778 1982"—a book by Asquith on oil well logging—the item location/call number browse command will produce hits on the LCC sequence beginning GF, which is at least near geology. (We cannot help remembering LC embarrassment when its computerized filing system did not suppress beginning articles in headings.) No doubt, this CLIO problem will be corrected.

Although Columbia has been a member of RLG since its inception and so possessed RLIN machine-readable cataloging data for about ten previous years, CLIO began its coverage as of January 1983, when LC inaugurated its index-register *NUC*. Retrospective input to CLIO was planned for cataloging since 1977. In the meantime, only new records for serials were to be added to CLIO. All bibliographic surrogates were for a while inserted in fuller RLIN style in the old card catalog, a reminder of the LC practice of duplicating the data in the new LC OPAC for its side-by-side card catalog.

As already suggested, vicissitudes abounded in Columbia University's introduction of CLIO. The discovery and removal of asbestos in campus tunnels that carried computer cables among Columbia libraries caused a delay. Then, in 1987, Biblio-Techniques, Inc., the Olympia, Washington, company that adapted WLN's software, went out of business "for financial reasons."[37] At its demise, Biblio-Techniques announced it was giving Columbia the source programs for CLIO. After more than a year, Columbia decided to adopt Northwestern Online Total Integrated System (NOTIS)[38] of Evanston, Illinois, for the OPAC software. Also, Columbia

37. "Biblio-Techniques, Inc. Ceases Business Operations," *Information Technology and Libraries* 6 (Mar. 1987):65; *1988 Encyclopedia of Information Systems and Services*, 8th ed., Amy Lucas and Annette Novello, eds., entry 241.

38. "NOTIS Becomes Separate, For-Profit Corporation," *Information Technology and Libraries* 6 (Dec. 1987):318; *1989 Encyclopedia of Information Systems and Services*, entry 1687.

gradually over more than a year would make the transition to the NOTIS design.

An advantage of NOTIS software was linking a library's cataloging, acquisitions, and circulation activities, so that—unlike in the old CLIO—a searcher could see the bibliographic record for an item in the library's collection along with its holdings and status on one screen display—which of the union catalog's libraries held the item and whether it was on order, in process, or out on circulation.

NOTIS was not the only computer organization offering OPAC design and implementation. Others included Carlyle Systems, Inc. of Emeryville, California; Geac Computers International, Inc. of Markham, Ontario; the aforementioned Utlas, of Canadian origin; and CLSI Inc. of Newtownville, Massachusetts.[39] Geac and CLSI had previously specialized in circulation automation. NOTIS software was being accepted for OPAC by other large academic libraries and library groups, including Harvard University and the City University of New York.[40] With the best of advice, probably after much study, Columbia had chosen Biblio-Techniques for its OPAC designer, a company that ceased operations after installing a public access catalog system. Not uncommon in the fast-changing world of information technology, Biblio-Techniques cessation made CLIO even more of a generic case than Columbia first imagined.

To summarize, the searching power of the present OPAC, as represented by CLIO, is not adequate for a comprehensive retrieval of bibliographic surrogates. Main entries have been abbreviated. Many access points offered by the MARC record have been omitted in OPAC search options; no provision has been made for cross-references, free-text search, and Boolean operations. Only trained practitioners with access to the full MARC records and authority files in a bibliographic utility database can approximate a thorough search and retrieval. At least NOTIS will bring Boolean search (though this type of search is somewhat slow) to OPAC capabilities.

However we may feel about the desirability of research on classification in automated search and retrieval of OPAC items, for either hierarchical browsing or pinpointing of very specific topics, this current emphasis on classification research suggests that American librarians have long neglected (and perhaps only subconsciously recognized) the full potential of this method of subject analysis as a revelatory device, not just a shelf-location aid.

39. *1989 Encyclopedia of Information Systems and Services*, entry 386 (Carlyle), 450 (CLSI).

40. "Library's Card Catalog to Go on Line in Fall," *Harvard University Gazette* 83 (May 13, 1988): 1, 4, 8. Information on the City University of New York and Columbia University is from interviews.

The professional literature has proposed that classification symbols are potentially valuable for automated topical browsing in OPACs and that research funds should be allotted to test them.[41] Most of the research on OPAC classification would incorporate the holdings' DDC, thus providing a DDC shelflist for subject search by end users and librarians. Subject search in this case usually means reading up (or down) the shelflist notation to broaden (or narrow) the subject and so increase recall and precision, maximizing the relevancy of the subject items retrieved.

Dewey is preferred by researchers of automated classification because of its "pure" numerical notation and its purported consistent hierarchical arrangement. Contrary to this preference, the Columbia collections are mostly classified by LCC, which does not have a "pure" numerical notation nor an easily read hierarchical arrangement. Although Columbia is switching to NOTIS for its OPAC software, NOTIS was created for DDC, not LCC, browsing.

Adding a shelflist to the OPAC is a step towards making the automated classed catalog accessible to the library patron, though the shelflist is still far from its ideal configuration. (Note the just described Item location/Call number browse in CLIO.) OCLC's 1988 purchase of the Forest Press, publisher of the DDC, and the OCLC plan to put DDC online, will probably mean that OPAC research on DDC will intensify, at the expense of LCC.[42]

Browsing the OPAC shelflist for any book on a subject brings to mind once more the differences between classification schemes and subject headings in their retrieval appropriateness and capabilities. Commonly unnoticed by researchers is the educational and enlightening value of following the classification scheme. On the shelves, in automated shelflists, or in the full text of the scheme itself, the classification scheme sorts out relationships within the world of knowledge. One may not agree with the scheme, but one always can benefit by its ideas. The practical obstacles to searching an automated shelflist, not to mention the development of an automated classed catalog, have been well detailed by Hill, who re-

41. A sampling of the copious documentation, previously uncited, includes: Elaine Fackenthal Svenonius, "Use of Classification in Online Retrieval," *Library Resources & Technical Services* 27 (Jan. 1983): 76–80; Janet Swan Hill, "Online Classification Number Access: Some Practical Considerations," *Journal of Academic Librarianship* 10 (Mar. 1984):17–22; "Group Launches Public Test of Online Dewey Decimal Data," *Library of Congress Information Bulletin* 44 (Mar. 11, 1985):46–47; Karen Markey and Anh Demeyer, "Dewey Decimal Classification Online Project: Integration of a Library Schedule and Index into the Subject Searching Capabilities of an Online Catalogue," *International Cataloguing* 14 (July/Sept. 1985): 31–34; Nancy J. Williamson, "Classification in Online Systems: Research and the North American Perspective," ibid., 29–31.

42. "OCLC Acquires Forest Press, Publisher of Dewey Classification," *Library Journal* 113 (Aug. 1988):19.

mains pessimistic about the early realization of automated classification for the OPAC.[43]

An informal brief test was made from present automated bibliographic records by this author to determine how subject retrieval by classification notation compares with keyword search of titles and also with—shades of Grace Osgood Kelley!—subject headings.[44] In this test a random selection from a subject authority was first made from the "Local government—Great Britain" listing in the January–December 1987 subject index of the *NUC*. Although the testing concerns subject retrieval by classification in OPACs, the records used are in microfiche. The 1987 *NUC* was chosen because most libraries with OPACs acquired at least some of the items it contains, and the subject index of the *NUC* is recent enough to include works made part of automated catalogs.

The eighteen titles in the *NUC* subject index under "Local government—Great Britain" were, in order of appearance:

Managing local socialism
The origin and development of local self-government in England and the United States . . . 1880 [microform]
Government by the people?
British life and institutions, 1973
Great Britain Committee of Inquiry into the Conduct of Local Authority Businesses. Local authority publicity
Local government and urban politics
Industrial democracy in local government
Local government management in the United States and United Kingdom
The local politics of race
Employee participation and local government
Local government in the modern state
New research in central-local relations
Kings of their counties
Government by consent
The new management of local government
Streamlining local government?
Urban political theory and the management of fiscal stress
A voice for your neighborhood

None of these titles contains both the phrases "Local government" and "Great Britain" for the geographical subdivision. So much for key-

43. Hill, "Online Classification Number Access."

44. Grace Osgood Kelley, *The Classification of Books: An Inquiry into Its Usefulness to the Reader* (New York: Wilson, 1937).

word search and retrieval of unenhanced titles! Of course, synonymous and related phrases could also be selected, but selecting them requires searchers to use subject authorities and to know the subject. (Subject headings with further subdivisions of "Local government—Great Britain" were omitted from this test.)

In the next step, the titles were examined in the register of the *NUC* to uncover all their tracings and, especially, to find which titles had "Local government—Great Britain" as their first subject heading. After some tiresome flipping of microfiches for different chronological parts of the 1987 Register, the eighteen main entries were found. Eleven main entries had "Local government—Great Britain" as their first subject heading; the remaining seven titles had the subject heading but not in first place. Six of the titles with the first-place subject heading had the LCC notation JS; three titles without the heading in first place also had JS. The Dewey notation for the titles with the first-place subject heading was 261.7 (one title); 320.441 (one title); 352.041 (three titles); and 658.3 (one title). Four works without the subject heading in first place had DDC assignments as follows: one title began with DDC 320, two titles with 352, and one with 354. Of the total eighteen titles, six had no LCC or DDC assigned. If LC still follows its policy of making the first subject heading the major topic of the work and matching that subject heading to its classification notation, combining LCC numbers for the sought subject heading in either first or following sequence will increase recall, but not precision. Using DDC for the same purpose would probably give the same result.

Even from this short experiment, deductions can be drawn. First, searching for the major subject content of books is more accurately pursued, as of now, through subject headings than title keywords and—to confirm Kelley—classification. The same subject heading may be applied to works with different classification symbols, though a modal classification, both in LCC and DDC, is ascertainable. This deduction leads to another: a correspondence between classification notation and subject heading is not to be expected, as Chan found in her study of LCC for automated search.[45]

Our brief test did not aim to compare the OPAC subject retrievability of LCC against that of DDC. The DDC notation did seem more scattered than the LCC, but consultation of the DDC relative index would perhaps heighten precision because selection of the notation could be more specific.

45. Lois Mai Chan, "Library of Congress Classification as an Online Retrieval Tool: Potentials and Limitations," *Information Technology and Libraries* 51 (Sept. 1986):185–86.

Markey discovered in her research on automated catalog use that searchers would like more related term (RT) suggestions.[46] One can only say that *LCSH* in print or online would provide numerous RT for search by subject headings.

In further regard to the Markey findings, one wonders if OPAC users might not benefit from and are unconsciously seeking terms not marked "RT" in *LCSH,* but somehow related to the context of the work. Only examination of a back-of-the-book index can currently supply these terms.

Much remains to be studied and done to maximize the power of subject headings. Searchers in automated analytical databases—discussed in Chapter 6—are already familiar with weighted index terms. Searching in computerized sources for works by their first subject headings or for works that combine various first subject headings would agree with LC policy on judging the most significant topics of the works. Manual coordinate subject search of this kind can be tedious, but its feasibility has been described.[47] Unfortunately, all MARC tags for topical subject headings are "Field 650," with their sequence unidentified. The descriptive cataloging tracings in MARC "Field 640" follow another LC sequence not as conducive to priority searching. Interestingly, when a library converts its printed catalog records to machine-readable format, it must number the LC tracings for each work so that the computer will not miss any of them.

It would be possible even now, using an automated system like RLIN, to search for works that satisfy Boolean commands for certain subject headings, but visually examining the main entries with their full tracings would be necessary to determine which subject headings were primary. Because MARC formats are under continuous official review, it is recommended for consistency's sake that only an officially standardized change in MARC-content coding be made. Local systems or libraries are not advised to change the MARC format on their own. Research and testing by accepted authorities are, however, surely indicated.

LC announced in mid-1986 that 150,000 MARC-formatted subject authorities from its *LCSH* would be made available in computerized form, to be updated weekly by current authority work.[48] According to the 1989

46. Karen Markey, "Integrating the Machine-Readable LCSH into Online Catalogs," *Information Technology and Libraries* 7 (Sept. 1988): 299–312.

47. Richard Joseph Hyman, *From Cutter to MARC: Access to the Unit Record* (Flushing, N.Y.: Queens College Press, 1977), 19. For a general discussion of postcoordinate search in the *NUC,* see Lois Mai Chan, *Library of Congress Subject Headings: Principles and Application,* 2nd ed. (Littleton, Colo.: Libraries Unlimited, 1986), 37–38, 184, 344, 356–57.

48. "MARC Distribution Service—Subject Authorities," *Cataloging Service Bulletin,* no. 32 (Spring 1986):71.

LC *MARC Distribution Services* catalog, the subject authority's headings and references begin with 1986; the *LCSH* with its updatings includes all headings and references in the LC catalogs.

At the 1987 American Library Association Annual Conference in San Francisco, a program entitled "Subject Authorities in the Online Environment" was sponsored by ALA's Library and Information Technology Association, Resources and Technical Services Division Cataloging and Classification Section, Association of College and Research Libraries, and Public Library Association. Early users of the computerized subject authority file (SAF), who used it chiefly for local cataloging, complained that the SAF was deficient as a thesaurus. It did not have a complete listing of *LCSH* subject headings. Its retention of the *LCSH* reference structure (though not the reference symbols) made determining the correct subject headings for a work difficult, and the SAF did not facilitate hierarchical searching and browsing. The program speakers recommended that the SAF be reformatted as a true thesaurus.[49]

Apart from the fact that a thesaurus is designed mainly for analytical access, following the reformatting recommendation would entail enormous expense and effort, as witness the differences between *LCSH* and the thesauruses of the Educational Resources Information Center and the Medical Literature Analysis and Retrieval System On-Line (MEDLINE). It is likely, however, that in the near future the four major bibliographic utilities described in this chapter will have loaded the SAF into their computerized catalogs.

The charges aired at the 1987 ALA Annual Conference were generalized in an article by Dykstra who objected to all LC thesaurus work and stated that *LCSH* had not been converted into a thesaurus because it still used subject headings, not terms.[50] As used by Dykstra, "term" appeared to be a near analogy to the linguist's "phoneme," except that instead of being a sound, the "term" is an irreducible unit of meaning that could be arranged hierarchically in a thesaurus.

With subject analysis the content can be verbalized to serve as both a subject heading, notably with subdivisions, and a classification term—

49. JoAnn K. Stewart, "Subject Authorities in the Online Environment," *LITA Newsletter*, no. 30 (Fall 1987):12–13. Stewart summarizes five papers given at the program during the 1987 ALA Annual Conference: Lois Mai Chan, "Functions of SAF"; Joanna Reed and Syd Jones, "Practical Considerations in Dealing with *LCSH* Tapes: A Vendor Perspective"; William A. Garrison, "Practical Considerations in Dealing with *LCSH* Tapes: A User Perspective"; Lizbeth Bishoff, "Public Access to an *LCSH*-Based Authority File"; Carol Mandel, "New Directions in Subject Authority Control: Multiple Vocabularies."

50. Mary Dykstra, "LC Subject Headings Disguised as a Thesaurus: Problems of Incompatible Purposes," *Library Journal* 113 (Mar. 1, 1988):42–46.

the "symbiosis" described by Ranganathan.[51] However, one must keep in mind, as this book reiterates, the different functions that subject headings and classification terms each perform.

Subject headings depend on the user's knowledge of the words employed—sometimes necessitating fluency in the nuances of a particular language. The classification term, ordinarily represented by a numeral or other symbol, is supposedly language neutral and can be translated without destroying the classificatory structure. A thesaurus tends to merge subject headings and classification terms, blurring as a result the distinctions of words and references. In a thesaurus, the main arrangement is alphabetical, but hierarchy is clearly shown and there are many scope (public) notes and cross-references, chiefly to show definitively which term is preferred in the subject analysis of an item. Since Cutter's codification of subject-heading practices, much effort has been expended on cross-references to implement the syndetic structure in a list of subject headings.

An examination of well-known thesauruses and subject-heading listings attests to the overlap of the two approaches to subject analysis. The U.S. National Library of Medicine (NLM) issues its *Medical Subject Headings (MeSH)* as used for its *Index Medicus* and other NLM publications and services, arranges these subject headings in hierarchical or "tree" order, and refers to them equally as subject headings, subject descriptors, and terms. Indeed, this hierarchical order is summarized in *MeSH* and in a separate publication, *MeSH-Tree Structures*.[52]

The *Art and Architecture Thesaurus (AAT)*, sponsored by the J. Paul Getty Trust as a component of its Getty Art History Information Program, includes a cumulative alphabetical index of all terms, a hierarchies listing, and an associated concepts register.[53] It is scheduled to go online, and is used by the staff of the Columbia University Avery Architectural and

51. S. R. Ranganathan, *Theory of Library Catalogue* (Madras: Madras Library Assoc., 1938), 77–198, especially 123.

52. *Index Medicus. Medical Subject Headings. Main Headings and Cross References Used in Index Medicus and National Library of Medicine Catalog*, 1963– (Washington: National Library of Medicine, 1983–), annual. Issued as part 2 of the January issue of *Index Medicus*; reprinted as part of *Cumulated Index Medicus*. For further detail, see Eugene P. Sheehy, comp., *Guide to Reference Books*, 10th ed. (Chicago: ALA, 1986), BE253–54. (Updatings in the January and July *College & Research Libraries*.) *Index Medicus. Medical Subject Headings. Tree Structures*, 1972– (Washington: National Library of Medicine, 1972–), annual. Companion to *Index Medicus Annotated Alphabetic List. Tree Annotations*; and *Permuted Subject Headings*. For the latest editions, consult the *Monthly Catalog of United States Government Publications*.

53. *Art and Architecture Thesaurus*, copyright held by the J. Paul Getty Trust of Malibu, California, and currently produced in computer-printout format at Williamstown, Massachusetts.

Fine Arts Library to select *subject headings* for its *Avery Index to Architectural Periodicals.*[54]

This examination of current thesauruses and subject-heading lists weakens Dykstra's definition of the thesaurus as a hierarchical arrangement of terms. It should be noted also that LC has not made an official announcement that it is changing its *LCSH* into a thesaurus. In the title of the recent LC publication, *LC Thesaurus for Graphic Materials: Topical Terms for Subject Access,*[55] LC used the word "thesaurus" consciously, but the publication has been criticized for not giving access to the hierarchies as *AAT* does. In summary, the intention of LC to convert its *LCSH* into thesaurus format remains unproven.

The citations in Chapter 4 to the editorial comments in the 11th edition of *LCSH* only confirm that the *LCSH* and its automated abbreviated edition, the SAF, were not to be considered "thesauruses."

The problems of automated catalog access seem more severe than those of printed access to bibliographic surrogates. Besides the near comprehensiveness of the latter, the *NUC* at least presented one approach to search and retrieval, though the approach could differ according to the latest descriptive cataloging and subject authorities. The single commonly used source for bibliographic surrogates was the *NUC* created by a centralized cataloging organization, LC. With the OPAC, the LC-supplied records can assume varied configurations. Copious cross-references in the pre-1983 *NUC* eased the burden of collocative search. In the *NUC* main entries the elements of the printed bibliographic record remained largely the same, as did their sequence. Librarians might be asked to explain the appearance of the ISBD or minor variations in abbreviations or typographical style. Even when the librarian on duty could not answer all such questions, the trained professional librarian, either from the readers' or technical services, could be called on for answers. Every librarian is now fair game with OPAC.

The online public access catalog presents strong challenges to the patron—and librarian. First, the bibliographic record is not always complete. LC abbreviates records usually only for items that are not ordinarily sought by the average patron.[56] OPAC, on the other hand, encourages

54. *Avery Index to Architectural Periodicals,* 1963–   (New York: Columbia University Libraries, Avery Architectural Library, 1963–   ), multiannual cumulations and *Supplements.* See Sheehy, *Guide,* EK55.

55. Elizabeth Betz Parker, *LC Thesaurus for Graphic Materials: Topical Terms for Subject Access* (Washington: Library of Congress Cataloging Distribution Service, 1987). A review by Amy E. Lucker appeared as "Subject Access to Graphics," *Library Journal* 113 (Feb. 1, 1988):48.

56. "Minimal-Level LC-MARC Records Added to OCLC Online Union Catalog," *OCLC Newsletter,* no. 171 (Jan./Feb. 1988):24; *Information Technology and Libraries* 7 (June 1988): 204.

shorter records for items that are sought by the average patron. Then, there is the lack of standardization for accessing the OPAC in different libraries. The displays of different OPAC systems can vary widely, also.

The LSP attempted to coordinate the utilities, though its efforts have directly aided the practitioner rather than the OPAC library patron. The aim of each OPAC system to present a transparent, user-friendly, menu-driven environment was laudable, though personal experience has revealed problems soluble only by a knowledgeable librarian.

The problems of automated analytical access, either for an individual database or for a system distributed by vendors like DIALOG or BRS, are even greater. (The analytical database producers and vendors are, to be sure, much less dependent on LC.) The profit motive of most database producers and distributors may have worked against standardization. The LSP has just begun to try to coordinate these many systems and their command languages, but the databases of the utilities come first. If the LSP succeeds in standardizing the many analytical databases, it will take a very long time, and one wonders if the results will ever trickle down to the library patron—still another justification for the continued existence of the professional librarian. The lack of standardization remains the *bête noire* of bibliographic organization in general and of automated search in particular. Chapter 7 discusses how some database producers are resorting to standardization.

It often appears that, with technological advances, we take one step forward only to take two steps back. To the aggravated problems of searching the analytical databases Chapter 6 is devoted.

6 AUTOMATED ANALYTICAL ACCESS

More than the other subjects discussed thus far, searching and retrieving computerized analytical information are continuously changing, both in technology and jargon—not to mention the effects bewildering business mergers and acquisitions have on them. Most texts on the subject are already outdated on publication, so their usefulness is drastically reduced. Some books on online searching are written "generically," that is, in terms so general that the changing details in the "real" world do not affect their accuracy. Furthermore, many books about online searching devote considerable space to the problems of personnel organization, staff administration, and budgeting and consequently neglect the nitty-gritty of the process itself. This chapter is mostly concerned with the "nuts and bolts" aspect of analytical information search and retrieval in the various databases. Readers should note that the text is based on data available at the time of writing and is very subject to change.

Unlike the bibliographic utilities and software producers, the database producers and distributors have as their chief activity supplying online information that is contained mostly in journal articles, though book and numeric data are also made available. Thousands of these databases, usually providing analytical access through surrogates, are in existence. Many are computerized versions of printed indexes that cover longer periods. Some computerized indexes, distributed by their creators or wholesale vendors, include more than their printed versions. A standard reference tool listing these databases is the *Encyclopedia of Information Systems and Services (EISS)*, as of 1989 in its ninth edition.[1] In this latest

1. *1989 Encyclopedia of Information Systems and Services*, 9th ed., Amy Lucas and Nan

edition the *EISS* has 2871 listings in its United States volume, and 1406 in its international volume. Most of the entries are for analytical databases, although the *EISS* also lists bibliographic utilities and software producers and distributors. The nondomestic databases are from about seventy countries. The 1985 *Computer-Readable Databases: A Directory and Data Sourcebook (C-RD)*, which does not list the library utilities or the software suppliers, includes 2,805 databases in 2,509 entries. It gives the number of databases in its various editions as: 301 in 1976, 528 in 1979, and 773 in 1982![2]

Both of these directories have useful descriptions. *C-RD* comes out in printed form less frequently than the *EISS*, but it enumerates criteria with which every potential database user should be familiar. Its database descriptions may be analyzed into five major groupings: (1) basic information; (2) subject matter and scope; (3) indexing, coding, and classification; (4) data elements present; and (5) user aids.

The first area, basic information, includes the name of database, with its acronym and, when available, former name and acronym; name of producer; frequency of database updates; time span covered; average number of items added per year; corresponding print products; commercial availability for lease, license, purchase and the medium in which provided; approximate number of items as of a set date preceding publication of the directory; language of database; names of the online timesharing organizations that process the database and make it available to the public; and names of the organizations processing the database for batch searching and for offering it to users.

The second, subject matter and scope of data in database, includes information from the producer's description, plus elements such as the date when the file was first made available in computer-readable form; the relationship of the database to other databases; and the language of the database sources. Also included for numeric databases are sources of data; data verification; available special features when given; and language of the database.

The third area, indexing, coding, and classification indicates the type and extent of subject analysis and indexing data (controlled words or

Soper, eds., 3 vols. (Detroit: Gale, 1989). Between editions of the *Encyclopedia* appears the paperbound supplement, *New Information Systems and Services*, first published in 1979. See also Eugene P. Sheehy, comp., *Guide to Reference Books*, 10th ed. (Chicago: ALA, 1986), EJ253. For updated additions to the *Guide*, see "Selected Reference Books of . . . " in the January and July issues of *College & Research Libraries*.

2. *Computer-Readable Databases*, 4th ed., 2 vols. ed. Martha E. Williams, (Chicago, ALA, 1985), viii. A new edition is planned every two years. See Sheehy, *Guide*, AB269. (A 5th ed., edited by Kathleen Young Marcaccio and Janice A. De Maggio, was published in 1989 by Gale of Detroit.)

phrases, subject and classification codes, chemical identifiers, text words from title and abstract, and personal name as subject). Chemical identifiers are terms or codes for chemical substances.

Fourth, data elements are given for bibliographic databases (author, title, publisher, date, etc.). The contents of numeric databases are detailed in the second area, subject matter and scope.

Finally, the user aids area lists the availability of database-oriented vocabularies, term lists, thesauruses, user manuals, and database documentation. The preceding are generally supplied by producers of word-oriented databases.

Indexes to *C-RD* include those to both volumes but printed in each volume: indexes for names, subjects, and names and addresses of producers and processors (vendors).[3] Similar indexes in the *EISS* incorporate seventeen categories for a typical entry, not always the same categories as *C-RD*. In both the *EISS* and *C-RD*, the descriptive data are largely contributed by the database producers and distributors.

A small number of these vendors supply subscribers through computer terminals that have access to hundreds of databases and thus become, like the bibliographic utility distributors of the LC MARC tapes, database wholesalers. Already, as shown in Chapter 5, the boundaries between the bibliographic utilities and the database wholesalers are blurring. OCLC tried unsuccessfully to offer gateway service to the BRS databases as well as to WILSONLINE, begun in 1984, and VU/TEXT of Philadelphia, Pennsylvania, begun in 1982. OCLC also has prepared, for BRS access, its EASI Reference database, which gives subject access to a recent selection from its OLUC.[4] RLIN announced at about the same time as OCLC that its gateway would access the DIALOG databases.[5]

The search options of the database producers and distributors are more numerous and sophisticated than those of the bibliographic utilities. Among the former, controlled classified vocabularies in thesauruses, free-text search, positional operators for subject words, and Boolean combination searches are common. Some of the database producers and distributors now offer full-text display and search, such as for encyclopedias—a development commented on below.

Some databases are produced and distributed by only a single organization. The full-text NEXIS, begun in 1980, contains descriptions of current events from newspapers, news and business magazines, etc., and LEXIS, begun in 1970, contains legal information. Both are produced

3. Ibid., xii–xvi.

4. *1989 EISS*, entry 2820 (WILSONLINE); 2751 (VU/TEXT); 1707 (EASI Reference Database).

5. Sheila S. Intner, "Editorial: On Falling from the Tree," *Library Resources & Technical Services* 31 (July/Sept. 1987): 205.

and distributed from Mead Data Central, Inc., of Dayton, Ohio.[6] Each of the database wholesale vendors strives to avoid duplicating its competitors' offerings. An obvious way to achieve this goal is to have exclusive rights for production or distribution of a database.

Analytical databases frequently specialize by subject area. PREDICASTS of Cleveland, Ohio, specializes in business; PsycINFO of Arlington, Virginia, focuses on psychology-related topics.[7]

Individual databases have different search commands and continuously changing structures. Contributing to this confusion are the almost daily additions of new sources by the database wholesalers. The wholesalers also provide a general search language, which, with some adjustments, is supposed to give sufficient access of a nonspecialized nature to all the databases distributed.

As with treatment of the major bibliographic utilities in Chapter 5, more attention is given in this chapter to the contents and search capabilities of the largest organization; the others are comparatively described and evaluated at less length.

The three major wholesale vendors of analytical online bibliographic information are, in descending order of size: DIALOG, BRS, and Pergamon ORBIT (On-Line Retrieval of Bibliographic Information Time Shared) InfoLine, Inc. According to the 1989 *EISS*, DIALOG services more than 300 databases; BRS, 150; and ORBIT, 90. DIALOG thus had about 150 more databases than BRS and 210 more than ORBIT, making DIALOG the OCLC of the analytical online information wholesalers.[8]

The chief aim and use of the databases serviced by DIALOG, BRS, and ORBIT are subject access to journal articles. Monographic items are not important in the inventory. Access is provided to parts of composite works, for example, those in the H. W. Wilson Company *Library Literature*, computerized since 1984 and available online from the producer or from BRS.[9] Numeric or nonbibliographic databases, individually designed and not employing the inverted indexing of bibliographic databases, are not ordinarily offered by the three major vendors. Numeric databases, such as those produced by General Electric Company of Rockville, Maryland, are often supplied with software and are used by businesses and industries to construct economic or production models and predictions. The principal wholesale vendor of numeric databases is Data Resources (DRI) of Washington, D.C., a subsidiary of McGraw-Hill, Inc., of New York, which offers, according to the 1989 *EISS*, thirty million series.[10]

6. *1989 EISS*, entry 1426 (NEXIS); 1423 (LEXIS).
7. Ibid., 1849 (PREDICASTS); 134 (PsycINFO).
8. Ibid., 667 (DIALOG); 321 (BRS); 1797 (ORBIT).
9. Sheehy, *Guide*, AB14.
10. *1989 EISS*, entry 877 (General Electric); 621 (Data Resources).

Most of the bibliographic databases in DIALOG, BRS, and ORBIT have printed counterparts; a few are online only; many are being offered on CD-ROM; and some give more access points in their computerized versions, such as the ERIC database. One of the most meticulously prepared indexes, ERIC is distributed by all three major vendors as well as the producer. MEDLINE (MEDLARS—Medical Literature Online) is recognized for its general excellence and thoroughness in providing worldwide coverage of the biomedical journal literature. It is available from the U.S. National Library of Medicine (the producer), DIALOG, and BRS.[11]

Counting vendors' duplication of databases through the 1989 *EISS* produces reasonably acceptable statistics. The three vendors' databases may have very similar names although the names may not refer to the same entity. The listings may also include sample databases for training and practice and subsets of already listed databases, and, of course, all the listings may not include the vendors' most recent additions of databases. Allowing for these problems, the figures may still be accepted as showing relative strengths.

According to this rough count, BRS overlaps with DIALOG by fifty databases, and with ORBIT, by twenty-five.[12] (Klingensmith and Duncan in 1984 listed nine databases serviced by all three vendors.[13]) According to the 1989 *EISS*, DIALOG produces or coproduces nine databases; BRS, five; and ORBIT, five. For low-cost training and practice files that are capsule versions of the originals, DIALOG supplies thirty; BRS, none; and ORBIT, three. DIALOG also offers classroom instruction programs for low-cost access by students at all levels to all disciplines.

DIALOG advertises unchallenged coverage of more topics than BRS or ORBIT. Coverage reports from each vendor, as provided in the 1989 *EISS*, are:

> DIALOG: Physical, life, applied, and social sciences, including agriculture and food sciences; education and the media; chemistry; biosciences and biomedicine, patents; medicine; environmental sciences; engineering and materials; business, management, company, financial and product information; citation indexing; sociology and linguistics; history, public affairs, and fine arts; current events and biography.
>
> BRS: Agriculture, biology, business, chemistry, computer science, economics, education, energy, engineering, environment,

11. Ibid., 2488 (MEDLARS); 2494 (MEDLINE).

12. Ibid., 667 (DIALOG); 321 (BRS); 1797 (ORBIT).

13. Patricia J. Klingensmith and Elizabeth E. Duncan, *Easy Access to DIALOG, ORBIT and BRS* (New York: M. Dekker, 1984), 193.

humanities, medicine, patents, psychology, physics, social sciences, and other areas.

ORBIT: Fields in science and technology; patents.[14]

Choosing among the three vendors (some libraries subscribe to more than one) will depend, obviously, on whether the included databases jibe with the specializations, hence patron needs, of the library or organization. If no specialization is required, relative costs, search options, and ease of access are given the priorities—resulting, perhaps, in a decision not to use any of these three wholesale vendors, but to choose some fairly unsophisticated databases instead. A special library or institution may decide on a service that is unavailable through the major wholesale vendors. All the above vendors can supply customized selective dissemination of information (SDI) files, but subject specialties are again a factor in choice. Private file services are also available.

DIALOG's Knowledge Index and BRS/After Dark services are oriented to the end user, not the professional searcher. Both are designed for personal computer (microcomputer) users, and they provide low-cost online access in nonprime time to a selected group of databases from the parent's inventories. These selected databases cover most disciplines, though Knowledge Index is weak in humanities indexes. Both are available to the user only after 6:00 P.M. local time or on weekends, and they offer direct or credit-card billing. The 1989 *EISS* lists sixty-one databases for DIALOG Knowledge Index and ninety-one for BRS/After Dark. An overlap of at least twenty-five databases is given.[15] As with the larger DIALOG and BRS services, the number of nonprime-time databases keeps increasing. Printed documentation, for example, self-instructional user manuals, are supplied by both services.

Neither BRS nor ORBIT denies the overwhelming quantity and varied subject matter of the DIALOG databases. DIALOG of Santa Monica, California, began in 1963 as an in-house research and development program to create space-age information handling. Not surprisingly, the program was part of the Lockheed Corporation, headquarters in Calabassa, California. In 1965 the DIALOG command language was developed under contract to the United States National Aeronautics and Space Agency (NASA). In 1978 commercial services began with three government files. In 1988 DIALOG, a wholly owned subsidiary of Lockheed, was sold to Knight-Ridder in Miami, Florida, which owns newspapers, television stations, and information services. In an announcement of the

14. *1989 EISS*, entry; 667 (DIALOG); 321 (BRS); 1797 (ORBIT).
15. Ibid., 671 (Knowledge Index); 322 (BRS/After Dark).

sale, DIALOG was described as the world's most extensive electronic information retrieval company, offering data from over 320 databases to over 91,000 subscribers in 86 countries. Knight-Ridder gave as a reason for its purchase that acquiring DIALOG would double the size of its Business Information Services Division.[16]

DIALOG acquires its machine-readable files from professional associations, publishers, government agencies, commercial organizations, and other sources, including self-produced files. (The acquisition policies of BRS are the same and probably ORBIT now, too.) The DIALOG system can be accessed by direct dial, telex, and through Telenet, Tymnet, Uninet, Datapac, and DIALOG's own Dialnet network. (Again, BRS and ORBIT access policies are similar to those of DIALOG.) Its gateway service allows DIALOG subscribers to access other databases. Its software permits full-text searching, Boolean searches, and "retrieval by specified elements."

Because of its many databases, DIALOG has had to publish copious documentation: overall system guides and instructions for the use of individual databases.[17] It has issued a *Brief Guide to DIALOG Searching* and the more comprehensive two-volume *Guide to DIALOG Searching*, the latter offering DIALOG system description and searching options as well as "bluesheets," which supply for each DIALOG database a one-page description of contents and access points. The three-volume *Guide to DIALOG-Databases* reproduces the bluesheet for each database and gives multipage documentation for every database in DIALOG File Number order. ERIC is File 1. DIALOG recommends that the user consult the bluesheet before searching a database.

DIALOG searchers can call up for display the indexes listed on the bluesheet for each database. The bluesheet basic index includes the suffix-coded fields, that is, the subjects. Because of its Schlagwort potential, the title field is included in the basic index. Added indexes on the bluesheet for each database contain prefix-coded, nonsubject fields. For ERIC DIALOG File 1, 17 fields and their prefixes are listed in the added indexes, for example, author, language, publication year. The only ERIC field in the added indexes that might also appear in the basic index is

16. Laura G. Harper, "A Comparative Review of BRS, DIALOG and ORBIT," *RSR Reference Services Review* 9 (Jan./Mar. 1981): 39–51; "Dialog Sold to Knight-Ridder," *Library Journal* 113 (Aug. 1988): 21.

17. Recent information on DIALOG is from the *1989 EISS* and DIALOG promotional materials. Searching examples are from: Lockheed Information Systems, *A Brief Guide to DIALOG Searching*, 2nd rev. ed., loose-leaf (Palo Alto, Calif.: Lockheed Missiles & Co., Information Systems, 1978–); idem., *Guide to DIALOG-Databases*, 3 vols., loose-leaf (Palo Alto, Calif.: Lockheed Information Systems, 1979–). Updating information for DIALOG appears in the monthly *DIALOG Chronolog*.

the ERIC rotated descriptors. Any search option in the indexes may be selected or expanded ("expand" is a browsing command to display the indexes of searchable items).

In its DIALINDEX (File 411), DIALOG provides a database including terms and postings from all prefix- and suffix-coded (subject) fields in all the individual databases. Since the databases in DIALINDEX are arranged by subject category, a single or combination of DIALOG databases can be selected by category, database label, or both. Often, more than one database is searched so that DIALINDEX is most useful for planning multidatabase search strategies for interdisciplinary subjects or for more comprehensive coverage of a single discipline.

DIALOG, like the other two major vendors, offers both Boolean and positional operations, thus vastly increasing its subject-searching power. Boolean search is a familiar device, though its AND and OR operators are the ones most heavily used. Of course, online Boolean search is restricted by the chronological coverage of databases. Automated and manual retrieval of single-subject or single-word terms, not requiring Boolean operators, is simpler and faster. DIALOG Boolean operators are applicable to individual terms or to sets of terms previously created through select commands, which in themselves may incorporate Boolean operators.

Positional operators reduce the false drops of Boolean search results because they specify the order of terms and their adjacency, that is, the maximum number of words between the sought terms. Positional operation also can set the frequency of term occurrence. In its 1984 Technical Memo 1 the *Guide to DIALOG Searching* emphasizes free-text searching as the use of truncation symbols and proximity operators for the creation of multiword search terms in select statements, though Boolean operators are also applicable. Especially in the employment of positional operators for free-text searching, it is important to limit the search to specific fields. Such limitation becomes extremely significant in searching full-text displays, which is discussed below.

Just as there is no "free lunch," there is no completely "free-text" search. Free-text search can result in matches only when the sought terms have been indexed by the system. Every significant subject word, the so-called keyword, in the title, abstract, or full text must be indexed to make free-text search feasible. Technical Memo 1 in the *Guide to DIALOG Searching* describes the DIALOG positional operators as follows.

> The NEAR operator (N) indicates that search terms must be next to each other or within a specified number of terms of each other, though not necessarily in the same order as the SELECT command. NOT proximity may be represented by: (NOT F),

> (NOT S), (NOT L), (NOT N) or (NOT nN), (NOT W) or (NOT nW)—which means, respectively, that all occurrences of Term A and Term B are to be retrieved when Term B is not: in the same field; in the same subfield (as defined by the database); in the same descriptor unit (as defined by the database); within specified adjacency on either side; immediately following within the specified number of terms.

As with Boolean operators, the proximity operator NOT is recommended by the *Guide* to be used only with caution since useful citations may be unwittingly eliminated. Several different proximity operators may be used in the same SELECT statement, but they are processed from left to right so that for search precision the more specific operator should appear first.

DIALOG, as well as BRS and ORBIT, stresses subject search and retrieval of analytical cataloging surrogates. Collocative retrieval of items by author is neither easy nor usually desired by searchers. None of the three major vendors has automated authority control for author names. An author may use full form of name or initials. DIALOG search commands for common names may yield so many possible citations that refinement or expansion of search strategy is usually needed, even to including a subject with which the name is associated—a LIMITing DIALOG search option similar to the simpler OCLC "search qualification."

A typical DIALOG search by author name may begin as

? s au=hirsh, ?

in which the first question mark is a system-supplied prompt, the "s" a SELECT command, and the second question mark the sign for unlimited truncation. This query may produce a DIALOG response that there are ten entries in the database under that name. The searcher can then refine the search as

? s au=hirsh, c ?

to which the system may respond that the last name with the initial applies to three entries. Unless coincidence plays a large role, the three entries will be relevant.

Adding a subject to the author's name is illustrated by the DIALOG command

? s au=jones ? AND solar( )energy

in which the proximity operator is ( ), formerly (W), requiring adjacent terms in strict word order. AND is a Boolean operator, which in DIALOG can be represented by lowercase letters or an asterisk. (Again, of the three Boolean operators—AND, OR, and NOT—the last is least used or advised.) Since most online databases begin coverage some years after their printed versions, one must reiterate that a fairly complete record of any author's production over a considerable period cannot be derived from computerized surrogates. For state-of-the-art information in the harder sciences, author collocation is probably not that important.

Printed journal article indexes ordinarily provide access by author and subject. Most online databases follow this pattern, adding subject access through free-text searching of keywords in titles and abstracts. Most of the database surrogates include abstracts. The following DIALOG subject search statement includes free-text search of ERIC abstracts:

? s mathematics( )program?/AB

which calls for selecting from the ERIC abstracts /AB the term "mathematics" immediately followed by the term "program," which has a limited truncation of one letter (one question mark) so as to retrieve also "programs."

A DIALOG ERIC single-word term subject search with a suffix-coded field limitation could be

? s Kansas/ID

in which /ID stands for an ERIC identifier, which can also be represented as /ID* or /IF or /IF*. This search statement should search all available ERIC abstracts for the appearance of "Kansas" and produce the appropriate citations.

A more complicated DIALOG subject search, including expand and select commands and Boolean operators, is shown in *A Brief Guide to DIALOG Searching*. The database used is the National Technical Information Service (NTIS), DIALOG File 6, and the subject is the multiword term, "bus fares." First, the Basic Index of NTIS is given the command

? EXPAND Fare

which produces thirteen terms and the number of entries in which they appear, from "E6 Fare 95 Items" through "E18 Fares (Transportation) 1 item." Among the expanded "Fare" terms are "E13 Fare (Forward

Area Refueling Equipment) 3 entries" and "E16 Fared Computer Code 4 entries." The searcher then commands

? s E6–E12, E14, E17–E18

which results in 152 items indicated for this Set 1. The searcher then issues the commands

? s Bus
? s Buses

which produces a record of 863 items for Bus (Set 2) and 595 items for Buses (Set 3). The next command is

? COMBINE 1 AND (2 or 3)

which yields Set 4 of sixty-eight items. The searcher then commands that Items 1 and 2 of Set 4 be typed out on the screen in Format 6, a short version of the records to be displayed for review:

? TYPE 4/6/1–2

There are eight formats (nine for a few databases), of which the fifth gives the complete citation including abstract. After deciding that the first two items displayed are relevant, the searcher commands that the sixty-eight items in Set 4 be printed in Format 5:

? PRINT 4/5/1–68

and the printouts will be mailed, generally on the next day. If the searcher has a high-speed terminal, say 1200 baud, the printing may well be done at the terminal to save more time.

Another example of free-text searching in the *Guide to DIALOG Searching*, Technical Memo 1 shows how the near operator (N) can be used. A search statement for retrieval in the National Newspaper Index database (DIALOG File 111) would read

? econom?(2N)recovery

in which the second question mark indicates unlimited truncation, and the number inserted before "N" specifies the maximum number of possible intervening words. Thus, "econom?(2N)recovery" will retrieve "economic recovery" or "recovery from economic troubles." The resultant

Set 1 contains 344 items that satisfy the free-text search statement. When the searcher commands

? TYPE 1/6/1,55

the first and fifty-fifth items of Set 1 will be displayed in Format 6 and will respectively show the database summaries: "Du Pont profit jumped by 61% in 2nd quarter; *economic recovery* and cuts in costs cited; firm lifts quarterly dividend by 7%" and "Ecuador reports *recovery* from *economic* troubles."

Although it was a feature of DIALOG and the other major vendors for many years, full-text display (though not technically a surrogate) for some databases is now being touted as an outstanding attraction for system subscribers. DIALOG promotional literature lists the benefits of searching full-text displays: immediate access to source information; access to footnotes, references, tables, etc.; efficient and flexible alternative to browsing in source documents; location and identification of specific named products, places, people, or other items not appearing in titles or indexing.

Among the DIALOG textual source databases are the *Academic American Encyclopedia, Everyman's Encyclopedia, Harvard Business Review Online, Moody's Corporate News*, and *World Affairs Report.* Directory source databases include *American Men and Women of Science, D & B Million Dollar Directory, Marquis Who's Who, Moody's Corporate Profiles*, and *Standard & Poor's Register—Biographical* and *Corporate.* The average text runs from 500 to 20,000 words per record, compared with an estimated 200 to 500 words per record in a DIALOG index-and-abstract database and an estimated 50 to 100 words per record in an index-only database. Searching full-text databases is not recommended by DIALOG for broad, general topics, but is said to be excellent for any mention of a person or company, memorable quotes, "buried" figures, latest jargon, or "buzz word" phrases.

The basic indexes of DIALOG full-text databases have words from fields like title, abstract, notes, descriptors, identifiers, and section headings, but also words from the text field. One sees immediately that full-text display is a step towards electronic publishing in the era of the paperless information society. The search techniques for full-text displays are mostly similar to those for bibliographic citations. In fact, limiting the preliminary search of full texts to their smaller fields, like titles and descriptors, is advised by DIALOG. When the full texts are searched, the proximity operators must be confined to the same sentence or paragraph. Introductory browsing of an entire text reduces searching usefulness. The bluesheets for full-text databases are particularly important, since they define the searchable subfield, usually a paragraph. (Perhaps full-text search should be called "partial text search.")

The bluesheet for AP News (DIALOG File 258), for example, points out that the suffix-coded field /TI restricts retrieval to the first paragraph and that relevance should be checked by reviewing in short format. The format options are defined in the bluesheet. The increasing availability of full texts is doubtless occasioned by greater computer storage capacity and accompanying lower storage costs. The expense of printing long texts, however, is of great concern to users, whose decision on whether to print—and what part of a long text to print—must be very carefully considered.

Particularly questionable in theory and practice are the online uses of proximity operators with full-text displays. Proximity operation depends either on words appearing within a short distance of each other or on the same word repeated at fairly close intervals. However, most writers are advised not to use the same word or words too closely together; synonyms or equivalent terms are recommended when the same or similar ideas are expressed. Proximity searching of related terms from the thesaurus soon becomes unrealistically time-consuming. Perhaps this problem has less impact in "noncreative" science and technology writing, where precision and standardized specificity are sought by writers and readers. In online searching of the literature of the "softer" disciplines, there is a real conflict between recommended and repetitious writing styles—not to mention poetic suggestive prose. Even when free-text searching is limited to the title, retrieval is hampered in "creative" writing by a fanciful title proper, which is often brought down to earth by the subtitle—a symptom of "colonitis" to which affliction this author is also susceptible. Perhaps most writers in the "harder" disciplines are less poetic in their choices of titles.

To approach another basic problem, many works are inappropriate for full-text display, even though they may be subjected to it. Encyclopedia texts, for example, lack illustrations, maps, and color as they are currently shown by computer. Perhaps newer developments in compact-disc technology will result in alphanumeric and graphic materials being accommodated in the same media unit.[18]

The benefits of speedy updating seem dubious for classic names or subjects like Thomas Carlyle or the alphabet in full-text display of encyclopedias. The latest technical information is, moreover, not usually found in monographs or encyclopedias. Many encyclopedias have annual

18. Francesca Z. Lunzer, "The Little Compact Disk Grows Up," *U.S. News & World Report*, 26 Dec. 1988/2 Jan. 1989, 114.

updating volumes that would appear to be better candidates for full-text display than the basic volumes.

Much of the online full-text information is more easily and cheaply retrieved from printed reference tools. As an example, DIALOG offers a full-text display of the winning horses in the Kentucky Derby. This information is similar to that in the printed *World Almanac*, which has a splendid table of contents where one may find the entry for Kentucky Derby.[19] It is often said that names and subjects mentioned "by the way" and not to be found in traditional indexes can be retrieved through free-text search of full-text displays. If the names and subjects are that peripheral to the main items discussed and indexed, one questions the utility of their being unearthed. A "hidden" subject seems to be contradictory to a relevancy.

The subject summarization and condensation of the abstract are intended substitutes (surrogates) for a full text, and indeed are a means of identifying the important topics dealt with significantly and thus revealing their potential relevance to searchers. The length and specificity of some abstracts may be criticized, especially if the abstracts are more indicative than informative, but the intellectual validity of abstracting remains unchallenged, especially if the abstracter knows current topical standardization.

Some texts are suitable for full-text display, such as legal decisions that are usually permanent in nature (*stare decicis*), or self-contained summaries of news in newspaper or magazine indexes, though printed sources give, possibly less conveniently, the same texts with longer retroactive coverage. However, many laypersons, even some practitioners, believe that full-text display coupled with free-text search options are the ultimate answer to any problems of subject retrieval and that they furnish painless access to hitherto unobtainable information. Unfortunately for such beliefs, apart from its limited automated retroactive reporting, free-text search is most effective not in browsing through long full texts, but when applied to specific and somewhat short fields like the title or abstract or summary. Free-text search of a specific full-text field, which is no longer than a subfield paragraph at most, is mandated for practical retrieval. In effect, free-text search of full texts becomes almost indistinguishable from controlled vocabulary searching of indexed words or phrases in particular fields of a bibliographic surrogate.

The time and expense in searching full-text displays, no matter what the searching methodologies or the number of subfields, must always be kept in mind, as must the often inconsequential results. To repeat, there

19. *World Almanac and Book of Facts*, 1868– . Annual. (New York: World Telegram, 1868–). Title and publisher vary. See Sheehy, *Guide*, AC87.

can be no free lunch: the final cost in time and money to search the paragraphs of a full text cannot be disregarded.

Again, one wonders if computerized search of database information, whether full-text or bibliographic surrogation, cannot often and sometimes more easily be accomplished through printed sources. Legal databases such as LEXIS certainly have had long-lived and more extensive printed predecessors. Subject search employing Boolean and proximity operators, especially in titles and abstracts, is indubitably useful for retrieving complex topical combinations reflected in the journal literature. Collocation by author or single subject is more expeditiously obtained from printed sources, especially when long-term records are involved. Apart from complicated subject searching in recent scientific and technical journal literature, the advantages of computerized access to database information are dubious. Speed and convenience can be attained through computers, but the universal applicability of online access is yet to be adequately demonstrated.

Modern housewives cannot be expected to abandon store-bought bread for old-fashioned home-baked loaves, nor can the perceived convenience and commercial success of the database vendors be wished away. If a moral is to be drawn, let it be not to throw out the baby with the bathwater. The older printed sources can be as important to searchers as babies to their parents. Home-baked bread may be a lost cause, but neither babies nor still useful hardcopy documents deserve that fate.

The preceding detailed descriptions of DIALOG searching techniques—and the general implications for retrieval—do not aim to detract from equally effective, sometimes more sophisticated strategies of BRS or ORBIT. It is undeniable, however, that DIALOG has many more databases than BRS or ORBIT, so that a choice of vendor may depend on the databases in demand by a particular institution. All the wholesale vendors publish updated listings of their databases, and the listings are available on request. Sometimes, a vendor decision is made because of only one database. A colleague told this writer in an interview that DIALOG was chosen by the academic library because it offered ERIC, even though the library owned its printed counterpart. Using the printed version was judged comparatively inconvenient by faculty and students. The other databases in the DIALOG repertoire could be used when necessary.

The history of ORBIT indicates a service unsure of its identity.[20] Formerly considered a rival of BRS for preeminence after DIALOG,

20. Recent information on ORBIT and BRS is from the *1989 EISS* and from ORBIT and BRS promotional materials; also the *Online* interviews with the presidents of ORBIT and BRS, the interviews to be referenced below. Detailed description of the ORBIT system

ORBIT has since withdrawn from the race. In 1986, Pergamon ORBIT InfoLine, Inc., McLean, Virginia, was formed after ORBIT was purchased from the System Development Corporation (SDC) ORBIT Search Service (offered by the SDC Information Services, a wholly owned subsidiary of the Burroughs Corporation). The ORBIT Search Service was to merge with that of Pergamon InfoLine Ltd., in London.[21]

In a 1987 interview with the president of Pergamon ORBIT InfoLine, the president stated that the purchase was made at a time when "SDC was losing interest in the ORBIT operation." In answer to a question on why SDC ORBIT, which had begun "on a level playing field" with DIALOG, had allowed DIALOG to outstrip it in size, the reply was that ORBIT was generally always concerned with government contracting and had developed its database inventory to suit its government clients.[22] (Earlier trade gossip was that the smaller size of SDC ORBIT, as compared with DIALOG, was the result of SDC insisting on exclusive control of its databases, which may be, from a different angle, the same reason given in the interview.)

The number and subject matter of ORBIT databases have already been given. At least before its 1986 sale, SDC ORBIT databases were topically most appropriate for government applications. Pergamon ORBIT InfoLine introduced gateways to BRS Information Technologies and the European Space Agency (ESA)/Information Retrieval Service (IRS). Of chief importance to ORBIT users was the new ORBIT's announced plan "to divide databases held by the InfoLine Search Service and the ORBIT service according to subject area. Eventually, InfoLine, London, will host business and related databases and the ORBIT Search Service in the United States will host scientific and technical databases." The

(prior to its 1986 purchase by the Pergamon Group of Companies) is in Harper, "A Comparative Review"; System Development Corporation, *ORBIT User Manual*, loose-leaf (Santa Monica, Calif.: SDC Search Service, 1982–); idem, *SDC Service Quick-Reference Guide*, loose-leaf (Santa Monica, Calif.: SDC Search Service, 1983–). Updating information for ORBIT was in the bimonthly *SDC Search Service Searchlight*. Detailed description of the BRS system is in Harper, "A Comparative Review Bibliographic Retrieval Services, Inc., *System Reference Manual, March 1981*, loose-leaf (Latham, N.Y.: The Services, 1981–) with updating information in the monthly *BRS Bulletin*. Similar guides and updating periodicals will undoubtedly be published by the new owners of ORBIT and BRS. *See also* Sara D. Knapp, *BRS Training Workbook: An Introduction with Practical Exercises from the ERIC Database* (Scotia, N.Y.: Bibliographical Retrieval Services, 1979).

21. "News Flash: Pergamon Buys SDC Orbit," *Information Today: The Newspaper for Users and Producers of Electronic Information Services* 3 (Oct. 1986): 2; Don Black, "Fact or Fiction: Pergamon Poised to Buy SDC Orbit?" ibid., 6, 26.

22. Jeffrey K. Pemberton and Helen A. Gordon, "ONLINE Interviews Jim Terragno," *Online: The Magazine of Online Information Systems* 11 (Nov. 1987): 15–22. The quoted remarks are from pages 17 and 18.

plan, later realized, was to transfer about 28 databases to the ORBIT Search Service, including Agricola, Aqualine, World Textile Abstracts.[23]

The public record of wholesale vendor activity for analytical information surrogates points to a strenuous expansion by BRS, which, like DIALOG, has ERIC. BRS is now ahead of ORBIT but still behind DIALOG in the number of its databases. BRS was a small academically oriented vendor service that became a major source of analytical database information for many kinds of users. Joint servicing of databases by BRS and OCLC is evidence of BRS's development.

BRS Information Technologies (formerly known as Bibliographic Retrieval Services) is a member of the Information Technology Group of Latham, New York, and it is, as noted above, second in size to DIALOG. Like ORBIT, BRS makes no claim to rival DIALOG in the number and variety of databases. In a 1988 interview, the chief executive officer of BRS commented that, unlike DIALOG, BRS was no supermarket but a group of boutiques. The chief executive officer emphasized the quality of BRS databases and its superior software for search and retrieval. The BRS forte, he stated, was information in business, science, education, or general reference. In biomedicine, BRS was already "quite comprehensive," and, indeed, over half of BRS business was in the life sciences.[24]

BRS began operations in 1977, originating as the State University of New York (SUNY) Biomedical Communications Network, using an IBM retrieval system. Almost 54 percent of its subscribers are academic libraries. "BRS has made a deliberate effort to tap the academic library market by offering access to a relatively small number of basic files and by establishing a unique fee structure that can slash volume users' costs by 60 percent."[25] The quantity and scope of the BRS databases have been given above. With its BRS/Afterdark, BRS has become a competitor of DIALOG with its Knowledge Index, both databases begun in 1982.

A quick inference from the descriptions thus far is that the searcher-intermediary can specialize only in a limited number of databases, usually confined to one or a few disciplines. The general search language of the wholesale vendor may give satisfactory introductory access to a family of

23. *1988 EISS*, 8th ed., ed. Amy Lucas and Annette Novello, (Detroit: Gale, 1988), entry 1727; *1989 EISS*, entry 1797. The quotation is from the *1988 EISS*. See also Jeffrey K. Pemberton, "What's Ahead for BRS? An Interview with P. James Terragno, President of Pergamon Orbit InfoLine," *Online: The Magazine of Online Information Systems* 13 (Mar. 1989): 57–60; Carol Tenopir, "Who Owns Whom?: Online Systems and Buyouts," *Library Journal* 114 (Apr. 1, 1989): 65–66.

24. Jeffrey K. Pemberton "ONLINE Interviews Marty Kahn, President BRS," *Online: the Magazine of Online Information Systems* 12 (Jan. 1988): 14. The entire interview is on pages 13–19.

25. Harper, "A Comparative Review," 39.

databases, particularly for end user searchers, but only the specialist searcher can exploit an individual database to its fullest potential. The specialist must not only be familiar with the database subject but also keep current with the constant changing of individual database contents, structure, and command language. Keeping up with the databases is like keeping up with the stock market, an unending and often an unsuccessful task even for those stockbrokers specializing in a few industry-related issues. Despite the recognition by wholesale vendors, such as the DIALOG bluesheets, of the need of searchers to be familiar with the peculiarities of databases, only experience (dare we say also "track record"?) with the database can build searcher competence and end user confidence. An instance of the need for the specialist searcher was represented in the 1988 offer by the Columbia University Library Search Service to provide cut-rate access to a limited number of users for popular databases in nonprime time for a limited period of searching *if* the searching was done by a trained librarian.[26]

Analytical database searching is now being offered by all types of libraries. One consequence is the melding of reader services and technical services functions, a consummation devoutly desired by this author and a theme reiterated throughout this book. The "free vs. fee" controversy seems to have abated, with most libraries—public and academic—supplying a basic no-charge search service, with longer and more complicated searches charged a fee based on vendor schedules. Libraries on the whole aim for cost recovery, not profitmaking.

The major vendors of database information—DIALOG, BRS and ORBIT—offer much the same search options, though the formulation of their search commands differs. Despite the demand for specialization in databases, the need remains for instruction in accessing *all* the major wholesale vendor systems. A useful comparative treatment of the search strategies and other options of the three vendors is Klingensmith and Duncan's 1984 *Easy Access to DIALOG, ORBIT, and BRS,* which lists similar service functions performed by the three:

Provision and viewing of individual and conglomerate indexes
Use of Boolean and proximity operators
Qualifying or limiting of searches by fields
Truncation of terms
Author searching by name only or with subject words
Reviewing of sets

26. Information from an interview with a reference librarian in the Columbia University Engineering and Science Library, October 27, 1988.

Online printing, with variations in the quantity of data to be included
Offline printing
Temporary or permanent saving of search statements or complete search strategies
SDI searching
Multidatabase searching
Subject and content categorization of databases
Online user information
Electronic mail
Printed documentation
Toll-free telephone help.[27]

Some authorities claim that the similar options of the three wholesalers make for transferability, that familiarity with the searching techniques of one vendor means an easy transition to using other database services. This claim is the basis for the book by Klingensmith and Duncan. Such an opinion is doubtful, if the reader has accepted the arguments of this writer. Just as it is more difficult for most people to be vocally fluent in many cognate languages, such as those of the Romance family, than in dissimilar ones like Japanese and Russian, it is hard to learn and remember different commands for the same kinds of searches in DIALOG, BRS, and ORBIT. For example, truncation of ORBIT terms is shown either by a colon or a hashmark, the first an unlimited truncation sign that can be embedded within a term or placed to its right. The hashmark is for limited truncation and can be put at either end of the term. The number of hashmarks indicates the maximum number of letters that can be added to the term. BRS truncation is symbolized by a dollar sign following the term. Limited BRS truncation is specified by following the dollar sign with a numeral to designate the maximum number of letters to be added. In DIALOG, the maximum number of letters to be added is shown by repeating the question mark the requisite number of times. Such differences can be mastered, though personal experience indicates that confusion or time-consuming consultation of documentation will be more likely. If the previously described LSP intersystem searching becomes applicable to analytical information database systems like those of DIALOG, BRS, and ORBIT (the opening of gateway systems is another problem), the need to learn these different database commands will be less crucial.

27. Klingensmith and Duncan, *Easy Access*. For an evaluation of instructional tools for searching databases, see Carol Tenopir, "Learning How to Search," *Library Journal* 112 (June 15, 1987): 54–55. All of Tenopir's regular articles in *Library Journal* focus on practical difficulties in searching databases.

Many advances in microcomputer technology are of greatest interest to the end user, but even library professionals should be aware that these advances affect basic library operations. The distinctions among minicomputers and microcomputers, dedicated terminals and microcomputers, "intelligent" and "dumb" terminals and microcomputers are being removed. Already, OCLC is providing access not only to its own database but also to those of vendors like DIALOG, BRS, and ORBIT. Developers of the OPAC anticipate remote access from personal computers (microcomputers) in dormitories, offices, or homes.

A development in microcomputer technology that can be of considerable benefit to the professional searcher, though chiefly designed for end users, is the front-end microcomputer. With the appropriate software, it can construct search strategies without the expense of experimenting with the databases themselves. Using the microcomputer front-end software, the searcher can save a tested search strategy and batch the prefabricated requests, not unlike the established technique of using a teletype machine: preparing messages to be sent without interruption at a convenient time. The database search formulated with front-end software can be accomplished without personal attendance at the keyboard, and the results prepared for review.[28]

If this chapter has shown anything, it is the lack of standardization by analytical database vendors and their wholesalers in protocols of search and retrieval. The LC Linked Systems Project (LSP) has as its general purpose giving users a switching capability to more than one database—a growing trend among computer searchers.[29] The LSP has been applied first to bibliographic utilities like OCLC and RLIN. An immediate related task has been to standardize the command languages of the various databases so that switching from one database to another does not mean memorizing different commands to achieve the same end.[30] Even with the bibliographic utilities, LSP success in standardization has been only partial.

The problem of standardizing analytical databases has been exacerbated by their numerous producers. If one were to bet on either commercial profit or intellectual unity, the former is more probable of winning. The challenge is to convince database producers and vendors that standardization will produce commercial profit.

28. Carol Tenopir, "Online Searching with a Microcomputer," *Library Journal* 110 (Mar. 15, 1985):42–43; idem, "Four Options for End User Searching," ibid., 111 (July 1986):56–57—especially the section entitled "Front-end software."

29. Carol A. Mandel, *Multiple Thesauri in Online Library Bibliographic Systems* (Washington: Library of Congress, 1987).

30. Richard W. McCoy, "The Linked Systems Project: Progress, Promise, Realities," *Library Journal* 111 (Oct. 1, 1986): 36–38.

The last chapter in this book chiefly reviews some outstanding problems of bibliographic organization as evidenced by previous chapters and the histories of recent research to solve them.

7 STATUS and NEEDS

If a major goal of this book has been achieved, the continued role of the trained information specialist (a.k.a. librarian) has been demonstrated. To justify this demonstration, librarians should understand the development of access to information through descriptive cataloging and subject analysis, and recognize its perpetuation. Early chapters have traced the organization of recorded knowledge to the first Western libraries. None of the bibliographic problems is new, nor are the solutions, some more successful than others. The distinction between technical and reader services in libraries is fast disappearing. The end user is not interested in a librarian's official function or title, only in the librarian's professional ability to locate information in answer to questions. That ability is based on merging bibliographic organization, the quintessence of librarianship, with reference work.

At least some of the information in this book should prove unfamiliar even to experienced practitioners. It is not this writer's intention to oppose unthinkingly automation of bibliographic organization. Resistance to technological change is professionally dangerous and ultimately self-defeating. Librarianship has seen a long history of opposition to modernization. The first manuscript codexes undoubtedly evoked the rancor of scroll lovers. Emergence of the Western printed book, which paid homage to the format and typography of the illuminated manuscript, was nevertheless protested by collectors and copyists. Since Gutenberg, printers of books have held sway, but are now fighting the inroads of computerization. Some veteran librarians express their fear of mechanization through stressing the benefits of reading the printed word and, along with some teachers, blame television, sound recordings of rock music, motion pictures—in fact, all nonbook media—for every ill of civilization.

If all the data that were required to respond to user demands were obtainable through mechanization—regardless of comparative costs—there would be less point in resistance. Whenever technology helps significantly in search and retrieval of needed information, the assistance is not to be spurned. Unfortunately, mechanization has not answered all our search and retrieval problems. The present chronological limitation of information databases is one reason not to discard older printed indexes nor to discontinue their necessary use.

The many frequent changes in printed descriptive cataloging codes are not only difficult for practitioners to keep up with, but almost incomprehensible to end users. Even when the older records, such as those from the *National Union Catalog (NUC)*, are converted to machine-readable form, and even when these records are changed according to the latest cataloging rules, the collocative role of the library's catalog or bibliography is impaired because of lack of authority control and copious cross-references. Practitioners and their clients confront a dearth of standardization as bibliographic organization differs in the same or various libraries.

Coordinate search in printed bibliographic surrogates can be tiresome, though not impossible. The task is made onerous by the Library of Congress (LC) omission of all tracings in the subject indexes to the post-1982 index-register *NUC* and in much of the *Library of Congress Catalogs: Subject Catalog*. The main entry must be consulted if all tracings are to be found. The realization of analytical subject access to journal literature has been much aided by printed journal indexes and, for later entries, by databases with sophisticated searching techniques, including using Boolean and positional operators. Abstracts that facilitate subject search are available in most database entries. The Wilson Company is issuing *Readers' Guide Abstracts* on microfiche, a contribution to noncomputerized reference work since the *Abstracts* were originally available online.[1]

It is almost universally agreed, however, that subject searching of databases is most appropriate for complicated combinations of multiple subjects with multiword terms. This kind of analytical subject access is best for current information in the harder sciences. For single-word subject searches or for author collocation, printed journal indexes may serve as well.

1. "New from the H. W. Wilson Company Fall 1988," *Wilson Library Bulletin* 62 (Sept. 1988): 80.

The lack of topical depth-analysis for monographic literature remains a major problem. Neither printed nor automated monograph indexes are of much use. Research continues, much of it subsidized, but the results are as yet unspectacular. Monograph indexes are still far from the depth-analysis of well-prepared back-of-the-book indexes. Perhaps, with the advantages of computerization, we should revitalize the *CumIndex* concept, which merges back-of-the-book indexes for different categories of subjects.[2]

Separate *CumIndex* databases may be required for subject and publication date, but the idea is technically feasible and certainly worth the effort. (The old battle cry of book indexers needs revival: no nonfiction book can be complete without a worthwhile index!) A subsidiary benefit of merging back-of-the-book indexes by subject category is its bibliometric comparative value: determining the relative prominence of topics in a discipline, as well as discovering the wordings for the same or similar subjects. The process could be of great help in updating subject-heading and classification authorities.

Classification has been advanced as potentially valuable for subject browsing in databases and online catalogs. (The Columbia Libraries Information Online (CLIO) catalog, as noted in Chapter 5, allows for browsing of call numbers.)[3] More hope for fruitful research could be held out if American librarians used classification for its subject-revelatory possibilities, that is, in a classified catalog, rather than chiefly as a shelf-location device. Experience with the classified catalog could provide a firmer basis for research. In any case, browsing of a printed classification scheme, either the Library of Congress Classification or the Dewey Decimal Classification (both ultimately to be online) is possible even now, and the structures of thesauruses and controlled vocabularies lend themselves to reading up and down a hierarchy. (We can disregard here theoretical objections to library classification in general.)

Cutter's syndetic apparatus for subject headings has been adopted with a vengeance by the thesaurus makers. A classification scheme index like the Relative Index of the DDC—often considered Dewey's greatest contribution to classification theory—offers numerous hierarchical references for investigation.

Research in applying classification to databases and OPACs should not be discouraged, even if present findings are not earthshaking. Unsuspected discoveries may be made. Preliminary survey results have un-

2. Frederick G. Kilgour, *The Library and Information Science CumIndex* (Los Altos, Calif.: R & D Press, 1976).

3. Columbia University Libraries, *Columbia Libraries Information Online (CLIO). Easy Access Pocket Card* (New York: The Libraries, 1985).

covered OPAC-user habits quite different from those previously found in card-catalog use studies, such as the subject-oriented desires of the OPAC users.[4] Perhaps more classification from OPACs would aid the user. Maybe OPAC-users ask themselves: "Why go to the bother of obtaining automated information, especially on subjects, unless newer or better means of retrieval are made possible?" Perhaps the classified catalog, more elaborate than the shelflist, could become part of the OPAC display. Entire classification schemes could also be installed.

Traditional classification, like traditional subject-heading work, is not designed for depth or coextensive coverage of monographic literature, but only for the general indication of important subjects treated in an important way. The principal function of classification is to group, not specify. The more classification symbols assigned a monograph (within reason), the better chance there is of including more of the major topics considered in a major way. (The multiple notations, along with classification references, for every monograph are important elements of the classified catalog.) Even the "specification" of Cutter's subject headings is not intended to give depth-analysis for every topic in the book. The Preserved Context Index System (PRECIS), regardless of its claimed superiority to *Library of Congress Subject Headings* does not equal the specificity of back-of-the-book indexing.[5] The problem of subject depth-analysis for noncomposite, nonfiction monographs stays tantalizing.

Research aimed at heightening the power of subject headings to reveal the principal topics of books should not be neglected. No doubt, much of the *LCSH* is outdated, its structure illogical, its wordings sometimes even offensive to groups in a democratic society. Too many researchers have only confirmed these already known facts. (Such researchers have apparently subscribed to the belief that one can make a silk purse out of a sow's ear.) Still, many years have gone into the construction of *LCSH*. Millions of books have been assigned LC subject headings. These headings constitute the national repository of monographic subject verbalizations, a repository deserving enrichment. Opportunities abound for making possible coordinate subject-heading search. This author has suggested research into weighted LC subject headings, but research is to be welcomed into any aspect of subject-heading potential for search and retrieval.

4. David F. Bishop, "CLR Online Public Access Catalog Study: Analysis of ARL User Responses," *Information Technology and Libraries* 2 (Sept. 1983):315–21; Karen Markey, "Thus Spake the OPAC User," ibid. 2 (Dec. 1983):381–87; Joseph R. Matthews and Gary S. Lawrence, "Further Analysis of the CLR Online Catalog Project," ibid. 3 (Dec. 1984):354–76.

5. Mary Dykstra, "The Lion That Squeaked: A Plea to the Library of Congress to Adopt the British PRECIS System, and to Reconsider the Decision to Overhaul the LC Subject Headings," *Library Journal* 103 (Sept. 1978):1570–72.

Related to the long-term promise of automated descriptive cataloging and subject analysis is the current research on artificial intelligence, specifically expert systems.[6] In theory, expert systems can accommodate any human decision from a discrete, closed number of choices. It is conceivable, for example, that the symptoms of different diseases in different parts of the body—already in printed volumes—can be collected and stored in computers, so that doctors may obtain diagnoses and treatment plans by matching patients' symptoms with those computerized. The interactive effects of drugs can also be computerized.

Alas, human decisions are frequently made in ways foreign to computerization: hunches, farfetched or intuitive conclusions, creative thinking, and imaginative leaps. If we have learned anything about computers, it is that all contingencies must be written out for computer programs, that computer technology requires everything spelled out, and that special provisions must be made to identify stochastic situations with which computers would need human help. One way that computers could deliver stochastic judgments is by appending a statistical tolerance, i.e., plus or minus permissible deviations.

Effective computer output depends on completely logical, quantifiable human input and on careful human monitoring. We have already noted computer difficulties in filing, which was supposed to suppress initial articles, and in CLIO OPAC browsing of call numbers. These errors arose from human input assumptions that are perfectly natural in the noncomputer world.

We have a long way to go toward standardizing the bibliographic record. Use of ISBDs and MARC formats is only a preliminary step. Continuous research on expert systems, most being conducted by nonlibrarian personnel, could help make the dream of automated cataloging and subject analysis come true. Librarians could build on LC experience with format recognition and automatic editing programs for MARC records. If publishers were willing and able to print subject abstracts and MARC records in their books, progress in artificial intelligence for bibliographic purposes could be hastened. The Cataloging-in-Publication (CIP) program might then have to be reevaluated.

The major problem characterizing the manifold difficulties of bibliographic organization and access could well be standardization. Concerns about standardization can quickly escalate into national (even international), political, economic, and cultural controversies. Practitioners com-

6. Philip Elmer-DeWitt, "How to Clone an Expert," *Time*, 2 Sept. 1985, 44; David E. Sanger, "Smart Machines Get Smarter," *New York Times*, 15 Dec. 1985, sec. F; Janice Woo, "Additional LITA Sessions. Expert Systems Not Yet Clones of Librarians," *American Libraries* 19 (Dec. 1988):934.

plain that the lack of standardization has adversely affected the structure and accessibility of bibliographic surrogates. Changing catalog codes have goaded some librarians to state publicly that the second edition of the *Anglo-American Cataloguing Rules* was unnecessary and that they hope it will be the last revision of bibliographic standards for the foreseeable future. The different editions of DDC and the endless changes in *LCSH* and LCC have always been targets for criticism. Somehow, the conflict between standardization and change must be reasonably reconciled.

In the display varieties and search options of the database vendors, we see the inevitable effects of the entrepreneurial American economy. Every vendor and producer are trying to maximize profitability by offering unduplicated databases and by adding more sophisticated search options. (The situation is the same for nonprofit organizations. Success brings emulation. In 1986 DIALOG offered electronic mail service after it was proven marketable by competitor vendors and in response to consumer demand.)

Not accidentally, the major database vendors present similar features in different ways. The search commands of the various bibliographic and analytical information database utilities all aim at the same targets in fundamentally the same way. Their different formulations avoid copyright infringement and resultant legal suits by competitors. Commercial vested interests have not been weakened by institutional mergers and exclusivity claims, e.g., the sale of UTLAS to Thomson International, Limited, and OCLC's copyright demands to protect its database against illegal downloading.

Individuality, encouraged by commercial suppliers and library predilections, has produced library online catalogs with custom-designed screen displays, search commands, and even purposes. Authorities' opinions on intersystem-searching skills transferability do not meet the needs of standardization nor apparently of realistic usage conditions. Libraries, usually for economic reasons and encouraged by *AACR2*'s permissiveness, used less than full MARC records in their initial machine conversion of bibliographic surrogates. They are now faced with the expense of upgrading these records for OPAC use: another aftereffect of unmet standardization needs.

International standardization was partially achieved years ago when LC spearheaded the campaign for a universal MARC format, called UNIMARC or SUPERMARC, which still allowed for national MARC formats but made possible their translation into the MARC formats of other countries. Efforts toward international standardization have also been pursued by the International Federation of Library Associations and Institutions (IFLA) and the Joint Steering Committee (JSC) for Revision of *AACR*, ending in *AACR* acceptance of the General ISBD. The ISBD(G), with individual ISBDs for specific types of material, has contributed to the IFLA program for Universal Bibliographic Control and its more hard-to-win Universal Availability of Publications. The ISBN and the ISSN were proposed by the Unesco and accepted as an optional cataloging addition by *AACR2* and LC.

LC wisely first concentrated on international network cooperation and then on the domestic network cooperation problems exacerbated by the major American bibliographic utilities and database vendors. In 1977 LC established its Office for Network Development (reorganized in June 1984 into a joint Network Development Office and MARC Standards Office), which with its Network Advisory Committee has published numerous discussion and network planning papers. A measure of national bibliographic cooperation was obtained when LC persuaded OCLC, the Research Libraries Group, and the Western Library Network to participate in its Linked Systems Project, which tries like the UNIMARC program to facilitate switching among the different bibliographic organizations. One publication of the LSP is *Linked Systems Project/Standard Network Interconnection Protocols (SNI).*[7] *SNI* is based on the Open Systems Interconnection Reference Model developed by the International Organization for Standardization. The earlier Conversion of Serials (CONSER) automated database project, originally financed in 1974 for two years through LC by the Council on Library Resources, has become a cooperative venture of OCLC, LC and the National Library of Canada. The willingness of OCLC to manage CONSER after LC was forced out of its management by financial shortage has paved the road to North American bibliographic standardization.[8] An additional factor in standardization is the availability to MARC subscribers of the LSP-assisted Name Authority Cooperative Project (NACO) database of almost two million names, which is being added to and updated by LC and cooperating libraries. On October 1, 1986, NACO was renamed the National Coordinated Cataloging Operations.[9]

7. Library of Congress, Cataloging Distribution Service, *Access '88: Catalogs and Technical Publications 1988* (Washington: The Library, 1988), 32.

8. Library of Congress, *Annual Report of the Librarian of Congress for the Fiscal Year Ending September 30, 1975* (Washington: The Library, 1976), 19; . . . *1976* (published 1977), xxvii–xxviii; . . . *1977* (published 1978), 55; Bohdan S. Wynar, *Introduction to Cataloging and Classification*, 7th ed. by Arlene Taylor Dowell (Littleton, Colo.: Libraries Unlimited, 1985), 533.

9. Library of Congress, *Annual Report . . . 1979* (Washington: The Library, 1980), 53–54;. . . *1980* (1981),64–65; Susan Baerg Epstein, "Automated Authority Control: A Hidden Timebomb? Part 1," *Library Journal* 110 (Nov. 1, 1985):36–37; "Part 2," ibid., 111 (Jan. 1986):55–56 (especially "Part 1"); "NACO (renamed on October 1, 1986, as National Coordinated Cataloging Operations)," *Library of Congress Information Bulletin* 46 (Dec. 12, 1987):21; Nadine L. Baer and Karl E. Johnson, "The State of Authority," *Information Technology and Libraries* 7 (June 1988):139–53.

Consensus is needed and being sought for a UNIMARC-type protocol that would allow searching of all major bibliographic and analytical database suppliers (the bibliographic utilities first) without users having to learn each system's command languages. It has not been possible to establish at once a complete transfer or exchange protocol, but beginning partial success has been gratifying. After all, only a limited number of Boolean operations exist, and they can be standardized at the start in a transfer or switching protocol.

The trend of bibliographic utilities to join with analytical database vendors, such as the Intelligent Gateway Service of OCLC and the sharing of its database with that of BRS mean that the problems of bibliographic standardization now involve all suppliers of automated information: catalog surrogates and informational analytical databases. As well recognized by LC, progress in bibliographic standardization requires the cooperation of agencies not directly connected with libraries, such as the Information Industry Association, as well as more closely related organizations like OCLC and DIALOG.

Practitioners uncomplainingly accept the assertion that libraries are comparatively small customers of the computerized information industry and thus are put last or ignored when commercial organizations decide on products and marketing plans. The library business may well be a comparatively small market segment for giant jobbers like DIALOG, ORBIT, or BRS but it is still a significant one. Much of the public gets its first or only contact with databases through public and academic libraries. Unsurprisingly, most database vendors provide special rates and programs to train future database searchers in library schools. After this beginning, jobbers should not forget these searchers. The later influence of these information professionals is not to be denied. Libraries, whether charging or not for their services, publicize the availability of database searching for their clients, a service for which the jobbers charge and are paid. Also, librarians as professional information specialists can advise database producers and suppliers on patron needs.

The standardization problems of the OPAC catalogs are just as serious, though not so evident.[10] A 1985 interview with executives of CLSI (formerly C L Systems, Inc.), best known for its automated library circulation systems, included the following exchange. The executives were asked, "How long will it be before online catalog systems can talk to each other—your system as well as other systems?" One executive answered that it

10. Stephen R. Salmon, "Characteristics of Online Public Catalogs," *Library Resources & Technical Services* 27 (Jan./Mar. 1983):36–37; Walt Crawford and others, *Bibliographic Displays in the Online Catalog* (White Plains, N.Y.: Knowledge Industry Publications, 1986); Walt Crawford, "Testing Bibliographic Displays for Online Catalogs," *Information Technology and Libraries* 6 (Mar. 1987):20–33.

would not become a reality before the 1990s, that the technology existed but that it was "a people process to bring all of that together."[11]

In trying to predict the future of American bibliographic standardization and compatible online interfaces, we have much less difficulty describing present technological means than foreseeing the "people process" that involves our unpredictable human character. Yet the campaign for bibliographic standards continues. One surprising, not to say startling, standardization has come from producers and vendors of CD-ROM players and discs. The challenge to standardization consists of proving that commercial profit and intellectual unity can coincide, and indeed, the two could be interactive. That challenge was acted on by the CD-ROM producers/vendors.

As usual, LC has pioneered with CD-ROM. Since 1978 it has investigated possible optical disc applications to library activities. It has supported since 1982 an Optical Disk Pilot Program, scheduled to end September 30, 1988.[12] With more than 80 million items in its collection, LC showed early interest in the use of optical discs for economical, space-saving storage. In 1982 it revamped its printed card production with its demand print system so that a master of the catalog card text on a digital compact disc could be laser printed on demand, obviating the batch storage and printing of millions of catalog cards. It has used video compact-disc technology to prepare a selective catalog of its prints and photographs collection. Also, in 1982 it commissioned a three-year study of how the new technology could be further employed at LC and, by implication, in other libraries.

LC has given no sign of letdown in developing the new medium. A July 28, 1987, press release, printed in the next day's *New York Times*,[13] announced that an outside contractor had created a new technology for LC involving a compact disc slightly larger than the commercial model for recorded sound that contained the entire LC collection of some 33 hours of spoken-word records made before 1910. The disc selections are accessed through a computerized index. (Various terms are used for the CD-ROM components. "Disk" is sometimes even used for "disc." A recent glossary or dictionary can clarify the terms.)

11. Brian Alley, "C L Systems, Inc.: A *Technicalities* Vendor Profile," *Technicalities* 5 (Sept. 1985):9.

12. Page Lewis, "Optical Disk Pilot Program Supported by Library of Congress," *Research Libraries in OCLC: A Quarterly*, no. 18 (Winter 1986): 10–11; Audrey Fischer and Tamara Swora, *Library of Congress Optical Disk Pilot Program, Optical Disk Print Pilot Project; Print Project Document Preparation and Input Report, Phase I, September 1984–December 1985* (Washington: Library of Congress, 1986). For authoritative accounts of all *Program* activities, see Library of Congress, *Annual Report of the Librarian of Congress*, beginning with the fiscal year 1982.

13. *New York Times*, 29 July 1987, sec. C.

In its 1988 *Access '88: Catalogs and Technical Publications*, LC announced it was experimenting with publishing the complete USMARC database, including name authorities, subject authorities, and bibliographic records on CD-ROM! If they are successfully applied at LC, the discs would be made publicly available.[14]

While LC was following this course, other libraries and institutions were testing and expanding the CD-ROM world. In 1986 the proselytical premiere issue of *CD-ROM Review*, marked "Display until October 1, 1986," was distributed. It listed more than seventy-five databases for purchase in compact-disc format. Some of the seventeen databases in the Library Subject Area included Standard & Poor's COMPUSTAT; Grolier's *Academic American Encyclopedia* (full text); Public Affairs Information Service's *PAIS International*; Library Corporation's LC MARC; Bowker's *Books in Print* and *Ulrich's International Periodicals Directory* (both full text); Utlas's DisCat (MARC, REMARC Cataloging) and DisCon (MARC, REMARC Conversion); and Cambridge Scientific Abstracts's MEDLINE.[15]

The great advantage of the compact disc is its large storage capacity, which dwarfs previous computer storage media. Current digital CD-ROMs can hold up to 550 megabytes of information on one side of a 4.72-inch disc, accommodating the equivalent of 1,500 floppy disks, a 28-megabyte hard disk, or 125,000 printed pages (500 books).[16]

An interview with the director of the Office of Research of OCLC, reported in 1988 but probably held in 1987, recorded the interviewer's comment preceding a question: "CD-ROM is bursting out all over right now."[17] In fact, the use of CD-ROM for bibliographic surrogates (and often for full-text display) has proliferated to the point of becoming a bandwagon on which librarians are afraid not to jump.

A 1988 minatory article by Pearce entitled "CD-ROM: Caveat Emptor" described a grant-subsidized experiment to use various CD-ROMs in a Columbia library.[18] The article undoubtedly referred to a much earlier trial. The subtitle expressed the reservations of the author, especially on the incompatible CD-ROMs, their contradictory program languages, and their numerous necessary players—in other words, the lack of CD-ROM standardization. Almost in response to this complaint ap-

14. Library of Congress, Cataloging Distribution Service, *Access '88: Catalogs and Technical Publications*, 1988, 4.

15. *CD-ROM Review*, 1986– (Peterborough, N.H.: CW Communications/Peterborough Inc., 1986–), 62–63.

16. Ibid., 4.

17. "Interview: Martin Dillon, Director of the OCLC Office of Research," *OCLC Newsletter*, no. 171 (Jan./Feb. 1988):23.

18. Karla J. Pearce, "CD-ROM: Caveat Emptor," *Library Journal* 113 (Feb. 1, 1988):37–38.

peared a rebuttal, consisting of the words "High Sierra," a format whose presence or absence was indicated for every CD-ROM database contained in the 1988 third edition of the *Optical Publishing Directory*, which listed over 200 publicly available CD databases.[19]

The categories in that *Directory* were name of product, producer's name, address and telephone number; original source; type (e.g., reference); format (e.g., CD-ROM); description (e.g., indexes available, topics covered, number of entries); High Sierra format? (yes or no); disc drive manufacturer; drive available with subscription? (yes or no); search software; update (times per year); configuration; and price.

In her article, "CD-ROM Database Update," Tenopir carefully explained High Sierra as referring to a group of computer manufacturers who proposed a standard dealing with CD-ROM volume and file structure and for player compatibility.[20] The standard was to be voted on by the National Information Standards Organization (NISO) for submission to the American National Standards Institute (ANSI). Tenopir held out the hope that, since the European Computer Manufacturers Association had proposed a similar standard, a compatible data structure standard could be approved by the International Standards Association and become the international CD-ROM standard.

Tenopir concluded by citing points of recent CD-ROM user surveys. Two of these points are worth noticing by this book's readers: (1) Users need computer literacy because it is more difficult to get the CD-ROM database up than it is to start online searching; and (2) Intermediaries will introduce end users to CD-ROM.[21]

The value of the High Sierra category is very high for potential purchasers and users of CD-ROM databases. Even before the CD-ROM standard was officially approved, database producers (following the policy of unity making commercial strength) were stressing compatibility of CD-ROM software and hardware—a movement not since weakened. Many of the CD-ROM databases have online equivalents. Now, if only the CD-ROM standard makers would behave similarly on standards for their analytical databases—the latter, of course, a concern of LC!

Early in 1988, Philips Company of the Netherlands and Sony Company of Japan distributed for comment to their CD licensees a standard for the CD-write once (CD-WO) format.[22] The companies had announced

19. *Optical Publishing Directory*, Richard A. Bowers, ed., 3rd ed. (Medford, N.J.: Learned Information, 1988). See also *CD-ROMS in Print 1988–1989*, 2nd ed. (Westport, Conn.: Meckler, 1988), which lists about the same number of CDs as the *Directory*.

20. Carol Tenopir, "CD-Rom Database Update," *Library Journal* 111 (Dec. 1986):71. The entire article appears on 70–71.

21. Ibid.

22. M. Yamamoto and H. Mons, "CD–Write Once: The Standard," *Optical Information Systems* 8 (Sept.–Oct. 1988):246–47.

in 1987 the preparation of such a standard—another example of the CD manufacturers' march to compatibility.

In the meantime, LC continued its own efforts towards standardization. McCallum, employed at LC, reported in late 1986 on standards submitted for reactions by the NISO, including: Computerized Serial Orders, Claims, Cancellations and Acknowledgments; Serial Issue and Article Identifiers; Holdings Statements for Non-Serial Items; and Common Command Language for Online Interactive Information Retrieval. Concerning this last standard, a principal topic of this chapter, McCallum commented: "With user support, the standard could be influential in bringing together the command syntaxes employed by database and system software providers."[23] This comment, by extension, could be applied to the reality of all standards—one must never forget that standards are not mandatory—and it confirms the not altogether sanguine opinion of the CLSI interviewee. Opponents to the imposition of standards have seemingly practical objections. Crawford of RLIN has written on the development of bibliographic standards and their pros and cons.[24]

The perhaps inescapable role of librarianship in relation to evolving technology has been reactive, not creative. Libraries have not been slow to adopt the latest advances in computerization, but they have yielded the creation of new computer hardware and software to other specialists. Unfortunately, as commentators have pointed out, librarianship has stood by while other professions more intimately connected to producing the new technology for profit have taken over much of the design and distribution of the automated information product. DIALOG, BRS, and ORBIT are now doing the job that many observers believe should have been undertaken by the library profession. Another effect of library distance from technological innovation has been that when automated systems are adopted by libraries, the systems exhibit old identification and retrieval techniques already known and refined by practitioners for the bibliographic organization of recorded knowledge.

On the other hand, many of the new library systems are of the "guinea pig" type imposed by suppliers without close knowledge of customer needs or functions. A gradual awakening of the library profession to the interrelationship of computerization and information has been shown by large academic libraries hiring permanent systems specialists and setting up of systems offices. In 1985 Columbia University announced that the functions of its vice-president and university librarian would encompass

23. Sally H. McCallum, "Standards," *RTSD Newsletter* 11 (no. 7, 1986):69–70. (The entire article is on 69–71.)

24. Walt Crawford, *Technical Standards: An Introduction for Libraries* (White Plains, N.Y.: Knowledge Publications, c1986).

administering the flow of all information, whether from books or computers.[25]

Because of the reactive nature of librarianship, technological progress operates on a separate level, though that progress directly or indirectly affects our bibliographic organization. Who would have thought it possible a decade or so ago that million-dollar mainframe computers, protected by environmental controls, would be replaced by increasingly smaller minicomputers and microcomputers that perform the same tasks at a fraction of the time and cost? When academic libraries first used computers for circulation, they had to rely on batch processing of data that was done at the university's main computer center during the late hours of the night after the more urgent computer work was completed. Circulation figures were thus not available for twenty-four hours. Today, with microcomputers feeding into a library's minicomputer console, online circulation data are immediately available.

Bibliographic organization waits on technological advances rather than initiates them. PRECIS would not have been invented without computer assistance, though PRECIS produces a printed subject listing. Cheaper and greater storage facilities have made possible the inclusion of more and more computerized bibliographic data, such as the full-text displays common among database vendors and producers.[26] The rapid development of optical compact disc technology has stimulated considerable changes in the supplying of cataloging and bibliographic information.

Some librarians have fought the rush to CD-ROM, chiefly because—disregarding standardization—they object to purchasing media for which updating is issued by the seller no more frequently than quarterly. Online databases are updated more quickly, and their convenience for users is at least as great.[27] One chief librarian in New York City gave this writer an unusual reason for adopting the CD-ROM for end users. That librarian felt that though CD-ROM could be considered an interim medium for the online database, it was important to offer students a fee-free opportunity to search automated information. The reactions of other librarians to this stand is that searching the CD-ROM databases is not fee-free, since the individual library must still pay the seller.

The necessary advances that optical compact-disc technology must make are already known if the CD is to meet the market challenge of

25. Columbia University, Office of Public Information, "Press Release," 16,731, Dec. 16, 1985; Judith Axler Turner, "Columbia U.'s Head Librarian Is Now Managing Academic Computing, Too," *Chronicle of Higher Education* 32 (Apr. 9, 1986):39–40.

26. Carol Tenopir, "Full-Text & Bibliographic Databases," *Library Journal* 110 (Nov. 15, 1985):62–63.

27. Idem, "Costs and Benefits of CD-ROM," ibid. 112 (Sept. 1, 1987):156–57.

competing computer-storage media. The struggle for standardization, that is, compatibility, has been detailed here. Subsequent improvements must incorporate features from the other storage media while preserving CD–unique advantages and adding features that are exclusive with CD.

One present limitation of CD-ROM would be removed if the discs could be erased.[28] Although erasability is a desirable marketing factor, it would reduce the compact disc's claims to indestructibility, that is, its archival quality for libraries, a claim already made for LC. The archival nature of the CD is, as earlier noted, still under investigation. The greater storage capacity of the compact disc will probably outweigh this theoretical contradiction of erasability. Perhaps both types of the CD could be offered.

CD capacity could be increased even more if both sides were usable. The different technologies needed for producing digital compact discs, e.g., full text for alphanumeric data, compared to compact videodiscs for graphic materials, should be made one or compatible so that text and pictures can be shown together. Progress on this problem is reported in Chapter 6.

The technological improvements required for optical compact discs have been given in detail because they illustrate that the current research into bibliographic organization is generally applied research rather than theoretical or sound-barrier breaking research. As this book has tried to show, the principles of bibliographic organization have not changed since ancient times. Perhaps we should be content with present research efforts to improve the application of these principles rather than trying to create new ones. However, some additional comments are necessary.

In research, even the applied type, the unexpected is always to be expected. For many years, the possible impact of optics technology on computerization has been discussed. It has been predicted that photons rather than electrons (light instead of electricity) could power incredibly fast computers. Experimentation is being actively pursued in America and Japan.[29] If successful, the outcome could mean radically different hardware, data storage, and search and retrieval commands. The future generation of computers—if generations are still being counted—might well be an evolutionary sport.

The interview with the director of the Office of Research of OCLC drew from him that the next "intense activity in the library community" would be the scholar's workstation, which combines faculty or student

28. "Erasable Optical Disc Fast Becoming Reality," *Online Newsletter: Information Intelligence* 9 (Feb. 1988):3–4.

29. Stephen Koepp, "And Now the Age of Light. Billions Are at Stake in the Race to Develop Optics Technology," *Time*, 6 Oct. 1986, 56–57.

microcomputers with networks, computerization of documents, and vocal input and output.[30]

"Workstation" has become a buzzword in current information technology, sometimes meaning any computer terminal used by searchers and retrievers. The scholar's workstation is reminiscent immediately of Bush's MEMEX, proposed in 1945 as "a scholar's desk-console housing an entire print library in microform and capable of displaying texts and building 'trails of references' at the push of a button."[31] Old wine in new bottles? Perhaps, though the medium for communication or surrogation has changed. Miniaturization, those "trails of references" indicating the presence of other sources, and scholarly self-sufficiency are still with us, though neither the MEMEX nor the scholar's workstation has yet become full reality.

A current topic in computer technology is hypertext, apparently an elaboration of the MEMEX trails of references. Hypertext is supposed to avoid the linear thinking (shades of McLuhan) of an author and to organize and thus make accessible the reader's instinctive reactions to texts. At the 1988 second Library and Information Technology Association (LITA) Conference in Boston, an entire program with more than one speaker dealt with the subject. Indeed, LITA has announced that it is developing standards for hypertext.[32] This early setting of standards for a bibliographic activity, before that activity becomes uncontrollable through habits or diffusion, should be applauded.

Recent personal intrusions into supposedly secure computer networks have resulted in media use of the word "virus" to describe such invasions of privacy. The anthropomorphization of the computer went unchallenged. A later use of WORM (Write Once Read Many) to describe how a human being found a way to insert a computer program, with instructions for replication, into the networks also went unchallenged in our professional press.[33] Only later did Susan Sontag, author of books on inappropriate metaphors for human diseases, state in an interview that

30. "Interview: Martin Dillon," 23.

31. Richard Joseph Hyman, *Shelf Access in Libraries* (Chicago: ALA, 1982), 130; Vannevar Bush, "As We May Think," *Atlantic Monthly* 176 (July 1945):101–8; James G. Rice, "The Dream of the Memex," *American Libraries* 19 (Jan. 1988):14–17.

32. Gordon Flagg, "Second LITA National Conference. Library Technology: An Interesting Mess?" *American Libraries* 19 (Dec. 1988):931; "Standards for Hypertext?" *RTSD Newsletter* 13, no. 6 (1988):4 of unpaged insert, before page 61.

33. The "virus" has been widely reported, e.g., Philip Elmer-DeWitt, "Invasion of the Data Snatchers! A 'Virus' Epidemic Strikes Terror in the Computer World," *Time*, 26 Sept. 1988, 62–67 (on the cover of the magazine is an illustration captioned "Computer Viruses"); idem, " 'The Kid Put Us Out of Action.' A Grad-School Whiz Injects a Virus into a Huge Computer Network," ibid., 14 Nov. 1988, 76; John Schwartz, "Big Bucks for Virus Killers. Data Security Heats Up," *Newsweek*, 28 Nov. 1988, 82.

"virus" was a metaphor which made the computer seem like a living thing.[34] Contrary to folk beliefs, Broadway drama, and the constant complaint that all errors are the fault of computers, the computer is not human but depends on human input for mechanical activation. The computer can do only what people tell it to do.

Every year, *Library Resources & Technical Services* publishes articles documenting the previous year's work in the technical services. The review of 1987 work in descriptive cataloging ended on a somewhat downbeat note: "With a few exceptions, the hints of last year that a new age of descriptive inquiry might be beginning have not proved true."[35]

This opinion might also extend to work in subject analysis.[36] At the ends of this book's chapters on current search and retrieval of surrogates (sometimes full-text), outstanding problems have been noted and some remedies and research needs outlined. For subject analysis in general, the point has been made and remade that neither subject headings nor classification can be expected to be permanent. Also, the failure of searchers to match their knowledge and expectations with the official subject authorities has always been with us and shows no sign of disappearing. Free-text search can sometimes help, but the like difficulties of matching search words with the author's writing persist. Making the best of an unfortunate situation, librarians (and library users) should expect failures, be willing to change their ideas and resultant vocabularies at any time, and hold on to outdated phraseology for the light shed on the recorded literature of the past.

Although mechanical developments are desirable and will affect bibliographic organization, it should be clear from the tenor of this book that only improvements based on respect for time-honored precedents in organizing recorded knowledge can result in increasingly effective search and retrieval. The output of any computerized system, as emphasized more than once, depends on the quality of the human planning and input. That input should reflect the knowledge of the unchanged principles of bibliographic organization. The trained professional librarian can and must survive—to end with the beginning of this chapter and book.

34. John Markoff, "Computers Are Starting to Seem More Like Living Things," *New York Times*, 19 Feb. 1989.

35. Janet Swan Hill, "The Year's Work in Descriptive Cataloging and . . . ," *Library Resources & Technical Services* 32 (July 1988):214. (The entire article is on pages 203–16.)

36. Diane Vizine-Goetz and Karen Markey, "Subject Access Literature, 1987," *Library Resources & Technical Services* (Oct. 1988):337–51.

SELECTED BIBLIOGRAPHY

To keep this bibliography to a tolerable size, the following selection criteria have been adopted. Most of the bibliography items are uncited in the text. They reflect a basic purpose of listing aids to the practical application of bibliographic organization, search, and retrieval. More recent commentaries have been included to represent the state of the art, while older works were selected that are of continuing validity.

Adequate data have been supplied in the book's notes to identify and retrieve cited publications. When a journal article has been cited only in part, indexes like *Library Literature* will yield complete pagination. As indicated throughout in the book and the notes, works like Eugene P. Sheehy's *Guide to Reference Books* provide detailed descriptions of the structure and printing history of most cited reference tools.

Dictionaries and Glossaries

The ALA Glossary of Library and Information Science. Heartsill Young, editor, with the assistance of Terry Berlanger. Chicago: ALA, 1983.

Harrod's Librarians' Glossary and Reference Book of Terms Used in Librarianship, Documentation and the Book Crafts. 6th ed. Compiled by Ray Prytherch. Brookfield, Vt.: Gower, 1987.

Hipgrave, Richard. *Computer Terms and Acronyms: A Dictionary.* London: Library Assoc., 1986. Distributed in the United States by ALA Publishing Services.

The Penguin Dictionary of Computers. Anthony Chandor, with John Graham and Robin Williamson. 3rd ed. Hammondsworth, Middlesex, England: Penguin, 1985.

The Penguin Dictionary of Microprocessors. Anthony Chandor. Hammondsworth, Middlesex, England: Penguin, 1981.

The Random House Dictionary of New Information Technology. A. J. Meadows; M. Gordon; A. Singleton, eds. New York: Random House, Vintage Books, 1983, c1982.

Sippl, Charles J. *Computer Dictionary.* 4th ed. Indianapolis, Ind.: Sams, 1985.

Stokes, Adrian V. *Concise Encyclopaedia of Information Technology.* 2nd ed. Aldershot, Hampshire, England: Gower Pub. Co., c1985.

General Textbooks

Chan, Lois Mai. *Cataloging and Classification: An Introduction.* New York: McGraw-Hill, c1981.

Taylor, Arlene G. *Cataloging with Copy: A Decision-Maker's Handbook.* 2nd ed. Littleton, Colo.: Libraries Unlimited, 1988.

Wynar, Bohdan S. *Introduction to Cataloging and Classification.* 7th ed. by Arlene Taylor Dowell. Littleton, Colo.: Libraries Unlimited, 1985.

Library of Congress Bibliographic Aids

Cataloging Service Bulletin, no. 1– , Summer 1978– . Washington: Library of Congress, 1978– . Succeeds Library of Congress. Processing Department. *Cataloging Service,* q.v. "An index to the *Cataloging Service Bulletin* numbers 1–36 (1987) is issued in annual cumulations and is a continuation of the *Index to the Library of Congress Cataloging Service Bulletins, 108–125 with Selected Items from Earlier Bulletins.* Available from Stanford University Libraries, Publications Sales Office, Stanford, CA 94305–2393."—*Access '88: Catalogs and Technical Publications,* 8.

CONSER Editing Guide. Prepared by the staff of the Serial Record Division under the direction of the CONSER Operations Coordinator. Loose-leaf. Washington: Library of Congress, 1986.

Hiatt, Robert M. "AACR2: Implementation Plans." *Library of Congress Information Bulletin* 37 (Nov. 17, 1978): 710–12.

"LC to Delay Adoption of AACR2 until Jan. 1, 1981." *American Libraries* 9 (Sept. 1978): 450.

Library of Congress. See also U.S. Library of Congress.

Library of Congress. Network Development and MARC Standards Office. *USMARC Authority Format.* Loose-leaf. Washington: The Library, 1987.

———. Processing Department. *Cataloging Service,* bulletins 1–125 (June 1945–Spring 1978). Washington: The Library, 1945–78. Superseded by *Cataloging Service Bulletin,* q.v. Reprint: *Bulletins 1–125, with a Comprehensive Subject Index.* 2 vols. Detroit: Gale, 1980. "An index to *Cataloging Service Bulletins 1–125,* (June 1945/Spring 1978), is available from Nancy B. Olson, Drawer 'U,' Lake Crystal, Minnesota 56055. An annual cumulative index to *Cata-*

loging Service Bulletin, beginning with no. 1 Summer, 1978, is also available."—*Access '88: Catalogs and Technical Publications*, 8.
———. ———. *Library of Congress Rule Interpretations*. Prepared under the direction of Robert M. Hiatt. Loose-leaf. Washington: The Library, 1988.
———. ———. *Subject Cataloging Manual: Shelflisting*. Loose-leaf. Washington: The Library, 1987.
———. ———. *Subject Cataloging Manual: Subject Headings*. Loose-leaf. Washington: The Library, 1985.
Rather, Lucia J. "AACR2 Options to Be Followed by the Library of Congress, Chapters 1–2, 12, 21–26." *Library of Congress Information Bulletin* 37 (July 21, 1978):422–28.
Tsung, Sally C., comp. *LC Rule Interpretations of AACR2*, Second Update—CSB 34–37. 2nd cum. ed. Loose-leaf. Metuchen, N.J.: Scarecrow, 1988. Previous cumulations were for CSB 1–27, published 1985; CSB 28–33, published 1987.
Tucker, Ben R. "AACR2 Options Proposed by the Library of Congress, Chapters 2–11." *Library of Congress Information Bulletin* 38 (Aug. 10, 1979): 307–16.
U.S. Library of Congress. See also Library of Congress.
U.S. Library of Congress. Descriptive Cataloging Division. *Synoptic Table of Rules: A Comparison of the A.L.A. Cataloging Rules for Author and Title Entries (1949) and the Code of Cataloging Rules [of Seymour Lubetzky]*. Prepared by Elizabeth Tate. Washington: The Library, 1959. (Lubetzky's *Code* was largely reflected in the *AACR*.)

Non-LC Bibliographic Aids

Bliss, Henry Evelyn. *A Bibliographic Classification, Extended by Systematic Schedules for Composite Specification and Notation*. New York: Wilson, 1940–1953. "The System published in 1935 has not been altered in this extended work, except in a few particulars."—preface.
Canaan, Judith Proctor. *Serial Cataloging: A Comparison of AACR1 and 2*. New York: New York Metropolitan Reference and Research Library Agency, 1980.
Classification Research Group (CRG). *A Classification of Library and Information Science*. Unpublished draft. London: CRG, 1971. The scheme is reproduced in part on the inside front cover of *Library Science Abstracts*.
Hagler, Ronald. *Where's That Rule? A Cross-Index of the Two Editions of the Anglo-American Cataloguing Rules, Incorporating a Commentary on the Second Edition and on Changes from Previous Cataloguing Standards*. Ottawa: Canadian Library Assoc., 1979.
Hoodless, Jean. *ALA Rules Correlated with Anglo-American Cataloging Rules*. Seattle: University of Washington Library, 1967.
A Manual of AACR2 Examples. Minnesota AACR2 Trainers. Lake Crystal, Minn.: Soldier Creek Press, c1981. Individual manuals for particular media and formats have been published (see below), some in editions following the first. Like all manuals issued by the Minnesota AACR2 Trainers, facsimiles of title

pages (or equivalents) are shown along with their *AACR2* cataloging records. Titles, names of compilers, and publication dates have varied for the various manuals. The manuals listed in this bibliography predate the *AACR2*, 1988 revision.

A Manual of AACR2 Examples for . . . . Ibid., 1980– . Manuals include those for: *Cartographic Materials*; *Early Printed Materials*; *Legal Materials*; *Liturgical Works and Sacred Scriptures*; *Manuscripts*; *Microcomputer Software and Video Games*; *Microforms*; *Motion Pictures and Videorecordings*; *Music and Sound Recordings of Music*; *Serials*; *Technical Reports*. (The various separate volumes above are in *The Complete Cataloguing Reference Set: Collected Manuals of the Minnesota AACR2 Trainers*. 2 vols. Edited by Nancy B. Olson and Edward Swanson. DeKalb, Ill.: Media Marketing Group/Minnesota Scholarly Press, 1988.)

A Manual of AACR2 Level 1 Examples. Minnesota AACR2 Trainers. Lake Crystal, Minn.: Soldier Creek Press, c1981.

A Manual of Advanced AACR2 Examples. Minnesota AACR2 Trainers. Lake Crystal, Minn.: Soldier Creek Press, c1982.

Maxwell, Margaret F. *Handbook for AACR2, 1988 Revision: Explaining and Illustrating Anglo-American Cataloguing Rules, Second Edition*. Chicago: ALA, c1989.

Verona, Eva. *Corporate Headings: Their Use in Library Catalogues and National Bibliographies: A Comparative and Critical Study*. London: IFLA Committee on Cataloguing, 1975.

Automated Searching

Authority Control in the Online Environment: Considerations and Practices. Edited by Barbara B. Tillett. New York: Haworth, 1989. ("A monograph published simultaneously as *Cataloging & Classification Quarterly*, Vol. 9, No. 3.")

Batt, Fred. *Online Searching for End Users: An Information Sourcebook*. Phoenix, Ariz.: Oryx, 1988.

Borgman, Christine L., Dineh Moghdam, and Patti K. Corbett. *Effective Online Searching: A Basic Text*. New York: M. Dekker, 1984.

Byerly, Greg. *Online and On-disc Searching: A Dictionary and Bibliographic Guide*. Littleton, Colo.: Libraries Unlimited, 1988.

Chan, Lois Mai, and Richard Pollard. *Thesauri Used in Online Databases: An Analytical Guide*. New York: Greenwood, 1988.

Choosing a Bibliographic Utility: User Views of Current Choices. Edited by Leslie R. Morris. New York: Neal-Schuman, 1989.

Directory of Online Databases. New York: Cuadra/Elsivier, 1980– . Quarterly. (Also available online.)

End-User Searching: Services and Providers. Edited by Martin Kesselman and Sarah B. Watstein. Chicago: ALA, 1988.

Fenichel, Carol H., and Thomas H. Hogan. *Online Searching: A Primer*. 2nd ed. Medford, N.J.: Learned Information, 1984.

Hawkins, Donald T. *Online Retrieval Bibliography, 1983–1986*. Medford, N.J.: Learned Information, 1986.

———. *Online Retrieval Bibliography, 1964–1982*. Medford, N.J.: Learned Information, 1982.

Humphrey, Susanne W., and Biagio John Melloni. *Databases: A Primer for Retrieving Information by Computer*. Englewood Cliffs, N.J.: Prentice-Hall, 1986.

Jensen, Patricia E. *Using OCLC: A How-to-Do It Manual for Libraries*. New York: Neal-Schuman, 1989.

Li, Tze-Chung. *An Introduction to Online Searching*. Westport, Conn.: Greenwood, 1985.

Mannheimer, Martha L. *OCLC: An Introduction to Searching and Input*. 2nd ed. New York: Neal-Schuman, 1986.

A Manual of AACR2 Examples Tagged and Coded Using the MARC Format. Minnesota AACR2 Trainers. Compiled by Julia C. Blixrud and Edward Swanson. Lake Crystal, Minn.: Soldier Creek Press, 1982.

Manual of Online Search Strategies. Edited by C. J. Armstrong and J. A. Large. Boston: G. K. Hall, 1988.

Markey, Karen, and Diane Vizine-Goetz. *Characteristics of Subject Authority Records in the Machine-Readable Library of Congress Subject Headings*. Research Report Series. Dublin, Ohio: OCLC, 1988.

Palmer, Roger C. *Online Reference and Information Retrieval*. 2nd ed. Littleton, Colo.: Libraries Unlimited, 1987.

Rollins, Stephen. "Computer Command Languages. The New Tower of Babel." *American Libraries* 14 (Apr. 1983): 233.

Roose, Tina. "Online Searching—Easier than You May Think." *Library Journal* 110 (Nov. 1, 1985): 38–39.

Subject Control in Online Catalogs. Edited by Robert P. Holley. New York: Haworth, 1989. ("A monograph published simultaneously as *Cataloging & Classification Quarterly*, Vol. 10, Nos. 1/2.")

Tenopir, Carol. "A Common Command Language," *Library Journal* 114 (May 1, 1989): 56–57.

———. "Dialog's Knowledge Index and BRS/After Dark: Database Searching on Personal Computers." Ibid. 108 (Mar. 1, 1983): 471–74.

———. "Searching by Controlled Vocabulary or Free Text?" Ibid. 112 (Nov. 15, 1987): 58–59.

Turpine, Geraldine. *Going Online 1987*. Medford, N.J.: Learned Information, 1988.

Commentaries

MONOGRAPHS AND COLLECTIONS

Bliss, Henry Evelyn. *The Organization of Knowledge in Libraries; and the Subject-Approach to Books*. New York: Wilson, 1933. (A "2nd ed. rev. and partly rewritten" was published in 1939.)

Crawford, Walt. *Patron Access: Issues for Online Catalogs*. Boston: G. K. Hall, 1987.

Expert Systems: Concepts and Applications. Edited by Charles Fenly and Howard Harris. Advances in Library Information Technology, no. 1. Washington: LC Cataloging Distribution Service, 1988.

Feinberg, Hilda. *Title Derivative Indexing Techniques; a Comparative Study*. Metuchen, N.J.: Scarecrow, 1973.

Foundations of Cataloging: A Sourcebook. Edited by Michael Carpenter and Elaine Svenonius. Littleton, Colo.: Libraries Unlimited, 1985.

Hyman, Richard Joseph. *Shelf Classification Research: Past, Present—Future?* Occasional Papers, no. 146. Champaign, Ill.: Graduate School of Library Service, University of Illinois at Urbana-Champaign, 1980.

The Impact of Online Catalogs. Edited by Joseph R. Matthews. New York: Neal-Schuman, 1986.

Kyle, Barbara Ruth Fuessli. *An Examination of Some of the Problems Involved in Drafting General Classifications and Some Proposals for Their Solution*. London: Social Sciences Documentation, 1958.

LaMontagne, Leo E. *American Library Classification, with Special Reference to the Library of Congress*. Hamden, Conn.: Shoestring Press, 1961.

Lancaster, F. W. *Vocabulary Control for Information Retrieval*. 2nd ed. Arlington, Va.: Information Resources Press, 1986.

Leavitt, Judith A. *CD-ROM Applications, Standards and Technology, Part II: A Selective Annotated Bibliography*. Library Hi Tech (LHT) Bibliography, vol. 3. Ann Arbor, Mich.: Pierian Press: 1988. "This selective annotated bibliography updates the bibliography on CD-ROM published in *Library Hi Tech* Bibliography, no. 2 (1987)." Vol. 4 is scheduled for 1989.

Lehnus, Donald J. *Comparison of Panizzi's 91 Rules and the AACR of 1967*. Occasional Papers, no. 105. Champaign, Ill.: Graduate School of Library Science, University of Illinois at Urbana-Champaign, 1972.

The Linked Systems Project: A Networking Tool for Libraries. Compiled and edited by Judith G. Fenly and Beacher Wiggins. OCLC Library, Information, and Computer Science series, no. 6. Dublin, Ohio: OCLC, 1988.

Markey, Karen. *Subject Access to Visual Resources Collections: A Model for Computer Construction of Thematic Catalogs*. Westport, Conn.: Greenwood, 1986.

Ranganathan, S. R. *The Colon Classification*. Rutgers Series on Systems for the Intellectual Organization of Information, vol. 4. New Brunswick, N.J.: Graduate School of Library Service, Rutgers, the State University, 1965.

Simonton, Wesley C., and Marilyn Jones McClaskey. *AACR/2 and the Catalog: Theory—Structure—Changes*. Littleton, Colo.: Libraries Unlimited, 1981.

Theory of Subject Analysis. Edited by Lois Mai Chan, Phyllis A. Richmond, and Elaine Svenonius. Littleton, Colo.: Libraries Unlimited, 1985.

Weiskamp, Keith, and Namir Shammas. *Mastering HyperTalk*. New York: Wiley, 1988.

PERIODICAL ARTICLES

Baer, Nadine L., and Karl E. Johnson. "The State of Authority." *Information Technology and Libraries* 7 (June 1988): 139–53.

Bevilacqua, Ann F. "Hypertext: Behind the Hype." *American Libraries* 20 (Feb. 1989): 158–59, 161–62.

Buckel, William L. "The Uniform Catalog." *Library Journal* 111 (Jan. 1986): 52–54.

Cochrane, Pauline Atherton, and Karen Markey. "Preparing for the Use of Classification in Online Cataloging Systems and in Online Catalogs." *Information Technology and Libraries* 4 (June 1985): 91–111.

Crawford, Walt. "Anyone for Optical Disques?" *LITA Newsletter*, no. 27 (Winter 1987): 4–5.

Gorman, Michael. "AACR2R: Editor's Perspective. *The Anglo-American Cataloguing Rules*, second edition, 1988 revision." *Library Resources & Technical Services* 33 (Apr. 1989): 181–86.

———. "The *Anglo-American Cataloguing Rules, Second Edition.*" *Library Resources & Technical Services* 22 (Summer 1978): 209–26.

Rosenberg, Victor. "The Scholar's Workstation." *College & Research Libraries News* 46 (Nov. 1985): 546–49.

Simonton, Wesley C. "Introduction to AACR2." *Library Resources & Technical Services* 23 (Summer 1979): 321–39.

Tuttle, Helen Welch. "From Cutter to Computer: Technical Services in Academic and Research Libraries, 1876–1976." *College & Research Libraries* 37 (Sept. 1976): 421–51.

Wilson, Patrick. "The Catalog as Access Mechanism: Background and Concepts." *Library Resources & Technical Services* 27 (Jan./Mar. 1983): 4–17. (Reprinted in *Foundations of Cataloging*, above under Commentaries—Monographs and Collections.)

Woo, Janice. "Additional LITA Sessions. Expert Systems Not Yet Clones of Librarians." *American Libraries* 19 (Dec. 1988): 934.

INDEX

Richard Joseph Hyman is a professor emeritus at Queens College, New York. Hyman was chairman of the Graduate School of Library and Information Science at Queens College from 1977–1984. Since his retirement in 1986, he has been a guest professor at Columbia University, Saint John's University, and Queens College. A member of the American Library Association, Hyman is listed in both *Who's Who in Library and Information Services* (ALA, 1982) and *Who's Who in America.*